GIFTS FROM AMIN

STUDIES IN IMMIGRATION AND CULTURE

ISSN 1914-1459

ROYDEN LOEWEN, SERIES EDITOR

GIFTS FROM AMIN
UGANDAN ASIAN REFUGEES IN CANADA

SHEZAN MUHAMMEDI

UNIVERSITY OF MANITOBA PRESS

Gifts from Amin: Ugandan Asian Refugees in Canada
© Shezan Muhammedi 2022

26   25   24   23   22   1   2   3   4   5

University of Manitoba Press
Winnipeg, Manitoba, Canada
Treaty 1 Territory
uofmpress.ca

Cataloguing data available from Library and Archives Canada
Studies in Immigration and Culture, ISSN 1914-1459 ; 18
ISBN 978-0-88755-283-0 (PAPER)
ISBN 978-0-88755-285-4 (PDF)
ISBN 978-0-88755-287-8 (EPUB)
ISBN 978-0-88755-289-2 (BOUND)

Cover photo by Roger St. Vincent with permission from Michael Molloy
Cover design by Kirk Warren
Interior design by Karen Armstrong

Printed in Canada

This book has been published with the help of a grant from the
Federation for the Humanities and Social Sciences, through the Awards
to Scholarly Publications Program, using funds provided by the
Social Sciences and Humanities Research Council of Canada.

The University of Manitoba Press acknowledges the financial support for
its publication program provided by the Government of Canada through
the Canada Book Fund, the Canada Council for the Arts, the Manitoba
Department of Sport, Culture, and Heritage, the Manitoba Arts Council,
and the Manitoba Book Publishing Tax Credit.

Funded by the Government of Canada | Canadä

CONTENTS

INTRODUCTION

On a brisk evening in late October 1972, my mother, grandmother, and two uncles arrived in Ottawa as refugees from Uganda. They were part of a larger movement of 7,550 Ugandan Asian refugees who were resettled across Canada from 1972 to 1974.[1] At the young age of nineteen, my mother became the principal applicant for the family's refugee status in Canada. As the only readily employable individual within the family, she was entrusted by the Canadian government to financially support her two younger brothers and her own mother. Decades later, with a cheerful smile, she recalled her first experiences of a true Canadian winter and her earliest interactions with Canadians. She explained her commute to the Canadian Imperial Bank of Commerce (CIBC) for work after only three days in Canada:

> When we woke up and it snowed that day, like everything was covered white. So everything looked different.... When I took a bus and went to the bank the day before, things looked differently. Because of the snow, everything looked different to me, and I didn't have winter boots, a winter coat. ...I got on the bus and I tried to follow [the route], and I got lost. So I was supposed to be at work at 8:30 or 9 a.m. and I didn't get there until 12 or 12:30 p.m.... [At the bank] I only knew one person, who [had] interviewed me. So when I got there, I saw her sitting in her office, so I just went to her and I was already blue and purple, like I was frozen. My

hands were frozen, my toes were frozen. . . . She asked me, "What happened? Did you get lost?" And I just started to cry and then she realized that I'm frozen, so she took me downstairs. . . . She made me a cup of tea, she put a blanket on me and gave me a piece of toast. And I was just sobbing away because I was so frozen and I didn't make it to work on the first day and I missed [making it to work on time], you know? And I was lost, and I didn't know how to get back to the hotel, I couldn't find this place, I didn't know who to call, so I was lost. I cried and cried and cried. . . . And then she says, "Why aren't you wearing your shoes? Why aren't you wearing your coat? Where is your scarf?" And I told her that I didn't have any. . . . Around four thirty or five o'clock I was supposed to finish work. She came to me and said, "We would like to see you downstairs before you go home." So when I went downstairs, the staff—during the day or lunch or whatever—they all went and bought me something warm. There was a scarf that somebody gave me. Somebody gave me gloves. They gave me a kettle to make tea for myself. They bought a few little things. They gave me a map. And so I was touched, I was touched that day.[2]

Her first days in Canada demonstrated one of the numerous ways that Ugandan Asian refugees experienced the Canadian spirit and climate. Ugandan Asian refugees were admitted to Canada under the Liberal government of Pierre Elliott Trudeau after being expelled from their homes by the president and military general of Uganda, Idi Amin. President Amin declared on 4 August 1972 that Uganda had no room for "the over 80,000 Asians holding British passports who are sabotaging Uganda's economy and encouraging corruption" and that he wanted to see power over Uganda's economy restored to the "hands of Uganda citizens, especially 'black Ugandans.'"[3] The expulsion decree forced the exodus of nearly every Ugandan of South Asian descent within only ninety days.

This was part of a larger campaign administered by Amin's regime involving mass violence perpetrated against hundreds of thousands of Ugandans. Three terror units responsible for mass violence were created under President Amin's rule: the State Research Bureau, the

Public Safety Unit, and the military police. In addition, *kondoism* was widespread. *Kondos* refers to bandits who arbitrarily confiscated goods or killed Ugandans either as members of the military or the general public who rented uniforms from military personnel. Under Amin's rule, from 1971 to 1979, hundreds of thousands of Ugandans died from the decentralized violence that took place due to *kondoism* and the terror units. Members of state security forces and soldiers were free to loot, smuggle, and blackmail Ugandans with little fear of being reprimanded by the state or being disciplined by their superiors. This encouraged supporters of Amin's regime to kill for not only economic gains but also for any other reason they deemed fit. There are numerous and less publicized accounts of individual soldiers conducting executions and loaning army uniforms to the public to extort money from Ugandans. The guise of *kondoism* shielded the violence of government soldiers and effectively legalized the killing squads of Amin as soldiers and the public could act with impunity. Acts of mass violence were carried out against Ugandans regardless of their ethnicity, religion, political affiliations, or economic situation. Estimates for those murdered under Amin's regime span from two hundred thousand to five hundred thousand Ugandans.[4]

When Amin announced the expulsion decree, Britain immediately called for aid from the Commonwealth community, including Canada, as it could not absorb large numbers of refugees due to heightened levels of racial antagonism in 1970s England. Many Ugandan Asians were previous or current British passport holders, and Amin vehemently argued they were "Britain's problem." A second request for help came directly to Canada's prime minister from Prince Shah Karim al-Husayni, Aga Khan IV, the spiritual leader of the Shia Nizari Ismaili Muslim community. Many Ismailis in Uganda were directly affected by the order, and the Aga Khan asked Trudeau, his close personal friend, to provide a safe haven for his community. The two requests for aid were echoed by the United Nations high commissioner for refugees, Prince Sadruddin (the uncle of Aga Khan IV), who pleaded with the international community to resettle those who were transported to refugee camps following the expulsion deadline of 8 November 1972.[5]

Canada answered the call for aid amid numerous concerns at home. The Cold War contest between capitalism and communism, a reformulation of Canadian identity after the Royal Commission on Bilingualism and Biculturalism, high rates of unemployment, shifting

attitudes towards human rights activism, and the official deracialization of Canadian immigration policy formed the backdrop for the
arrival of nearly eight thousand Ugandan Asian refugees by the end
of 1974. The United Kingdom claimed responsibility for almost thirty thousand Ugandan Asians who held British passports. However,
it would not admit Ugandan Asians who had opted out of British
citizenship during Ugandan independence in 1962 in exchange for
becoming Ugandan nationals. Therefore, the Canadian government
prioritized resettling those who became stateless when their Ugandan
citizenship was revoked under Idi Amin's regime. Canada became the
single largest recipient of stateless Ugandan Asians, marking one of
the largest resettlements of non-European and non-white refugees in
the nation's history up to 1974.[6] Additionally, the arrival of Ugandan
Asians marked the first major resettlement of a predominantly Muslim
group of refugees in Canada.[7]

   This book explores how Ugandan Asian refugees transitioned into
Canadian citizens and their personal constructions of identity and sense
of belonging. Understanding the historical context of their expulsion
from Uganda, the multiple influences behind the Canadian government's decision to help them, and their lives in Canada after fifty years
of resettlement provides insight on the relationships between public
policy, refugee resettlement, and integration in the twentieth century.
Similar to other refugee communities who arrived in Canada during
the postwar period, Ugandan Asian refugees were not passive recipients
of international aid. They navigated various bureaucratic processes to
secure safe passage to Canada, applied for family reunification, and
made concerted efforts to integrate—and often give back—to Canadian
society. By co-opting reception centres as a space for building social
bonds and supporting integration, seeking immediate employment to
raise capital to support the sponsorship of family members, submitting letters to the Canadian government to request reunification with
family members overseas, and demonstrating the importance of having
family members in Canada during the resettlement process, Ugandan
Asian refugees reshaped government policies on refugee resettlement.
The abundant use of oral histories throughout the book highlights the
agency of migrants as they interacted with evolving geopolitical landscapes. While Canada and other nation-states hold sovereignty over
who is, and more importantly who is not, admitted into their borders,

migrants participate in complex relationships between themselves and the international community.

The term "Ugandan Asian" is historically rooted and is used throughout the book. Prior to the partition of India in 1947, political leaders and media in East Africa used the term "Asian" to describe anyone from the Indian subcontinent. Later, "Asian" came to mean anyone from India, Pakistan, Goa, or Bangladesh. Although the label erodes the cultural and religious plurality of such individuals living in East Africa, it was purposefully used to categorize all members of this minority community. Within Uganda and other parts of East Africa, those of South Asian descent were also commonly referred to as *muhindis*, a Swahili word for Indians used in both a colloquial and pejorative manner that was largely replaced by the catch-all term "Asian." As the community became increasingly rooted within Uganda, scholars and the international media began to refer to these individuals as Ugandan Asians, signifying their attachments and affiliations to the country while noting their ancestral connections to the Indian subcontinent.

Ugandan Asians who resettled in Canada were not initially considered refugees based on the criteria outlined in the United Nations 1951 Convention Relating to the Status of Refugees and the subsequent 1967 Protocol Relating to the Status of Refugees. Although Ugandan Asians possessed a "well-founded fear of being persecuted for reasons of race, religion, nationality, membership of a particular social group or political opinion," they were not "outside the country of [their] nationality."[8] The Canadian government purposefully refrained from classifying Ugandan Asians as refugees to avoid having to use relaxed selection criteria when screening applicants for resettlement and to appease anti-Asian sentiment in Canada. Government documents instead use the terms "Ugandan expellees" or "Ugandan Asian expellees" to refer to the community. However, once Ugandan Asians arrived in Canada, they were labelled as refugees by the Canadian media and public since they faced persecution and were officially outside their country of origin.[9] Eventually, government officials embraced the term and acknowledged their de facto status as refugees.[10]

The Canadian government's reluctance to label Ugandan Asians as refugees reveals how the term "refugee" is highly politicized. Refugee scholars have noted how the term is subjective and often manipulated to reflect various "social, economic, political, as well as historical contingencies."[11] Ugandan Asians underwent a "refugeeing process," where state actors co-opted the term "refugee" when portraying the benevolence of the Canadian government on the international stage. While refugee historian Laura Madokoro rightly problematizes the use of the term and opts to use the more inclusive "migrant" in her exploration of Chinese migrants during the Cold War,[12] I have chosen to keep the word "refugee" to reflect how Ugandan Asians describe themselves. All forty-nine oral history participants in the book self-identified as refugees. Various commemorative events, literature produced by members of the Ugandan Asian community, and the Uganda Collection at Carleton University (an archive focused on Ugandan Asian refugees) further make evident that the term "refugee" is an essential component of their identity.[13] For example, four major Ugandan Asian authors—Peter Nazareth, Shenaaz Nanji, Tasneem Jamal, and Mahmood Mamdani—have produced fiction and nonfiction literature that firmly entrenches the linkages between Ugandan Asians and the term "refugee." To respect the historical development of the term "Ugandan Asian refugee," references to the community evolve throughout this book. In the early chapters, covering the period prior to the expulsion announcement, I use the term "Ugandan Asians." When discussing the expulsion, I refer to them as "Ugandan Asian expellees." Finally, in the remaining chapters following their international resettlement, I describe them as "Ugandan Asian refugees."

Four central themes are presented throughout the book. The first theme explores how Ugandan Asians developed a strong sense of attachment to East Africa and challenged the rigidity of the three-tiered race and class hierarchy embedded in Uganda during colonial rule. Despite being labelled as recent migrants by Idi Amin's military regime or indentured labourers who "forgot to go home," many Ugandan Asians viewed themselves as citizens of Uganda. The second theme asserts that the Canadian government's decision to admit Ugandan Asian expellees was based on a duality of opportunism and humanitarianism. On the one hand, Canada responded to the expulsion decree due to appeals for assistance from the British government, the high commissioner for refugees, and His Highness the Aga Khan IV alongside knowledge that most expellees were highly educated, skilled entrepreneurs and professionals. On the other hand, accepting Ugandan Asian expellees, as Prime Minister Trudeau stated, reinforced the nation's commitment to the "ideals of human dignity, social justice and the principle of multi-racialism."[14] The prime minister's remarks also reflect how government officials branded various groups of refugees in the postwar period. Canadian refugee historian Jan Raska's work on the twelve thousand Czechoslovak refugees who arrived in 1968 shows how federal officials described incoming refugees as "a small gold mine of talent" while also seeing the resettlement as a Canadian commitment to international humanitarianism.[15] Internal government documents reveal how the same rhetoric was used during the resettlement of Ugandan Asians.

The third theme reviews how the integration of Ugandan Asian refugees was facilitated by collaborative efforts from the Canadian government and public combined with the willingness of refugees to make Canada their permanent home. Scholarship within migration studies consistently emphasizes that integration is a two-way process that requires efforts from the host community as well as newcomers to create pathways to belonging.[16] The final theme investigates the transition of Ugandan Asian refugees to active Canadian citizens. Through numerous commitments to voluntarism, political participation, and assertions of their allegiance and ties to Canada, all forty-nine of the interviewed refugees expressed a strong sense of being Canadian. Although their identities are situated within a complex web of national, religious, and ethnic affiliations, participants consistently asserted that they are Canadians. In oral histories Ugandan Asian refugees articulate their belief in Canadian values, including free speech, democracy, and respect for diversity, and they have established a formal archive at Carleton University to reaffirm their existence within the Canadian historical narrative. These findings surrounding the resettlement, integration, and identities of Ugandan Asian refugees break new ground within the historiography of Canadian immigration.

The earliest scholarly works exploring migration to Canada, published from the 1930s to 1960s, captured the past experiences of immigrants and settlers from Western Europe. Beginning in the 1970s, new works emerged to challenge the myth of European settlers as the primary founders of Canada and the stereotyping of various immigrant communities such as the Doukhobors and Mennonites. Beyond the inclusion of race, ethnicity, class, and gendered perspectives on immigration, the use of oral histories and the incorporation of migrant agency significantly contributed to how historians captured the experiences of newcomers. By the turn of the twenty-first century, migration scholars were arguing that factors such as race, ethnicity, class, and gender were compounded by internal and external power dynamics, within and outside of their respective communities, and structural forces within society that complicate the historical record. For example, historian Dirk Hoerder used collections of personal memoirs, diary entries, and private writings of newcomers to demonstrate how everyday casual interactions between newcomers and Canadians (e.g., at local community events, church gatherings, or in the workplace), not race and ethnicity alone, define inclusion and integration for immigrants.[17] Historian Franca Iacovetta uses the concept of "gatekeepers" to argue that integration is not a straightforward process of interaction between immigrants and Canadians that can transcend racial and ethnic barriers. Gatekeepers include a vast array of individuals who participate in formal areas of migration, such as government officials, social workers, and family experts, as well as others including journalists and popular writers.[18] This book reveals that although ethnic identities remain fluid, many Ugandan Asian refugees did experience some form of discrimination in Canada, affirming Iacovetta's conception of gatekeepers, as refugees interacted with a multitude of individuals who either welcomed or hesitated to accept their participation in Canadian society.

Coinciding with the development of Canadian immigration history, refugee studies emerged in the 1970s to address the distinction between refugees and immigrants. Historian Gerald E. Dirks contends that Canada viewed refugees as permanent settlers and that their admission to the country depended on the political and economic context.[19] In the postwar years, Canadian immigration policy was directly influenced by the postwar economic boom and need for more labourers, calls from the public for humane policies to resettle European displaced persons and refugees fleeing oppressive communist, socialist, and authoritarian regimes, and a preference for British and other European migrants with limited acceptance of people from Asia, Africa, and the Caribbean. Refugees were admitted based on the prevailing issues within Canada through orders-in-council, executive discretion, and ministerial orders, as the country did not have a separate admission policy for refugees until the 1976 Immigration Act.

Refugee historians Marlene Epp, Laura Madokoro, and Jan Raska articulate how citizen activism, international human rights, and compassion shaped postwar resettlement efforts but did not trump Canada's requirement for newcomers to integrate economically and socially. Xenophobia, race thinking, and political biases informed which refugee communities were deemed admissible under the guise of the country's "absorptive capacity" for newcomers.[20] This book problematizes what Madokoro correctly identifies as the conventional narrative of immigration in Canada after 1967—that of an uncontested transition towards open and race-neutral immigration policy.[21] Against a background of shifting policies and sustained requirements for new arrivals to possess high levels of human capital, thousands of refugees were resettled in Canada following the Second World War.

The rise of authoritarian regimes along with Cold War proxy conflicts led to the global displacement of hundreds of thousands of people. From the mid-1950s to the 1980s, roughly eighty thousand Indochinese, forty thousand Hungarian, twelve thousand Czechoslovak, seven thousand Chilean, and three hundred Tibetan refugees arrived in Canada.[22] I aim to build on previous historical investigations of these refugee groups, which are part of the Canadian historical narrative on refugee resettlement in the postwar era.[23] Raska documents various arrivals of refugees from Czechoslovakia starting in the late 1940s. He identifies how Prague Spring refugees were admitted to Canada based on their high levels of education, language abilities, experience in the professions—similar to the Ugandan Asian community—and their conformity to anticommunist values. Most importantly, Raska's work acknowledges that refugees who arrived in 1968 expressed their affinity for prodemocratic values not only to appease the government and the public but also to demonstrate their own beliefs in liberty and freedom.[24] Unlike the Czechoslovak refugees, Ugandan Asian refugees did not have a base of compatriots living in Canada. Although there were Kenyans and Tanzanians of South Asian descent living in Canada in the 1970s, they had only recently arrived, in the late 1960s. Collectively, these communities would define conceptions of identity for East Africans of South Asian descent living in Canada. Tibetan refugees also gained entry to Canada under the premise of being able to quickly integrate into the labour market. Government officials screened applicants for high levels of motivation and "good character" in what Raska argues was Canada's test case for non-European refugees who could readily adapt to life in Canada in a short period.[25] Each of these resettlements set precedents for forthcoming initiatives but were individually shaped by the historical context. A consistent fluctuation between open and restrictive policies guided each response to global crises that were influenced by the local and international geopolitical contexts. The fundamental debate within these scholarly works relates to Canada's motivations for resettling specific groups of refugees.

Historian Robert Keyserlingk's edited volume on Hungarian refugees brilliantly engages the debate by questioning the altruistic nature of the Canadian government's decision to admit refugees.[26] The various authors contest the notion that Canada's refugee policy was based solely on the economic and political climate of the 1950s. Refugee scholar, Howard Adelman argues that Hungarian refugee resettlement was motivated by humanitarianism but also reinforced Canada's identity as a European settler nation, occurred alongside favourable economic conditions, and supported the global fight against communism. Historians Gerald E. Dirks and Nandor Fred Dreisziger argue that there was a strict screening process during the resettlement initiative to ensure that none of the refugees were Nazi sympathizers or communists. A disproportionate number of Hungarians who came to Canada were young, well educated, and highly skilled. On the one hand, humanitarianism is revered as the ultimate motivation for refugee resettlement in Canada. On the other, scholarly works on each of the resettlements from 1950 to 1980 describe the ulterior motives of the Canadian government. Be it a reluctance to admit certain individuals based on Cold War rhetoric, or an intentional overrepresentation of young, highly skilled, and highly educated refugees, Canadian refugee policy is not a clear act of altruism.

Specialists on refugee policy argue that decisions to admit refugees are predicated on additional factors relating to international human rights and concerns over national security. Political scientist Christopher G. Anderson argues that two dominant ideologies dictated the response of the Canadian government to refugee crises from Confederation until the formal deracialization of the country's immigration policy in 1967.[27] At times, concerns for international human rights overrode nativist concerns based on unemployment and citizen rights, enabling refugees to be admitted to Canada. This represents what Anderson calls the liberal internationalist discourse. The opposite occurred during the Depression and Second World War, reflecting the supremacy of the second ideology, known as the liberal nationalist discourse. Suha Diab argues that questions of national security and humanitarianism informed refugee policy during the Uganda crisis of 1972 and the 1973 overthrow of Chile's Unidad Popular (Popular Unity), a coalition of leftist parties.[28] Diab concludes that admission to Canada is subject to the security and humanitarian impulses of government officials, leading to a rapid response to Ugandan Asian refugees based on humanitarianism and a significantly delayed admission of "communist" or "socialist" Chilean refugees based on security concerns. The securitization of Canadian refugee policy continues today based on conceptions of global terrorism in a post-9/11 world.

These categories of analysis provide useful frameworks for interrogating allegations that the Canadian government was "skimming the cream of the crop" with regards to the resettlement of Ugandan Asian refugees.[29] Some scholars argue that Canada was not on a "mission of mercy" and that the country received a disproportionate number of young refugees while failing to accept more challenging refugee cases.[30] In this book I conclude that these charges were accurate to some degree, reflecting the debate over Canadian refugee policy and its predication on the duality of opportunism and humanitarianism. The dialogue on refugee resettlement continues in this book with an interrogation of Canada's decision to respond to the plight of Ugandan Asian refugees, as well as other refugee groups, as such decisions are dictated by a multitude of factors that range from compassion to pragmatism.

Academic studies on Ugandan Asian refugees have focused on their resettlement in the United Kingdom and identities as British Ugandan Asians, digital expressions of memory, and their resettlement and initial adjustment in Canada up until 1974. The late Dr. Vali Jamal was unable to complete a seven-volume overview of the displacement and resettlement of Ugandan Asians, including where the diaspora lives today. None of his work has been published to date and does note engage with significant archival research from a Canadian perspective on the resettlement of Ugandan Asian refugees in Canada or make significant use of oral history interviews. Consequently, there is only one academic book dedicated to exploring the historical context of Ugandan Asian refugees. It focuses on those who went to the United Kingdom and is also severely dated, as it was written in 1975.[31] There are several articles by historian Margret Frenz, who interrogates the memories, identities, and multiple affiliations of refugees who trace their ancestry to Goa, including those who reside in Toronto and England.[32] Other scholars have investigated the complexities and fluidity of Ugandan Asian identities in the United Kingdom along with their attachments to material culture, which physically embody their attachments to East Africa.[33] Academic studies provide insight on conceptions of memory as well as constructions of identity among those who settled in the United Kingdom and elsewhere.

Two theses, written in 1974 and 1981, address the experiences of Ugandan Asian refugees in Canada from a sociological perspective. The first study used long-form questionnaires completed by thirty-three Ugandan Asian refugees living in Calgary. Benson Chukwuma Morah concluded that by 1974, Ugandan Asian refugees were moderately assimilated into Canada despite being in the country for only a few months.[34] This work provides insight on the initial experiences of the refugee community in Calgary; however, the measures used to assess integration are based on sociological analyses pertaining to rates of employment and education. Further, the study draws conclusions based on a small sample size specific to Calgary and does not include any oral interviews with refugees. The second study focuses on the sociological question of whether ethnic or nonethnic factors are salient when understanding how migrants resettle, using the specific case study of nonvoluntary migrants.[35] Cecil Pereira amalgamated the responses of survey participants and ultimately concluded that ethnicosity (measured by food, festivals celebrated, language spoken at home, etc.) did not affect resettlement. However, he did identify that job discrimination, downward labour market integration, and job dissatisfaction were prevalent among Ugandan Asian refugees in Canada.

In addition to these academic publications, other works have been written by members of the Ugandan Asian refugee community. Several novelists explored their individual perceptions of the expulsion, the political context in Uganda, their upbringing and childhood experiences, and their subsequent resettlement in Canada and the United Kingdom.[36] Other community members described their life histories through cookbooks, articulating their multiple identities through delicacies that are infused with tastes of the past.[37] Literature from the community identifies how migration from South Asia to Uganda and onwards to Canada and other places infused their cuisine with spices and tastes that reflect their shifting histories. These sources provide invaluable insight on the life histories of Ugandan Asian refugees and are incorporated throughout the book.

Conceptions of the Ugandan Asian refugee community are continuously being created and recreated. This book explores the complexities of the Ugandan Asian refugee community and how their identities have evolved over time. Examining their sense of self broadens understandings of integration as a multifaceted concept that involves interactions between Ugandan Asians and Canadians. This book aims to emphasize the role of transnationalism in the historical creation of diaspora communities. Historical experiences inform present-day ideas of belonging and sense of attachment to Canada. Additionally, the Ugandan Asian refugee community represents several cultural, religious, and national affiliations, which are further complicated by personal identity construction. Scholars who specialize in exploring these concepts articulate that identity is fluid, socially constructed, contested, and continuously reassembled.[38] Building on sociologist Stuart Hall's conception of identity, this book reinforces the significance of history, as opposed to biology, as a fundamental element of how Ugandan Asian refugees express who they are. While their membership in the Canadian community is challenged on many fronts, Ugandan Asian refugees in Canada have consistently asserted their place within society and see it as an intrinsic part of their identity. Essayist Neil Bissoondath contends that identity is personal but that racial and cultural differences have become amplified under Canada's multiculturalism policy, establishing an attitude of tolerance towards minority rights. Multiculturalism fails to consider how identities are highly subjective and develop across generations, and often leads to generalizations about diverse communities.[39] The framework of identity construction is essential for reclaiming the numerous affiliations and personal expressions of self for Ugandan Asian refugees, which are captured through the extensive use of oral histories.

Interviews captured the intimate and personal narratives of Ugandan Asian refugees. Oral histories advance our understanding of human agency alongside the relationship between the individual and the social being.[40] Those who were expelled from Uganda experienced trauma, and oral histories can promote closure and peace, offering a potential healing process.[41] Oral history practitioners in the field of trauma note that the opportunity to discuss traumatic events in a safe atmosphere with an empathetic and engaged listener can provide a pathway to healing by allowing interviewees to dissociate themselves from the impacts of trauma on the human psyche. This approach to oral interviews was critical to ensuring that Ugandan Asian refugees felt comfortable at all times and were given ample time to reflect on their personal recollections. Several participants described moments of distress, fear, anxiety, uncertainty, and violence during the expulsion period in Uganda. Participants were not forced to divulge any details that they did not feel comfortable sharing. At times of discomfort, I halted the audio recording, resuming it only when the interviewee consented to continue. Thus, interviewees were able to explore their historical experiences of trauma on their own terms, reflecting the importance of using a life history approach when conducting interviews with survivors of trauma. Encouraging Ugandan Asian refugees to exert their agency in this kind of setting helps us to understand the resilient ways in which they have restructured their lives since the expulsion period.[42]

A fundamental approach I took to empowering interviewees was to remind every participant at the beginning of the interview process that we could take breaks, pause the audio recording, and erase any portions of the tape that left them uncomfortable. Historian Alexander Freund explores how some professional historians are wary of this process, especially with regards to participants wishing to speak off the record or long silences, and argues that participants should be encouraged to continue.[43] However, adhering to the practices of shared authority posited by oral historian Michael Frisch, particularly the call for interviewers to be sensitive to the requests of participants, I chose to embrace off-the-record discussions and silences.[44] During the recording process, silences were contemplative, authoritative, or purposeful tools used by Ugandan Asian refugees to assert their agency over their own oral histories. At the outset of this project, I was prepared as a researcher to give complete authority to the narrators during the interview process. What they chose to keep on tape was up to them, as I was not on a quest for the "perfect interview" unobstructed by silences or off-the-record details.

Oral histories contest, complicate, and question established narratives on Ugandan Asians in both East Africa and Canada. Their recollections of the expulsion refute President Amin's claims that Ugandan Asians had failed to integrate socially with Ugandan Africans, as they recounted strong attachments and affiliations to East Africa. Remembering family members who refused to leave Uganda or describing in detail their devastation upon being forcibly removed, interviewees expressed their ties to the country. Oral histories also provide evidence of how in some instances, Ugandan Asians (friends and relatives of interviewees) exploited Ugandan Africans and sabotaged the economy, whereas others engaged in rigorous philanthropy and contributed to the development of the country. Another significant discovery through oral history interviews is the varying degrees of antagonism levied against the Ugandan Asian community by government and military officials during the ninety-day expulsion period. Previous studies dismissed reports in British newspapers of widespread physical and verbal harassment as rumours as well as the purposeful distortion of events by the media as a means of garnering further support for resettling refugees in the United Kingdom. Interviewees recounted the realities of the ninety-day expulsion period, which recaptured the plight of Ugandan Asians during this time.

Oral histories with Ugandan Asian refugees also bring to light insights into their resettlement and identities in Canada that contradict government reports. Several researchers have concluded that Ugandan Asians obtained employment within Canada at a rapid pace; however, interviewees outlined various instances of employment discrimination. A lack of "Canadian experience" or Western credentials disenfranchised many refugees, who were underemployed based on their occupational expertise. Government surveys of Ugandan Asians also failed to capture racialized interactions between Canadians and Ugandan Asian refugees. Racial antagonism towards South Asians was particularly prevalent in 1970s Canada, as noted by historians and anthropologists Hugh Johnston, Norman Buchignani, Doreen Marie Indra, and Ram Srivastava, and oral history participants recounted numerous examples of verbal harassment.[45] In some cases, confrontations escalated into physical harassment. Conversely, interviewees also recalled how Canadians extended a helping hand when they first arrived. These grassroots efforts by Canadians to create inclusive pathways into Canadian society were not captured in archival records at Library and Archives Canada or other material sources.

Interviews also demonstrated the myriad of ways in which Ugandan Asians identify themselves in Canada today. Personal assertions of identity remained elusive in broader collections of materials, as state bodies and scholars failed to capture Ugandan Asians' expressions of self within the Canadian context. Interviewees revealed the multiple affiliations of Ugandan Asian refugees and explained what being Canadian means to them. Without these in-depth oral histories, the project would not be able to critically engage with the established narratives of Ugandan Asians' social exclusivity in Uganda, harassment by Ugandan government, various forms of discrimination following resettlement in Canada, and the complexities of identity within the community.

Oral historian Steven High's methodological framework promotes the dissemination of knowledge throughout the refugee community and the broader Canadian public and is the most appropriate means of creating an inclusive approach to oral history.[46] Unfortunately, given the nature of this project, it was not feasible to involve each participant in the writing process. Potential delays in adjusting transcripts and approvals for each chapter would have hampered my ability to complete the dissertation on time, and the use of visual recording equipment posed major ethics challenges, ultimately prohibiting the use of High's methodology. Fortunately, through a collaboration with Carleton University and its Ugandan Asian refugee archive, I hope to embrace the true values and merits of sharing authority, as the collection of oral interviews will continue through the university's archival team. Twenty oral histories from this book have been donated to the Uganda Collection to promote the sharing of authority. The archive allows participants to amend any portion of their interviews, arrange follow-up interviews to supply additional context, and determine if their interview should be made open to the public online or for in-archival use only. All those who wished to donate their oral histories to Carleton University signed consent forms agreeing to the permanent preservation of their interviews for subsequent generations.

I conducted oral history interviews with forty-nine participants from June 2014 to October 2015. All participants were born in Uganda and eventually resettled in Canada. I also conducted interviews with two leading immigration officials for Canada who were on the ground in Kampala during the expulsion period. Roger St. Vincent was the head of the visa office in Beirut and was responsible for running operations in Uganda, and Michael Molloy, who also worked in the Beirut office, served as St. Vincent's second in command. Interviews were held across Canada in the following cities: Calgary, Edmonton, Kitchener, Montreal, Ottawa, Toronto, and Vancouver. They ranged in length from forty-five minutes to three hours and took place in a variety of locations, including local religious institutions, coffee shops, restaurants, and personal residences. All participants reached out to me due to recommendations from other participants and word of mouth by various community members.

A broad array of individuals participated in the study, including thirty-one men and eighteen women. They arrived in Canada at different ages, the youngest at six and the oldest at forty-five years old. In terms of religion, the group was relatively diverse, with thirty-five Ismaili Muslims, nine Christian Goans, four Hindus, and one member of the Ithna-Asheri Muslim community. Unfortunately, due to limited connections and their smaller representation within the overall resettlement population, no Sikh, Parsi, or other members of the Muslim community (e.g., Sunni Muslims, Bohras, Ahmadiyyas) participated in the research project. The Ismaili Muslim community is slightly overrepresented in the study, reflecting 71 percent of the overall sample but accounting for roughly 65 percent of the Ugandan Asian refugee community in Canada, according to the only reliable statistics about those who arrived via chartered Canadian aircraft.[47] There was also a lack of participants who were over the age of thirty-five upon arrival. This is in part because the older population has passed away or has medical considerations, and in part because of Canada's preference to admit younger Ugandan Asian expellees. The concentration of interviews with individuals who were sixteen to twenty-five years old upon arrival is related to the personal reasons they chose to participate in the study, as most were nearing retirement or had already retired at the time they were interviewed. As they concluded their formal work lives, many participants looked back on their time in Canada and wished to share their personal life histories. I did not aim to make generalizations about the community as a whole based on the sample of interviews. Instead, this oral history collection is but a first step towards recapturing the lived experiences of Ugandan Asian refugees in Canada, and it will continue through Carleton University's Uganda Collection.

To fortify participants' agency in the research process, I purposefully remained flexible and open to the multiple directions taken by interviewees as they narrated their life histories.[48] My position as a young, male, Ismaili Muslim, academic, and child of a Ugandan Asian refugee offered several benefits but also shaped the construction of interviews. Given the expulsion occurred in 1972, all of the participants were well into their fifties and beyond and often interpreted the interview as an opportunity to relay community-based historical experiences to the second generation. I addressed the vast majority of participants as "auntie" and "uncle" as sign of respect, which built trust but also blurred the lines between being an academic researcher and being a curious youngster seeking to learn and listen to stories from distant relatives who have recently reconnected. Many participants responded to this form of cultural respect by referring to me as *beta* (son) or *dickro* (son), which are common terms of endearment in Hindi, Urdu, and Gujarati used to refer to someone who is not one's biological child. These intergenerational discussions and transmissions of knowledge sparked important conversations in the interviews. As a male researcher, I expected to encounter differences in authority and power where male participants would feel they had greater freedom to recount their life histories and women would feel more inhibited, especially when being addressed by a stranger.[49] However, throughout the process there was no appreciable difference between male and female participants, who privileged my identity as a curious youth over my gender.

At the beginning of each interview, a significant portion of time was spent discussing the origins of the study and hearing about the participant's personal interests and life anecdotes. This was crucial to establishing a relaxed atmosphere and building trust between the interviewees and me, which occurred rather quickly because the majority of participants felt a direct connection to me based on my family's roots in Uganda. Participants immediately tried to place my mother's family in their own networks. Most interviewees asked, "What was her last name?" or "Where was she born?" followed by a comment like "Oh she was from Mbarara. I had a cousin that lived there." Interactions were kept casual in nature and were often described by participants as a "nice chai and chat." More stories came after the interviews had formally concluded, as participants offered meals or an additional cup of chai and snacks. I have not included these specific recollections in the book, as they are outside the license given to me by the interviewees. As mutual friendships formed, I needed to balance the fostering of solidarity with participants with the responsibilities of academic research and the creation of an ethical relationship with narrators of the past. This situation is one that oral historians must commonly navigate.

This book informs policymakers, academics, and the public in regards to future refugee resettlement programs in Canada. Displaced people represent one of the most disenfranchised and marginalized groups in the current geopolitical climate. Given the ongoing political conflicts, rising levels of inequality, climate change, and other disasters, revisiting past resettlements in our nation's history is critical to informing current policies, reception efforts, and public consciousness related to those fleeing persecution. One limitation of the book is the resettlement bias, as it does not review displaced people who are not provided with international resettlement opportunities. Unfortunately, only 1 percent of recognized refugees by the United Nations High Commissioner for Refugees (UNHCR) are resettled abroad.[50] By capturing the voices of refugees, I aim to challenge the rhetoric used by politicians who keep displaced peoples "over there." Refugee scholars agree that Western governments purposefully reframe asylum seekers approaching their borders as "economic migrants," "illegal or undocumented," "queue jumpers," and "bogus refugees."[51] Reducing the experiences of refugees to matters of state policy, border control, and public opinion fundamentally severs the shared human connections between refugees and citizens. Consequently, this study used life histories abundantly as a means of capturing the hopes, dreams, and aspirations of Ugandan Asian refugees alongside their fears, struggles, and traumas of displacement. Focusing on the human aspects of their life histories invigorates our understanding of the refugee experience while reminding us of our shared human bonds.

The current global political landscape has tarnished the humanitarian impulse behind providing refuge for displaced peoples. Politicians have leveraged this vulnerable population in a ploy to garner votes for their respective parties. As refugee scholar Emma Haddad outlines, politicians participate in "organized hypocrisy" where "states create refugees, then fail to take responsibility for them."[52] My book is but one small step towards a deeper understanding of refugee resettlement, and it situates Ugandan Asian refugees within the Canadian historical record as Canadian citizens. Fifty years after the expulsion decree, the global community can begin to understand why former governor general of Canada Adrienne Clarkson describes Ugandan Asian refugees in Canada as "a present from Idi Amin."[53] I hope this book helps readers begin to explore how, as Ugandan Asian refugee Aziz put it, "even the Canadian government, even the people, they really helped us to be what we are."[54]

CHAPTER 1

ROUTES AND ROOTS:
Exploring the History of South Asians in Uganda

*It is the Indian trader who, penetrating and maintaining himself
in all sorts of places to which no white man would go or in which
no white man could earn a living, has more than anyone else
developed the early beginnings of trade and opened up the first
slender means of communication.*

Winston Churchill, *My African Journey*, 1908

*As Nyerere [president of Tanzania] once put it, if the people of
Uganda thought they were in the frying pan during Obote's time,
they knew they were in the fire proper during Amin's.*

Tony Avirgan and Martha Honey, *War in Uganda:
The Legacy of Idi Amin*, 1982

South Asians have a prominent historical legacy within East Africa.
Migration from the Indian subcontinent to East Africa increased
significantly after the 1840s with three principal groups of migrants,
including merchants and traders, indentured labourers, and civil servants. As the community continued to grow within Kenya, Tanzania,
and Uganda, South Asians sent word back home of the numerous
opportunities available in East Africa, encouraging further migration.
Solidifying their roots in Uganda, South Asians began to fervently
build schools, hospitals, prayer halls, and community centres. The
majority of these institutional structures were based on religious and
regional affiliations in South Asia. British imperialism, along with

divide-and-conquer strategies implemented by colonialists, enticed South Asians to segregate themselves from the local Ugandan African populations. The "colonial sandwich" that placed white colonialists at the top, brown merchants in the middle, and labouring black Africans at the bottom legitimized racial segregation within all facets of Ugandan society. However, the rigid race and class hierarchy within Uganda was not impermeable. Numerous oral histories and major philanthropic activities conducted by Ugandan Asians for the benefit of all Ugandans show a blurring of the layers within the colonial sandwich. This chapter refutes the dominant discourse of segregation within the historiography of Ugandan Asians to demonstrate how interactions between members of Ugandan society were not strictly limited to the colonial race and class hierarchy.

Following the Second World War, colonial powers in East Africa prepared to leave the region. The structures left in place from colonialism allowed the South Asian community to take control of the economy. Due to their privileged position within the race and class hierarchy in Uganda, Ugandan Asians replaced Europeans as "brown colonialists." However, rising pan-Africanism, decolonization, and major independence movements in Kenya, Tanzania, and Uganda placed the Ugandan Asian community in a precarious situation. As countries in East Africa secured independence, their respective South Asian communities were offered opportunities to become formal citizens of their countries of residence. South Asians were left with a difficult choice. Their first option was to embrace the limitations of becoming citizens in East Africa, which would require a formal revocation of their status as British subjects. The second option was to apply for British citizenship, demonstrating their allegiance to the colonialists. Opting for British citizenship reinforced perceptions among East Africans that South Asians were colonial collaborators.

The governments of East Africa made efforts to Africanize local economies, and Ugandan Asians who were British citizens faced various nationalization programs and trade licensing impediments that curtailed their dominance in the regional economy. An initial reluctance to limit European and Ugandan Asian control of the economy under the first president of Uganda, Dr. Milton Obote, had led to increased general antagonism towards Ugandan Asians, who were viewed as the principal exploiters of Ugandan Africans. Both Kenya and Tanzania addressed their "Asian problem" through socialist or nationalist practices aimed at putting control of the economy into the hands of their citizens, which effectively disenfranchised their Asian communities. President Idi Amin, however, had his own solution to the "Asian problem."

Ugandan History (1840–1972)

Two major precolonial features that carried into twentieth-century Uganda are ethnic diversity and the kingdoms of Buganda, Toro, Ankole, Bunyoro, and Busoga. The five kingdoms had their own institutions and cultural heritage, along with a strong sense of solidarity. Particular ethnic groups lived in each of these precolonial states, intensifying state allegiance. Under its colonial divide-and-conquer strategy, Britain subdivided areas to foster ethnic tensions. For example, in districts mainly composed of a single ethnic group such as the Bukedi, Kigezi, Teso, or Toro, the British created additional counties and subcounties based on minor differences in traditions and cultural practices. Historian Martin R. Doornbos argues that Ugandan tribes were thus manufactured by the colonialists.[1] Officially, Uganda has recognized at least thirty-one subgroups of various ethnicities that derive from either the Bantu or Nilotic tradition. The Bantu people reside primarily in southern Uganda while the Nilotic people are from the north. Several characteristics and customs differentiate the two groups, including diet, cash crops cultivated, physical features, and traditional social organization. Highlighting the rich linguistic and ethnic diversity of the country, during the 1980s Uganda Radio was broadcast in fifteen languages, and twenty newspapers were printed in eight languages.[2]

British influence did not arrive in East Africa until the mid-nineteenth century. Colonialists first settled along the coast of Zanzibar, then moved deeper inland into Tanzania, Kenya, and Uganda. Their presence and development in East Africa are marked by the creation of a commercial presence through the Imperial British East Africa Company in 1888 and a political presence by creating the East Africa Protectorate in 1894.[3] Upon their arrival in what would become Uganda, the colonialists created an alliance with the people of Buganda, whose territory bordered Lake Victoria. Buganda was recognized as an individual kingdom on the condition that it would remain faithful to British authorities. The Uganda Agreement of 1900 stated that the king of Buganda (known as the *kabaka*) and his senior leadership had autonomy over state affairs along with privileged access to land rights. The initial favouritism bestowed upon the people of Buganda by the British colonialists later created one of the largest barriers to Ugandan nationalism, as the kabaka and his community were unwilling to part with their exalted status.

Shifts in Ugandans' socioeconomic status paved the way for the rise of nationalism throughout the twentieth century. Scholars argue that higher incomes generated from improved cultivation of cash crops, such as coffee and cotton, expanded formal education, better social benefits, and increasing Ugandan self-awareness led to greater participation in political parties.[4] Decolonization also took root in the early twentieth century, as Ugandans advocated for more political, economic, and social control over their affairs. However, the development of Uganda's political parties emphasized social cleavages that persisted in the postindependence era. The three major political parties followed regional and religious affiliations. The Uganda People's Congress (UPC) was composed of northwestern Ugandans, who were primarily Protestants, the Democratic Party represented the Catholics of the remaining regions of Uganda, and the Kebaka Yekka was the sole political party for the people of Buganda.[5]

By the time of the 1962 general election, ethnicity had begun to play a more pivotal role in Ugandan politics than religion did.[6] The colonial method of divide and conquer left many Ugandans more attuned to local rulers. This effectively undermined the power of the central government as Ugandans continued to pledge their allegiance to the five precolonial states instead of the three major political parties. Although elections became a prominent event in the daily lives of Ugandans, political parties sought to capitalize on existing social cleavages to rally support.[7] Uganda's independence coalesced under unique circumstances, given the relationship of the five kingdoms, one of which was an independent state (Buganda). While Buganda possessed a federal relationship with the central governing state, the four other kingdoms of Ankole, Toro, Bunyoro, and Busoga were given quasi-federal powers, leaving the remainder of the country to be run by local administrations.[8] Uganda declared independence on 1 March 1962 with Democratic Party leader Benedicto Kiwanuka named as the first prime minister. In new elections held the following month, Kiwanuka was replaced by Dr. Milton Obote, who had formed a coalition between the UPC and Kebaka Yekka.[9]

The emphasis and exploitation of ethnic cleavages by Uganda's second government brought ethnicity to the fore of Ugandan society. Prime Minister Obote leveraged the remnants of the colonial administration for his party's political gain. First, he needed to address the issue of Buganda's status as a separate state within Uganda. This was no simple feat, as his victory over Kiwanuka had depended on a partnership with Kebaka Yekka, ultimately requiring him to declare the kabaka, Mutesa II, as Uganda's first constitutional president.[10] For the first four years of independence, a silent struggle for power between Obote and Mutesa II ensued.[11] The basis of the "Buganda problem" was the kingdom's economic dominance, but Obote changed the political landscape of the entire country through the suppression of Bugunda.

In 1966 Obote provoked Mutesa II into expelling the central government out of Buganda. He did so by requesting support from the British army to quell a mutiny in Buganda and by returning to the kingdom of Bunyoro two counties that had been given by the British to Buganda. After the kebaka expelled the central government, Obote retaliated by declaring a state of emergency in Buganda and sending the army, along with its military general, Idi Amin, to occupy the kingdom.[12] The state of emergency lasted until 1971 and allowed Obote and the central government to directly control Buganda. In 1967 Obote created a unitary constitution, which abolished the five kingdoms and established the Second Republic of Uganda.[13] The first executive president of the Second Republic was, unsurprisingly, Dr. Milton Obote. To further consolidate power, Obote removed any members of the UPC who were no longer loyal to him, banned all political parties except for the UPC, killed those who opposed the UPC, nationalized the economy, and began to rely heavily on his own tribe, the Langi, and the closely related Acholi tribe for political and military support.[14] In an attempt to solve the economic woes of the country, Obote created the Common Man's Charter, which was approved by the UPC on 19 December 1969, along with the Move to the Left program.[15] In 1970 he issued the Nakivubo Pronouncements, which mandated that the government would control at least 60 percent of all the foreign companies in the country, including financial institutions and mining operations.[16]

These decrees were political measures to siphon earnings towards groups affiliated with Obote's government, and they largely failed to distribute wealth throughout the country. These policies impacted the

Ugandan Asian community in a variety of ways and established the basis for Idi Amin's rise to power.

Idi Amin in Power

Throughout Obote's leadership his right-hand military commander was General Idi Amin. They eliminated several political rivals and killed hundreds of anti-Obote supporters. Tensions between Obote and Amin arose in the late 1960s when Obote and his supporters accused Amin of murdering his chief political rival, Brigadier Pierino Yere Okoya, and misappropriating government funds.[17] Amin overthrew Obote on 25 January 1971 in a military coup while Obote was attending the Commonwealth Summit in Singapore. By the time of the coup, Obote had effectively thwarted ethnic and economic unity in Uganda. Poor economic policies along with Obote's biased recruitment of Acholi and Langi people in the army and the civil service made it extremely difficult for Ugandans to form an alternative source of power.[18] The coup was welcomed by many, especially by the people of Buganda, who were marginalized under Obote's rule. However, as Julius Nyerere, president of Tanzania from 1964 to 1985, exclaimed, "If the people of Uganda thought they were in the frying pan during Obote's time, they knew they were in the fire proper during Amin's."[19]

Immediately following the coup, Amin began to gain political support by reversing some of Obote's unpopular public policies. He lifted the state of emergency in Buganda, released more than fifteen hundred political prisoners back into society, and allowed the body of former kabaka Mutesa II to be brought from London for a proper burial at the Kasubi Tombs in Uganda.[20] He also reduced state ownership under Obote's socialist program from 60 percent to 49 percent. To appease various religious groups and strengthen his political support, he created a department of religious affairs and made donations of 100,000 shillings to the various heads of the Muslim, Catholic, and Protestant faiths in Uganda.[21] Amin portrayed himself as a fellow Ugandan in contrast to the British-educated Obote, who required a translator wherever he went in Uganda. The new president spoke Bantu languages (Luganda and broken Swahili) and Sudanic languages (Kakwa, Lugbara, Lendu, Logo, and Madi), as well as Lwo (Alur) and Kinubi.[22] During his first year in power, Amin drove his Land Rover to several public events, including sports matches, and interacted with local Ugandans.[23]

Unsurprisingly, Amin favoured his army, as it was responsible for bringing him to power. Similar to Obote's biased recruitment of his fellow Langi and Acholi tribesmen, Amin drew from his own tribe, the Kakwa of West Nile district and others from southern Sudan and northwest Zaire.[24] To protect himself from those who were loyal to Obote, he began to ethnically cleanse the Ugandan army of recruits from Lango and Acholi. Two examples of these atrocities include the explosion of the Makindye barracks in March 1971, which killed 30 Acholi and Langi soldiers, and the execution of 150 to 500 Acholi and Langi soldiers from the Simba Battalion in July 1971.[25] Against the backdrop of anti-colonial sentiments, Amin made Swahili the official language of the country and fervently sought to ensure that black Ugandans controlled the economy.[26] During Obote's leadership, the government let Ugandan Asians remain in control of the economy, despite its socialist program of 60 percent state ownership. Instead of redistributing wealth to encourage the development of a black Ugandan commercial class, Obote allowed Europeans and Asians to further penetrate the agricultural and industrial markets.[27] His primary motive for promoting non-Ugandan businesses pertained to his preferential treatment of the Langi and Acholi peoples. Obote was initially hesitant to implement "Africanization" economic policies because this would place the majority of businesses in the hands of the people of Buganda. With high levels of education and business acumen, the people of Buganda were well suited for controlling the Ugandan economy.[28] However, both the Common Man's Charter and Nakivubo Pronouncements in the late 1960s and early 1970s exemplified efforts to promote left-leaning programs that increased the Ugandan government's control over the economy.[29] President Amin's final reform immediately after seizing power in 1971 was to return control of the economy to black Ugandans. Despite the prominent historical legacy of South Asians in East Africa, they were expelled from Uganda, irrespective of their citizenship, because of their market dominance and social exclusivity.

Historical Roots of the South Asian Community in Uganda

The earliest migration to East Africa from the Indian subcontinent dates to the ninth century. Various Arab and Indian communities participated in a growing network of trade throughout the Indian Ocean and the Arabian Peninsula. Some scholars even trace the roots of Indian trade with East Africa to the second century, describing accounts of a Greek pilot ship that engaged with both Arab and Indian merchants along the eastern coast of Africa.[30] For centuries Indian merchants were the main suppliers of a variety of goods in addition to being importers of ivory, gold, iron, incense, and slaves. The African slave trade, in particular, illustrated the growth in commercial transactions between India and Africa.[31] By the fifteenth century, the king of Bengal was in possession of eight thousand African slaves.[32] Consequently, South Asians had already established themselves in East Africa as traders and shopkeepers well before British colonial rule and the greater "scramble for Africa" in the 1800s. These trading networks became advantageous for the large influx of South Asians who migrated to the region in the latter half of the nineteenth century. Indeed, the Arabic word *sahil*, meaning boundary or coast, gave rise to the term *swahili*—"people of the coast"—reflecting the vast Arab presence in the littoral cities of Mombasa and Zanzibar.[33] It is crucial to note that the populations of coastal towns, such as Mombasa, included those from the coastal community, the African interior, South Asia, and the Arabian Peninsula before the appearance of Europeans in the region. As noted by historical anthropologist Zulfikar Hirji, for centuries prior to the arrival of European colonialists, intermarriage and cooperation between these diverse groups of people for political, social, and economic reasons occurred throughout the region.[34] The region's rich multiculturalism substantiates the deeper historical roots of the South Asian community in East Africa.

In the 1840s South Asians migrating to East Africa primarily went to Zanzibar, seeking economic prosperity as commercial traders. The archipelago had come under Arab control and in 1841, the sultan of Oman, Seyyid Said, moved his capital there.[35] Under his leadership, South Asians were placed in administerial positions relating to finance, amplifying their dominance within trade, shopkeeping, and moneylending. The sultan's decision to give them preferential treatment set a crucial precedent for the British, who would also entrust them with administrative positions during the creation of colonial governments throughout East Africa. The sultan also granted religious freedoms to South Asians and thus promoted the migration of all religious groups from the Indian subcontinent. His liberal policies increased the South Asian population in Zanzibar from three hundred to four hundred in the early 1800s to nearly six thousand in 1866.[36] The success of these migrants led more South Asians—mostly from Gujarat, Mumbai, Punjab, and Karachi—to Zanzibar and farther inland. Members of the former Portuguese colony of Goa also moved to East Africa. Relatively few Goans who initially migrated fell within the merchant class; the rest were shop owners, employers, or government officials in Zanzibar.[37]

These regions served as the main sources of migration from South Asia to East Africa. The migration patterns of South Asians replicated those of the British colonialists. This is in part due to British protection that was extended to all Indian migrants, as India was under colonial rule in the nineteenth century. Another motivating factor for migration from South Asia was the deteriorating access to arable land, food, and employment opportunities. The geographical proximity of the two regions also promoted migration to East Africa. Most importantly, the bulk of South Asian migration to Uganda was voluntary, selective, and spontaneous. Most individuals could only finance their journey by taking a loan or convincing a relative living in Uganda to put up the money and work with the family to pay back their loan. Although merchants and traders made up the majority of migrants to Uganda, two other notable groups turned to it as a land of opportunity.[38]

The second major group of migrants consisted of indentured labourers known colloquially as coolies (the term comes from the Hindi word *quli*, which means labourer). They did not arrive until European colonization in the 1840s, when thousands of labourers were needed to construct railway systems in both Kenya and Uganda. During the five years it took to build the Uganda Railway (1896–1901), 32,000 Indian workers were recruited, of which 6,724 decided to stay in East Africa.[39] The migration of indentured labourers in conjunction with other groups of South Asians was encouraged by the British colonial government in India. It passed the Indian Emigration Act of 1883, permitting the legal movement of South Asians throughout East Africa without any restrictions.[40] The relatively small number of indentured labourers who chose to remain in East Africa formed the basis of the myth that all South Asians living in Uganda at the time of the expulsion order were descendants of the railway workers "who forgot to go home." Those who did return home brought stories back from East Africa about economic opportunities and promoted further migration from the Indian subcontinent.

The final category of migrants consisted of government officials brought by British colonialists to replicate the bureaucratic systems of colonial rule established in India. The British government's recruitment campaign facilitated the voluntary migration of Goans to East Africa, as they sought to create an inexpensive colonial administration by avoiding the use of British administrators. More than half of those recruited for the colonial government in Uganda were Goans.[41] Although the vast majority of Goans worked in the public sector, some took up positions as shopkeepers, tailors, cooks, and stewards. In fact, Goans played a crucial role in the tailoring industry and were even responsible for creating one of Uganda's most popular forms of dress known as the *gomesi* or *busuuti*. Designed by the Goan tailor A.G. Gomes, it is a cross between the Indian *sari* and the local Ugandan *pusuti*. Ultimately, Goans were predominantly public service workers or specialized artisans. Historian Margret Frenz argues that it is difficult to specify the number of Goans who migrated to Uganda, since available census data is scattered. The census included Goans as a separate category from 1911 to 1948 but grouped them in broader categories such as Asian, Portuguese, Indian, and Christian from the 1950s onwards. Estimates place the total Goan population in Uganda at three thousand in the 1970s.[42]

Goans who worked for the Ugandan civil service were granted an additional benefit of a paid six-month vacation to Goa every four years.[43] It is imperative to note that the earlier generations of Goans who opted to take advantage of this perk ultimately planned to retire in their respective villages back in Goa. Returning to live in Goa was a prominent practice among the early migrants as well as older Goans. The paid leave and the desire to retire in Goa reinforced ideas about the impermanence of South Asian migration to Uganda and emphasized the vested interests of Asians abroad, which Amin harnessed to justify his expulsion decree. Although not everyone in Uganda's Goan community wished to return to Goa, the perception of their impermanence was extended to all Asians, who were framed as foreigners or indentured labourers who forgot to return home. The three main categories of post-1840 South Asian migration demonstrate the various motivations that led people to relocate to East Africa.

Establishment of the Ugandan Asian Community

Once the railways were constructed, merchants from the coastal towns of Mombasa and Zanzibar used their privileged economic positions to create shops along the route. They travelled farther inland within Kenya, Tanzania, and Uganda while motivating friends and relatives from the subcontinent to take advantage of rising demands for trade and commerce. The vast majority of South Asians arrived in Uganda after the railway reached Kisumu near Lake Victoria. Under these circumstances, South Asians served as middlemen between the colonialists and the local population of Ugandan Africans. Their skills and expertise in economics, stemming from their favoured position in Zanzibar, facilitated trade and commerce in a pioneer society where the indigenous population was unable to leverage Indian Ocean trading networks to supply goods and lacked interest in the shopkeeping industry. The entrepreneurs who had originally installed themselves as merchants would eventually come to dominate the Ugandan economy. By the First World War, Asians could be found in many East African urban centres, including Mombasa, Dar-es-Salaam, Nairobi, and Kampala. The majority of these migrants came from northern India or Goa. Many Gujarati- and Kutchi-speaking tradesmen chose to remain in East Africa and encouraged their family and friends to set up new businesses in Kenya, Tanzania, and Uganda.

Initially, Asian migrants set up small shops or *dukas* in which they sold modest quantities of exotic consumer goods to farmers and in return purchased food items. They worked long hours and lived frugally in order to save as much money as possible. Maria, an oral history participant, described many *dukawallahs* (shop owners) as hard workers: "They would open at seven in the morning and they would work until ten at night. Like any time the Africans wanted, they knew they could go and get service."[44] Many of these small shops were opened in remote areas of Uganda, which created new markets for consumer goods. Asians became so prominent in trade and commerce through these dukas that in many regions of Uganda, currency was referred to as "arupia," a term derived from the Indian rupee. In a typical duka, the store was at the front of the building. Behind it were the living quarters of the shop owner, either within the same building or in a separate structure. Maria's husband Edmond recalled how his "father had property and all in Jinja. He had shops in the front like a plaza or whatever you call it, four or five shops. And at the back we were staying, not part of the building but he had a separate [unit] . . . like a bungalow."[45] Many Asians employed family members to reduce costs and increase savings, particularly in the more remote regions of Uganda. Pioneers who set up shops in smaller communities faced the realities of a more isolated life. Azim's family's business had "a gas station and . . . a retail shop, more like a 7/11, and they also, also sold products to all the smaller little shops around . . . the community. So my dad would drive probably one hundred miles taking orders—filled his truck, his small truck—and deliver, and then he would replenish the order from a city called Mbale. And we were actually in Majanji, we were right on the shores of Mbale."[46]

As dukawallahs prospered, many chose to open a new store in another region, often run by a close friend or family member. Historians Peter G. Forster, Michael Hitchcock, and F. Lyimo argue that such communal and business norms strengthened each other, and a breach of trust would lead to immediate termination of employment and public shaming within the community.[47] The economic success of the dukawallahs generated conflict among Ugandan Africans, who criticized their practices and viewed them as self-interested, corrupt, obsessed with turning a profit, and unpatriotic. Over time, the clustering of Asians in shop owning would diminish in the face of competition from local Ugandans. By the 1950s, the majority of retail traders throughout Uganda were Ugandan Africans. As dukas became less prominent among the Asian community, their decline was counteracted by the rising development of the wholesale and manufacturing business sectors, beginning in the early 1900s.

Cotton became a major cash crop in Uganda in the early 1900s, and Asians served as middlemen between English cotton ginners and Ugandan African cotton farmers. As the cotton industry expanded, there was an increasing shortage of cotton ginners, which provided an ideal opportunity for Asians to become cotton ginners themselves. Eventually, due to their knowledge of the local market, they undercut European sales and dominated the cotton ginning industry. In 1931 Ugandan Asians owned 155 out of 194 cotton ginneries in the region.[48] Asians also responded to modern demands in the market by becoming *fundis* (artisans), while handling import and export demands as dukawallahs and by working as bookkeepers for other shops and ginneries. Asian wholesalers dominated the Ugandan economy from the turn of the twentieth century through to the postindependence era. By the end of the Second World War, Ugandan Asians controlled the retail, wholesale, and manufacturing industries in the country. Although they accounted for 1 percent of the population, they continued to earn one-quarter of the national income (see Table 1).

Table 1. African and Non-African Income in Uganda in 1959, 1964, and 1967 (Million Shillings)

Income	Year		
	1959	1964	1967
African income	1,458	1,880	2,359
Non-African income	705	937	1,166
Total GDP	2,163	2,817	3,525

Source: Reproduced from Vali Jamal, "Asians in Uganda, 1880–1972: Inequality and Expulsion," *Economic History Review* 29, no. 4 (1976): 612.

Continued financial success encouraged further migration. The number of Ugandan Asians rose from 5,604 in 1921 to 77,400 in 1961.[49] By the early 1970s, Asians controlled an estimated 80 to 90 percent of Ugandan trade and owned nearly 80 percent of the commercial sector.[50]

Examples of early Asian pioneers demonstrate their participation in different areas of the Ugandan economy as well as the heterogeneity of the Ugandan Asian population. Allidina Visram is one of the most well known. Arriving in Uganda just before the turn of the century, Visram quickly installed himself as a cotton ginner and began experimenting with a large variety of imported crops for plantations. Using his early connections to a fellow Ismaili from Gujarat, Haji Paroo, Visram set the standard for other dukawallahs, who replicated his strategy of partnering with the British to build several dukas offering banking facilities along the railway lines. By 1910, Visram had created successful coconut oil, sesame oil, jaggery, and even hardboard manufacturing plants in both Uganda and Mombasa. By the year of his death in 1916, he had established a vast industrial, trading, and plantation empire, which included over 170 stores.[51] Other pioneers also became active within the economies of mainland East Africa. Augustino de Figueiredo migrated from Goa and opened a shop in the former capital of Uganda, Entebbe, in 1902. He initially sold a variety of goods but most importantly offered a tailoring section. Recognizing the demand for clothing in Uganda, he recruited forty additional tailors and opened new shops in Kampala and Jinja. Fazal Abdulla from the Shia Bohra Muslim community established the second major tailoring operation in Uganda in 1910. Many others from various religious and regional communities participated in the growing Ugandan economy by manufacturing goods, from furniture and upholstery for vehicles to soap, ghee, and safari tents.[52]

Two of the most famous Asian entrepreneurs were Nanji Kalidas Mehta and Muljibhai Prabhudas Madhvani. They were Hindus belonging to the Lohana caste (primarily a merchant class) who migrated from small villages in Saurashtra, a district of Gujarat. Both men established prominent economic empires that involved not only industrial production and manufacturing but also agriculture. Arriving in Uganda in the early 1900s, Mehta and Madhvani entered the agricultural sector after achieving initial success in cotton ginning. In 1924 Mehta built Uganda's first sugar factory, located in Lugazi between Jinja and Kampala. Paralleling the success of Mehta, Madhvani established another sugar empire based in Kakira, just six miles from Jinja. By the time of Madhvani's death in 1958, he had not only created his own company, but also diversified his economic interests by producing jaggery, refined sugar, oil, soap, maize, and many other products. As these pioneers demonstrate, numerous religious and regional groups from the Indian subcontinent were essential to Uganda's economic development. Industries were not dominated by a specific religious community, and as a whole Asians prospered in Uganda. As the numbers of migrants continued to grow, along with their success, Asians began to enter professions that often required a post-secondary degree.[53]

As the Asian migrant populations who arrived in the late 1800s moved into their second and third generations in East Africa, they transitioned to obtaining specialized training and university degrees, primarily in the fields of economics, business, law, medicine, and engineering. Historian Robert G. Gregory argues that this expansion into the secondary professions enabled the Asian community to further advance its economic enterprises through management skills and collaboration with international companies.[54] Asians were not only present in the major industries but also in crucial occupations in law, medicine, and teaching (see Table 2).

Table 2. Asian Representation by Occupational Sector in 1968

Sector	Country (%)		
	Kenya	Tanzania	Uganda
Agriculture	...	9	12
Commerce and finance	34	30	30
Manufacturing and industry	17	20	20
Public service	22	14	14
Transport and communications	17	15	12
Other services	10	12	12

Source: Reproduced from Desh Gupta, "South Asians in East Africa: Achievement and Discrimination," *South Asia: Journal of South Asian Studies* 21, no. 1 (January 1998): 130.

For example, it was a Ugandan Asian lawyer, Anil Clerk, who defended the first president of Uganda, Milton Obote, and later the next president, Idi Amin, in court. The presidents sought to clear their names of any associations with manipulation of postindependence politics.[55] Asians were also some of the first medical professionals, including dentists and pharmacists, in East Africa. They served all members of Ugandan society regardless of their private or public employment status.

With respect to teaching, Uganda followed the predominant trend throughout East Africa that saw an increased demand for teachers coinciding with the rapid construction of schools beginning in the 1920s. Some Ugandan Asians studied abroad in the United Kingdom and returned to become schoolteachers in Uganda. Delphine, for example, said, "Fortunately, they were thrilled to have me back in Uganda to teach and I did start off in an elementary school. That's what I was trained for, to be an elementary schoolteacher. But they thought I was overqualified, so I started teaching at the Shimoni teacher training college. So really I was teaching students to become teachers. They didn't call us quite professors, because I wasn't a professor, but they called us tutors."[56] Ugandan Asians established themselves throughout the country, not only in various urban and rural communities but also in a wide array of occupations. Their dominance within the business sector along with their infiltration into the secondary professions secured their position in the middle to upper classes of Ugandan society. This was facilitated by their privileged position under British rule, when they were actively placed as a buffer between the colonialists and local Ugandans.

The Colonial Sandwich

The three-tiered race and class hierarchy implemented by the British imperialists originated at the very beginnings of European imperial expansion in East Africa. With the creation of the British East Indian Company, and the eventual establishment of the East Africa Protectorate (the future country of Kenya) in 1894, the British colonialists had a firm presence in the region. As noted previously, Zanzibar served as an early example of the preference among imperialists for Asians to be employed as civil servants and merchants. The racialized system of colonial Uganda divided society into three distinct groups. Upper-class British imperialists were at the top, middle- to upper-class commercial Asians were in the middle, and the remaining Ugandans were at the bottom. This created a racial hierarchy of white, brown, and black. A Kenyan Asian immigrant to Canada in the 1970s, N. Rahemtulla, described the racialized colonial atmosphere as follows: "The black man was ignorant and lazy, the white man the master and a superior being as he would have us believe. I, the Asian, was neither. I had no choice but to work like crazy or face starvation."[57] Rahemtulla's comments allude to the many ways in which false notions of East Africans as "ignorant and lazy" were also held by some members of the South Asian community. The colonial sandwich was predicated on European notions of race, class, ethnicity, and religion and was used as a means of maintaining British hegemony and white supremacy throughout the East Africa. Divide-and-rule tactics deployed by the imperialist system reinforced the middle-class position of Ugandan Asians, which not only intensified their minority status but also amplified their position as a mercantile class. Since their privileging in Zanzibar, Asians continued to be preferred as the primary merchants and traders in East Africa.

The ability of Ugandan Africans to participate in import–export trade was purposefully repressed as a means of solidifying class divisions within society. Ultimately, this gave rise to a process in which local Ugandans consistently interacted with Asians in all commercial relations. African historian Semakula Kiwanuka argues that "the only real and significant contacts between the races were those in the market place: between seller and buyer, between trader and customer and between master and servant."[58] This was further exacerbated in the civil service sector, frustrating local Ugandans and promoting ethnic conflict between Asians and Africans.[59] For example, the colonial administration forced Ugandan Africans to go through Ugandan Asian clerks in order to gain access to European officers. This meant that any grievances faced by Ugandan Africans, including those related to poor treatment from Ugandan Asian employers and limited employability within the government as designed by the imperialists, forced them to go through the Ugandan Asian clerks first. Inevitably, this placed Ugandan Asians in an uncomfortable position within the country's bureaucracy. The race and class hierarchy was a means of protecting European imperialists from any local resistance.

By manipulating the economic and social system to their advantage, colonialists devised a societal structure where the minority Ugandan Asian population was viewed as the perpetrators of exploitative policies. Since Asians were positioned as a buffer between the British and the indigenous population, animosity was directed toward the Asian community as opposed to the true perpetrators of exploitation. Ugandan Asians did benefit from the colonial system though. At a bureaucratic level they quashed grievances from Ugandan Africans while others continued to exploit labourers in manufacturing and agricultural businesses.[60] These sentiments extended throughout East Africa in the 1900s and were used by various newly independent governments as a means of justifying discriminatory policies towards the Asian community. Within Uganda in particular, these tensions led to the popular idea that "he is rich because he is an Asian and I am poor because I am an African."[61] This would serve as one of the most convincing justifications for Idi Amin's expulsion decree in 1972.

The colonial sandwich played a crucial role in the economic structures of Uganda before independence and was embedded in society in numerous ways. Segregation manifested itself through separate

bathrooms for each racial group in the civil service sector, which
progressed to separate schools, hospitals, and residential neighbourhoods. Segregation spread throughout society and every aspect of life
to the extent that when a Ugandan Asian chose to donate blood they
"were taken to the Red Cross' Indian Blood Bank."[62] Racial divisions
went as far as sporting competitions, where Europeans played field
hockey against South Asian and African teams. The Lowis Cup, later
called the pentangular games, is indicative of how sporting teams
were further subdivided based not only on national origin but religious and regional affiliations. The Lowis Cup was awarded annually
to the winners of a five-team cricket tournament in Kampala that was
initiated by Uganda's Goan community and later extended to include
other sports such as field hockey and badminton. Jalal described
playing in the tournament, recalling that "it used to be what they
called the pentangular games. Indians or Hindus, Muslims, Goans,
Africans, and Europeans [were the teams]. Now because Indians
were so powerful, they broke it up into Muslims, Goans, and Indians,
meaning Hindus. So the five ethnic groups, we would play cricket
. . . as a tournament and I happened to get selected to play cricket
for the Uganda Muslims."[63] These five teams recruited other players
from areas such as Mbarara, Mbale, Masaka, and Jinja, where local
leagues were also divided by region and religion.

According to some scholars, these subdivisions were further amplified by self-segregation and beliefs of cultural superiority among
Ugandan Asians.[64] Sociologist Benson Chukwuma Morah offers
the most detailed account regarding such beliefs. He argues that the
lack of rich cultural traditions in Uganda from the Asian perspective
along with the reluctance of Africans to embrace and appreciate the
practices brought by Asians troubled members of the community,
as they believed they were the bearers of a rich cultural tradition.[65]
To build on this critique, Morah identifies how Ugandan Africans
did not observe any dietary restrictions associated with religion and
thus were seen to lack any form of ritualistic purity. Other scholars
articulate how Asians wanted to be left to their own communities
as a means of pursuing their traditional ways. Historian Michael
Twaddle points to the institutionalization of various Asian communities through self-imposed segregation as they constructed their
own cemeteries, schools, and recreation centres along with places

of community care and worship.[66] Furthermore, Morah extends his argument of cultural superiority to include ideologies of racial superiority, asserting that Asians "did not hide their disdain for the African physiognomy and person; coming from a cultural tradition where everything 'fair' is synonymous with 'handsome,' 'good looking,' and everything dark synonymous with 'ugliness,' 'low caste,' 'not fit for contact,' 'loose morals' and 'excellence in sexual dalliance.'"[67] As these scholars argue, some Asians viewed themselves as above Africans, as evidenced by the growing presence of separate institutions and perceptions of superior cultural and religious customs. Given these beliefs, many local Ugandans began to hold negative views of the Asian community, who dominated commercial relations and looked down upon Ugandan society.

Tensions between the two communities were heightened throughout the mid-twentieth century to the point that Ugandan Africans commonly expressed their frustrations in local media. For example, opinion pieces during the expulsion period would depict Asians as "those parasites who suckle at Uganda, our mother" or address them as "you bloody Indian."[68] General animosity towards Asians in East Africa dates to the beginning of imperialism in the region. British colonialists described the Asian community as "crafty, money-making, cunning . . . the local Jew; unscrupulous and single-minded in the pursuit of gain; a user of false weights and measures, a receiver of stolen goods, and a 'Banyan' contemplating his account book."[69] Ugandan historian Dent Ocaya-Lakidi argues that these views would inevitably be internalized by East Africans socialized through the British education system in the Uganda Protectorate. While Ugandan Africans lacked political power during the colonial period, they did not refrain from identifying the "Asian problem." An opinion piece from the early 1920s captures the growing discontent and foreshadows the expulsion decree, stating, "As we have no power to command Indians to get out of our country, we must protest and dispute every inch of the way so that they shall not get what they want in our country."[70] This would form the basis for rising tensions between the Asian and African communities in Uganda.

Another critical moment for preindependence relations between the two groups was the boycott of Asian goods in 1959. This stemmed from a deeper historical plight among the people of Buganda, one of Uganda's five traditional kingdoms, who were given a privileged position by the colonial administration in relation to the other kingdoms, and who had launched an earlier campaign against the Asians in the mid-1930s. The Young Baganda Association charged the Asian community with inhibiting the upward mobility of Ugandan Africans, arguing that "Indians of this type [merchant and business class] are the very people who . . . occupy positions which should have afforded outlets to Africans."[71] By 1959 the Uganda National Movement—comprised largely of the rising black middle class in Buganda—had removed approximately half of the Asian businessmen from Buganda using violence and intimidation. In response, the colonial government arrested several leading officials in the Uganda National Movement, banned the party, and threatened to sanction Buganda until its king, Mutesa II, issued a formal apology condemning the party's actions.[72] The position of Asians in Uganda became increasingly more contentious at the dawn of Uganda's independence.

Once independence was achieved in 1962, the grievances of Ugandan African traders subject to Asian monopolies in the commercial industry continued under the rule of President Obote. To respond to these grievances, in 1966 Obote created the Produce Marketing Board (PMB), which appointed Ugandan Africans in the bureaucracy to control the purchasing and selling of agricultural goods.[73] In an attempt to circumvent the dominance of Asian sellers, the board's role was to establish fair prices and returns for the urban working class and peasantry in Uganda by setting price controls. However, due to limited assets, the board was unable to hold on to their stock for long periods and were forced to resell their acquired goods back to the Asians at a modest profit. In turn, enterprising Asian businessmen continued purchasing agricultural products from the board and maximized monopoly profits. This led to a triple burden of exploitation for Ugandan growers, who were subject to poor returns on their initial produce, bought by agricultural cooperatives and the Produce Marketing Board, which sought quick returns on their purchases, and inflated prices created by the Asian monopolies. The failure of the newly independent government to provide any tangible solution to the "Asian problem" during the initial years of independence would serve as a motivating factor behind President Obote's aggressive socialist campaign in the late 1960s. However, these main conflicts did not deter Ugandan Asians from participating in local politics, both before and after independence, or from fostering positive relationships with Ugandan Africans.

In the years following the conclusion of the First World War, Ugandan Asians sought representative appointments within the Legislative Council of Uganda. All members of the Legislative Council were Europeans. To respond to grievances from the Asian community but also maintain the colonial system, the governor appointed only one Asian for every two European members. The Asian community then boycotted the Legislative Council for five years.[74] Clashes between the colonial government and the Asian community continued beyond the interwar period as Asians fought for proportional representation. The community's subdivisions along religious and regional lines persisted in their political efforts, and no unified South Asian political organization emerged. Instead, several political groups with distinct vested interests were created. The first was the Kampala Indian Association, founded in 1908 by a group of local businessmen to serve as a rallying point for all Asians living in the major city. The second was the Central Council of Indian Associations (CCIA), founded in 1921 with the intent of being the premier representative body for all Asians living throughout Uganda. It would also serve as a lobbying group for Asian social, economic, political, and educational interests. The Indian Merchants' Chamber, established in 1924, aimed to influence colonial policies on economic practices and major business deals.[75] As each of the newly created groups possessed various special interests, they were unable to effectively lobby the colonial government for representative political control. These organizations also competed with the rising political consciousness of Ugandan Africans.

On the eve of independence throughout East Africa, many South Asian leaders sought to reaffirm their privileged position. After the 1959 boycott of Asian goods in Buganda, some business leaders felt threatened by the increase in African nationalism. Under these conditions, the CCIA demanded constitutional safeguards as a means of maintaining a specific South Asian voice within the political sphere. However, its conservative views ran counter to the majority of Asians, who strongly sympathized with African nationalists fighting for self-determination. Considering the recent establishment of self-rule

within the Indian subcontinent, the CCIA was seen as hypocritical
by many Asians in the community. These sentiments were articulated
through the 1958 creation of the Uganda Action Group (UAG) by
a group of young Asians. The group's primary goal was to dispel the
ideology of the "old guard" of Asian leadership within Uganda and
lobby for the admittance of Asians within African political parties.
The UAG vehemently opposed having reserved minority seats for
Asians within the National Assembly and opted for a more inclusive
approach to politics that was devoid of racially based representation.
Ultimately, the UAG persuaded the Legislative Council and others
in the Asian community that the CCIA was actually against "special
representation" for Asians and that "adequate representation on the
Legislative Council for non-Africans should be secured by their full
participation."[76] However, early attempts by the Asian community
to support African nationalism did not last during Uganda's first
years of independence. The UAG was unable to garner significant
support from the Ugandan Asian and African communities and
subsequently fizzled out. It is evident that Asians did attempt to
support African nationalism; however, their status as "colonial collaborators" and their advantaged economic positions, alongside their
perceived self-imposed social exclusivity, diminished these efforts.
They did not succeed in altering perceptions of their engagement
in economic exploitation and avoiding the traditional scapegoating
of the Asian community in Uganda. The remnants of colonial rule
prevented Asians and Africans from uniting politically.

Despite the failed attempts of the Asian community to participate
politically in Uganda, members did make several major contributions
to Ugandan society, improving the livelihoods of all Ugandans. The
vast majority of philanthropy practised by the Asian community came
in the form of schooling or the extension of social services for all
people living in East Africa. The rapid construction of schools that
began in the 1920s took place within each of the racial communities
in Uganda, but in the Asian community the schools were segregated
along religious and regional lines. Initially, most of the Asian schools
offered curricula that focused on religious instruction and language
retention (primarily Gujarati or Konkani for the Goan community),
and incorporated material that focused on the Indian subcontinent
in the subjects of history and geography. Eventually these privately

funded initiatives received government funding. In 1959, before independence, the majority of the seventy-seven primary schools in Uganda were technically open to all but were largely attended by Asian students.[77] By the early years of independence, however, these schools accepted all students. For example, the Allidina Visram High School accepted students of all backgrounds starting in the early 1960s, and hired its first African faculty member in 1965 and its first African headmaster in 1970. Asian conceptions of inclusivity cannot entirely account for the growth of diversity in schools though. Many Ugandan Asians were aware that with the coming of independence one of the first elements of society to change would be racially seg-regated schools. Further, not all institutions in Uganda had remained rigidly segregated along racial lines; there were exceptions to the rule. Based on the principles of brotherhood among all believers, Muslim religious institutions tended to be open to all Muslim students. For instance, the Bohra Muslim community opened its first school in Kisumu, Uganda, in 1929 for Africans, Arabs, and Asians; by 1937, 90 percent of the students were Ugandan Africans.[78]

Undoubtedly, the Madhvanis and the Mehtas, two of the most prominent Ugandan Asian business families, made significant con-tributions to the schooling of both Asian and African children. Both families established schools—from nursery to secondary schools— for their employees' families. The Madhvani family also opened the Muljibhai College of Commerce in Kampala in 1950 to educate and train Ugandan Africans in business management and other technical skills. Graduates were hired into management positions within the Madhvani company structure.[79] Beyond these contributions, the leader of the Ismaili Muslim community, Aga Khan III, founded the East African Muslim Welfare Society in an attempt to break down racial barriers between Muslims and to reinforce a pan-Islamic identity. Ismailis remained the key contributors to the organization, which was ultimately responsible for building seventy-five schools, sixty-three mosques, a training college, and a technical school from 1945 to 1957.[80] Furthermore, many members of the Asian com-munity engaged in philanthropic and humanitarian efforts with their African labourers on a microscale. Historian Phillip Gregory argues that Asians who developed close relationships with Ugandan Africans often subsidized their school fees.[81] These efforts mirrored the overall philanthropic sentiment among Asian communities in East Africa; culturally, charitable giving within their means was considered a duty. Ugandan Asians' attempted political involvement and philanthropic works, alongside evidence from oral histories, challenged the rigid race and class hierarchy.

Although there remained a stark divide between the Asian and African communities, the colonial hierarchy was not impermeable. Several scholars have debated the impacts of the rigid race and class structure in Uganda. For example, historian Desh Gupta argues that a significant proportion of Ugandan Asians came to view the country as their permanent home, as demonstrated by the increased percentage of spouses who lived with their partners, which increased from just 20 percent in 1911 to upwards of 50 percent by 1931.[82] Furthermore, Asians did not reside only in the major urban areas of Uganda. Communities such as the Ismailis, as well as other Muslim, Hindu, Sikh, and Christian communities, inhabited various regions within Uganda. For example, in a Ugandan Asian autobiography, Noordin Somji outlines how in the 1950s and 1960s he visited numerous Ismaili religious schools throughout Uganda, including in Jinja, Mbale, Soroti, Lira, Kaberamaido, Gulu, Masaka, Mbarara, Fort Portal, and Kisumu, as well as smaller towns such as Mubende, Mityana, Nagalama, Kikandwa, Wobulenzi, Masindi Port, and Murchison Falls.[83]

Another indication that Asians were moving towards a Ugandan identity was the greater levels of fluency in both English and Swahili among the younger generations. Historian J.S. Mangat maintains that exposure to an urbanized environment, school systems based on Western models, and improved standards of living led to shifts in dietary habits, dress, and language among Ugandan Asians.[84] A study conducted just before the expulsion decree in Uganda found that approximately 74 percent of respondents preferred to remain in Uganda as opposed to returning to India.[85] The transition whereby Asians came to view themselves as East Africans challenges the conception of distinct boundaries between the Asian and African communities held by some scholars. Despite rhetoric used by the colonialists and Idi Amin's regime, few Asians returned to India to retire; a significant majority of them considered themselves to be permanent residents of East Africa.

Several Ugandan Asian novelists, including Bahadur Tejani, Peter Nazareth, and Shenaaz Nanji complicate the realities of the colonial sandwich in their work. In his 1971 novel, *Day After Tomorrow*, Tejani questions the sense of belonging of South Asian migrants living in East Africa by denouncing their in-group exclusivity, incomplete integration into society, and propagation of separate South Asian cultural and religious affiliations. His work falls in line with those scholars who are critical of the South Asian community for allegedly opting for self-imposed segregation. The emotional pain of many Ugandan Asian expellees is articulated in Nazareth's 1972 novel, *In a Brown Mantle*. As the protagonist bids farewell to Uganda while on a plane to London, he exclaims, "Goodbye, Mother Africa . . . your bastard son loved you."[86] Nazareth's protagonist truly experiences a sense of belonging in Africa and feels betrayed upon expulsion. Nanji's *Child of Dandelions* firmly expresses the deep attachments to Uganda held by some members of the Asian community. The grandfather of the main character in the novel explains that he and his African partner cannot leave Uganda: "The Kasenda earth is soaked with my blood, my sweat, and my tears. My farms, the coffee beans, they're part of who I am. This is home. Halima and I cannot leave our home."[87] These authors collectively affirm the ambiguity of colonial race relations in Uganda and illuminate the multifaceted connections between Ugandan Asians and Ugandan Africans. Their fictional works demonstrate the two major arguments presented by scholars regarding interactions between the two communities: Ugandan Asians either firmly adhered to the racial and class-based divides, or they cultivated relationships with Ugandan Africans and truly identified with Uganda as their homeland.

Oral histories I conducted with Ugandan Asian refugees in Canada also problematize the lived realities of the colonial hierarchy. As a former civil servant, John N. argued that in the 1960s and 1970s, "There was very little discrimination against Asians. . . . If you were a Ugandan, whatever colour you were, you got treatment. I went to university. The country paid for my whole education. They even gave us some money for books and so on. We never had to pay a thing. They even gave us pocket money. . . . They didn't say 'oh you were an Asian, you can afford more.' . . . When it comes to jobs, they [Ugandan Africans in the government] never discriminated against us. So in the government there was loads of people of Indian origin, and Goans were very big in the civil service."[88] In his oral testimony, John N. identified instances where Ugandan Asians and Ugandan Africans had cordial relations before the expulsion decree. This re-affirmed attachments to Uganda while challenging the conception of a divisive race- and class-based hierarchy. Other interviewees explained how some community members did hold prejudicial views of Ugandan Africans.

> Karim: But he [Father] was such a diehard, and I think one of the things that I would say to you, what has even been more painful in my life is to watch my dad suffer through the fact that this country [Uganda] really let him down. He invest-ed in this country heart, soul, everything, ok? To the point where there were other Asians who were sending money into other countries [but] my dad never did. He came here with twenty-three dollars and that's all. There's no sort of. . . .
>
> Interviewer: Offshore bank account.
>
> Karim: No, there's nothing. You know, his own brothers . . . had offshore money. He believed in this country and he be-lieved this country would never do this to him. But it did.[89]

Karim's remarks show the intricacies of race relations in Uganda. The colonialist structure of divide and rule was effective to a certain extent, but it by no means impacted Ugandan Asians universally. Some Ugandan Asians felt tied directly to the country and integrated consciously into Ugandan society, and others remained cautious or reluctant to embrace it. A testimony from Sikandar, an oral history participant quoted under a pseudonym, showcases some of the abuse against Ugandan Africans, supplementing the scholarly views of Asian self-segregation and prejudice:

> Some of the things we did there was wrong. We treated them [Ugandan Africans] very bad. I've seen people finish eating food and what is leftover they were giving to their houseboys. Everybody did that and everybody is denying it! My brother once told me, he said, "How can we do this? We make the guy sign for five shillings forty cents and you pay

him three shillings." I said, "That's slavery." You know what was the answer? If he doesn't want a job, his brother will take it. What an attitude! How did I feel when I was treated in Canada working [from] eight [o'clock] to eight [o'clock] and getting paid for eight hours, don't they realize that? But part of it was lots of us were exploiting the country.[90]

Sikandar's testimony provides direct insight into the exploitation of the local population, reinforcing criticisms of the Ugandan Asian community as brown colonialists who replaced the British. Other oral history participants also described prejudicial attitudes towards Ugandan Africans among the Ugandan Asian community. Considering the factors that initially brought South Asians to Uganda, their economic dominance in the country, and the complex realities of the colonial sandwich, Ugandan independence would present Ugandan Asians with a dilemma, especially with regards to citizenship.

Ugandan Independence

The issue of Ugandan citizenship arose in October 1962 when section 7 of the newly formed constitution declared that "all persons born in Uganda who were citizens of the United Kingdom and Colonies, or British protected persons, should become citizens of Uganda on 9 October 1962."[91] Additional provisions within the 1962 constitution outlined four major concepts regarding citizenship. First, second- and third-generation British Asians automatically became Ugandan citizens because they had at least one parent or grandparent who was born in Uganda. Second, all those born after 9 October 1962 were considered citizens. Third, only British-protected persons or naturalized British citizens were eligible to apply for citizenship. This meant people who held Indian or Pakistani citizenship were ineligible. Finally, those who wished to become Ugandan citizens needed to apply within two years. The most pertinent feature of the new citizenship regulations was the requirement for individuals to submit proof they had renounced their British citizenship within three months of securing Ugandan citizenship. Those who failed to produce sufficient evidence were considered noncitizens and rendered illegal.

The British authorities would not effectively revoke a person's citizenship until they received proof of a passport newly acquired from

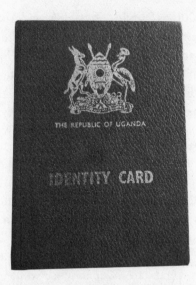

Figure 1. Red identity or *kipande* cards that all Ugandan Asians carried with them after the census verification in the 1970s. Image credit: © Shezan Muhammedi.

another country. Although this provision was meant to protect UK citizens abroad, it made the acquisition of a valid Ugandan passport far more difficult. Ugandan Asians navigated a convoluted citizenship process between the Ugandan and UK governments. First, they needed to submit their newly acquired Ugandan passports to the UK. Second, they needed official confirmation from the UK government that they were giving up their British citizenship, which they received via a letter sent from the UK Home Office. Third, they had to forward the letter to the Ugandan authorities to show they had renounced their British citizenship. All three steps had to be completed within three months, which was incredibly difficult given bureaucratic delays and lengthy mailing procedures.

The question of citizenship raised difficult political and personal questions for Ugandan Asians, most of whom held British passports. What were the expectations of Ugandan citizens with regards to their loyalty and allegiance? Were they to put their South Asian identity before or after their Ugandan identity? Those who had sided with independence movements were seen by Ugandan Africans as opportunistic and simply taking advantage of independence for social and economic benefits. On the other hand, those who had collaborated with the

Europeans were accused of disloyalty and hindering African aspirations for self-government. Regardless of their position, legal scholar Meir Amor argues, all Asians were discriminated against on racial grounds.[92] Nonetheless, it was clear that for the newly independent East African governments, discrimination was based on citizenship rather than race as a legitimate means of dealing with the Asian minority. To make matters worse for the Asian community, the East African governments were pushing towards Africanization policies to promote black African national identity and return economic and political control to black East Africans. The move towards Africanization in both the public and private sectors, the need to make a decision about citizenship, and the continuous scapegoating of the Asian community created a major dilemma for Asians living in East Africa.

Asian subcommunities responded differently to the new legislation. Ismaili Muslims overwhelmingly adopted Ugandan citizenship, presumably based on the guidance of their spiritual leader, the Aga Khan IV, who advised the community to acquire Ugandan citizenship to reduce tensions with local Ugandans.[93] Other subcommunities were placed in a rather difficult position. The Goans were predominantly civil servants. As employees of the colonial government, they faced a clear conflict of interest in terms of making any formal and public endorsements or criticisms of the new legislation. As more aggressive Africanization policies were implemented throughout Uganda, many business owners opted to become citizens. For example, with the creation of the 1969 Trade Licensing Act, companies or firms within Uganda would be considered locally owned only if at least 50 percent of the capital or property was owned by a citizen.[94] These pressures continued to mount against Ugandan Asian business owners under the country's first two presidents.

Uganda's first president (1962–1971), Dr. Milton Obote, made several attempts to put control of the economy into the hands of Ugandans. The Trade and Licensing Act, for example, made it obligatory for all noncitizens—mainly the Asians who had opted for British citizenship during Ugandan independence—to acquire a valid licence and demonstrate possession of £4,000 in liquid capital. This was a direct attack on the small-scale dukawallahs, who did not possess such assets. The Asian response to the act was to allow levels of essential supplies to fall, causing an immediate rise in pricing.

They increased their marginal profits and deposited their funds abroad. Responding to government legislation on trade by exploiting consumers with higher prices demonstrated the ways in which some Ugandan Asian participated in economic sabotage. Some also bribed government officials to allow them to continue to do business without a licence, and hired Ugandan Africans to act as frontmen so their shops appeared to be owned by the local population. In some instances, through their control of real estate, Asians inhibited the aspirations of Ugandan Africans who sought to become urban entrepreneurs.[95] Obote also championed the Move to the Left program and 60 percent government ownership of major foreign companies as outlined in the 1970 Nakivubo Pronouncements.[96]

Instead of redistributing newly acquired wealth towards the Ugandan business class and encouraging the development of a black Ugandan commercial class, Obote allowed Europeans and Asians to further penetrate the agricultural and industrial markets. His primary motive for promoting non-Ugandan businesses pertained to his preferential treatment of the Langi and Acholi peoples. Obote was initially against the Africanization of the Ugandan economy, because it would leave the majority of businesses in the hands of the Baganda (the people of Buganda), who were the most educated Ugandans. He let the Europeans and Asians retain economic control until the late 1960s and '70s, when he issued the Common Man's Charter and Nakivubo Pronouncements. The next president of Uganda, Major General Idi Amin, would seek to rectify the grievances of the Baganda and other tribes and return economic control of the country to Ugandan Africans. Taking his cues from Kenya and Tanzania, Amin set his sights on dealing with the "Asian problem."

Major nationalization programs took place in postindependence Kenya and Tanzania in the late 1960s to restore economic control to black Africans. Similar to Uganda, Kenya used the rhetoric of Africanization when taking economic control from the Asian community, whereas Tanzania rallied behind the socialist cause. Six years after Tanzania secured independence came President Nyerere's Arusha Declaration of 5 February 1967.[97] The goal of the program was to return the means of production to Tanzanians, and it led to the immediate nationalization of several industries, including all banks and insurance companies, several import–export organizations, and majority ownership of all industrial companies. Tanzania opted to avoid the perilous realm of racial politics and firmly established its nationalization program as a socialist measure. The country's citizenship practices at the time of independence replicated those of Uganda by providing Asians with an opportunity to choose local citizenship or reaffirm their British nationality. However, Tanzania did not force those who applied for citizenship to show proof of renunciation of their British citizenship, ultimately making it easier for them to opt for citizenship. This resulted in approximately sixty thousand Asians becoming citizens of Tanzania.[98]

President Nyerere argued that socialism could not be carried out on a policy of racialism. "Like water and oil, they never mix," he said. "I am absolutely certain that if we distinguish between the Indians who are exploiters and those who are exploited, and if we resolve to treat the exploited the same way as other workers they will help us to implement our policies of socialism and self-reliance."[99] Although it was made clear that nationalization policies were targeted at "exploiters," they inherently affected the entire Asian community. Furthermore, the Tanzanian government granted immigration officials the power to expel any noncitizens from the country, leading to the deportation of three hundred Asians in 1967.[100] Tanzania's nationalization program led large numbers of the Asian community to leave the country, but it was not rooted in any overt form of racial discrimination.

Four years after Kenyan independence, a new immigration act forced all European and Asian residents who had not become Kenyan citizens to apply for work permits to remain in the country. Although permits could be renewed on an annual basis, noncitizens needed to sufficiently prove that no Kenyan citizen was qualified to carry out the specified mode of labour. This was not considered to be a racial law, as it targeted those who were not Kenyan citizens, much in the same way that Obote's Move to the Left program only targeted non-Ugandan citizens. It was a systemic way for the Kenyan government to deal with the "Asian problem" without creating a form of obvious discrimination, which Uganda subsequently replicated in the 1969 Trade Licensing Act. In 1967 only 70,000 of the total 190,000 Asians in Kenya had accepted Kenyan citizenship.[101] Kenya's 1967 Immigration Act, enacted on 1 December, prompted 15,000 Asians to leave the country in 1968.[102]

Editorial comments in Kenyan newspapers articulated the general
feelings of animosity towards the Asian community that accompanied
the new nationalization policies: "One way or the other, Asians in
Kenya must be made to modify their unscrupulous trade attitudes at
once. We cannot brag about building a harmonious multi-racial state
amidst trade turbulency [*sic*]. . . . Whatever the future will be, the Asian
community has nothing to grumble about; the present trend, whether
good or bad, is the harvest of seeds sown by themselves."[103] Both major
forms of legislation implemented in Kenya and Tanzania would ultimately have adverse effects on the freedom of Commonwealth citizens
to immigrate to Britain.

In early 1968, as the three major East African countries dealt
with their respective Asian populations by implementing socialist or
Africanization policies, the number of migrants moving from East
Africa to the United Kingdom increased dramatically. Typically,
Britain received three thousand East African immigrants per year,
but it was faced with six thousand arrivals within the first two months
of 1968.[104] Nativist sentiments in Britain were considerably high as
decolonization led to rising numbers of migrants arriving in the country. Politicians such as conservative members of Parliament Sir Cyril
Osborne and Enoch Powell openly expressed unapologetically racist
sentiments. Osborne attacked those who supported increased levels
of Commonwealth immigration in a 1964 newspaper and argued that
"those who oppose the slogan 'Keep Britain White' should answer the
question, do they want to turn it black? If unlimited immigration were
allowed, we should ultimately become a chocolate-coloured, Afro-
Asian mixed society. That I do not want."[105] By the end of February
1968, the British government made a significant amendment to the
Commonwealth Immigration Act of 1962.[106] The updated legislation
prevented migrants whose parents and grandparents were not naturalized British citizens, largely from former British colonies, from
migrating to the United Kingdom, mirroring the same amendments
made to Ugandan citizenship in 1964. The position of the British in
conjunction with the policies enacted in other areas of East Africa
served as possible models for dealing with the Asian minority population in Uganda. However, Amin found his own way.

Amin overthrew Obote on 25 January 1971.[107] He announced an
eighteen-point memorandum on Radio Uganda justifying his military

coup. Initially, the coup was welcomed by many, especially by the Baganda, who had experienced extreme hardships under the rule of Obote. Asians also favoured Amin, as they hoped for a restoration of previous economic conditions. Oral history participant Amin V. recalled how "the Asian community was flabbergasted that 'things are going to happen now, they are going to be in our favour'... I guess for a year it was, and then everything went haywire.... That first year when Idi Amin was there I don't think anybody had any problems."[108]

The first sign of Amin's plan for expulsion came in October 1971, when he ordered a verification of the official census data on the Asian community. According to the 1969 census figures, 74,308 Asians were in the country, of which 25,657 were citizens and 48,651 were not.[109] The verification process mandated that every member of the Asian community report their citizenship status to the government. From that point onwards, all Ugandan Asians were required to carry census receipts. Those who did not present themselves for verification forfeited their rights to live in Uganda in what was referred to by Ugandan Asian historian Hasu H. Patel as the "cattle count."[110] No official numbers were ever released after the verification, and the Ugandan government continued to operate using the 1969 census numbers. There was some early indication during the census verification that drastic measures would be taken towards the Asian community. According to local media outlets, this process clearly demarcated "who is a citizen and who is not," and "the declared Asian citizen of Uganda might have to start taking a hard look at the practical aspects of what is really meant by being integrated into the greater population."[111]

Towards the end of Amin's first year in power, he began to curtail the effects of a Ugandan Asian–dominated market. On 7 December 1971 he called for a meeting with leaders of the Ugandan Asian community to articulate his government's grievances against the Ugandan Asian community. In his speech at the Indian conference, he brought three distinct issues to the fore, underscoring his major claims of economic sabotage and social exclusivity by the Asian community. First, Amin criticized Ugandan Asians who attained a professional degree with state funds but chose to work outside of the public service. Citing several statistical reports, he argued that of the 417 Ugandan Asian engineers who received state scholarships from 1962 to 1968, only 20 currently worked for the government. Furthermore, 217 Ugandan Asian doctors and 96 Ugandan Asian lawyers had received similar funding in the same period, and only 15 and 18, respectively, were working for the government.[112] Tying the exploitation of state-offered benefits to specific critiques of the "commercial and tax malpractices of the Asian traders and businessmen,"[113] Amin depicted the Asian community as disloyal. "We are, for instance, aware of the fact that some Asians are the most notorious people in the abuse of our exchange and control regulations," he said. "Some of you are known to export goods and not to bring the foreign exchange back into Uganda. On the other hand, some of you are known to undervalue exports and overvalue imports in order to keep the difference in values in your overseas accounts. Another malpractice for which many of you are notorious is that of smuggling commodities like sugar, maize, hoes etc. from Uganda to the neighbouring territories."[114] Price gouging by Asian business owners after the 1969 Trade Licensing Act substantiated Amin's accusations of economic sabotage. The oral histories from Karim and Sikandar also provide some substantiation.

According to Amin, Ugandan Asians had "no interest in this country beyond the aim of making as much of a profit as possible and at all costs" and he promised that "if any businessman is found smuggling or hoarding goods in this country, such businessman should not expect any mercy and he will permanently lose his trading license whether he is a citizen of this country or not."[115] A crucial element in this portion of his speech is the reference to loose principles of citizenship. Amin was not afraid to revoke a trading licence regardless of the holder's status. He extended his theme of malpractice to include a charge of nepotism against Asian business owners. When prompted by officials to employ Ugandan Africans in higher positions, Ugandan Asians used locals as "mere window-dressing," Amin said, and "those Africans whom you have employed, although they earn fat salaries, know next to nothing as far as the secrets of your enterprises are concerned."[116] Amin argued that Ugandan Africans lacked any real authority or ability to conduct any form of business, demonstrating the failure of Ugandan Asians to trust their fellow Ugandans.

Amin also attacked the failure of Ugandan Asians to integrate socially with Ugandan Africans, primarily in terms of a reluctance to intermarry. Although there were some instances of intermarriage, a general reluctance to engage in this practice prevailed within the Ugandan

Asian community. As historian Gardner Thompson argues, "Ismaili girls reacted in horror at the suggestion for accelerated intermarriage made at the Asian Conference convened by President Amin in December 1971 ... for the community, not only racial but religious integrity would have been lost."[117] Amin said the community had "continued to live in a world of its own; for example, African males have hardly been able to marry Asian females. The facts reveal that there are only six. And even then, all the six married these women when they were abroad, and not here in Uganda."[118] For Amin, intermarriage was a direct measure of good faith among the Ugandan Asian community. Ugandan Asians, he said, were at fault for the hostility directed at them: "it is you yourselves, through your refusal to integrate with Africans in this country, who have created this feeling towards you by the Africans."[119]

Beyond intermarriage, Amin revisited the issue of Asians who had not opted for Ugandan citizenship. He articulated in his speech that anyone who obtained citizenship before the coup under lawful measures could rest assured that their passports would be recognized. However, he made specific reference to those who may have forged their documents or obtained them through illegal measures. The citizenship status of Ugandan Asians remained precarious, as it was within the purview of government officials to arbitrarily decide whether any form of documentation was acquired legitimately. The president took this opportunity to lament Ugandan Asians who did not opt for citizenship and argued that "my Government is disturbed because it is clear that many of you have not shown sufficient faith in Uganda citizenship. . . . Therefore I will remind you that, if there is any blame which you might later on wish to bring against my Government about your citizenship, the persons responsible for any confusion were yourselves."[120] Again, the blame was placed on the Ugandan Asian community. Amin's speech portrayed the reluctance of some Asians to adopt Ugandan citizenship as a manifestation of the entire community's disloyalty. For Amin, all Ugandan Asians, regardless of their citizenship status, had taken advantage of the local community. At no point did he mention the colonial government's favouritism towards the Ugandan Asian community as a source of tarnished relations between the communities.

The Ugandan Asian leaders in attendance at the meeting responded openly to Amin's grievances. The Indian conference had three major outcomes for the Ugandan Asian community. First, the racialized issue of black Ugandans making a claim for the Africanization of the country's economy came into focus. Second, there was no differentiation between citizen and noncitizen Ugandan Asians, showing for the first time that formal citizenship in Uganda was a loose concept. Last, Amin unintentionally united Ugandan Asians regardless of their citizenship status, social position, ethnicity, or religious background. They did not stand idly by as Amin criticized the community and fuelled animosity towards them. During the conference, they said that Amin's regime was spreading "false, malicious, and inflammatory and racial propaganda levelled against the Asians in the new media."[121] Their response to Amin's allegations also justified their opposition to intermarriage, stating that "opposition to inter-caste, inter-tribal, inter-communal, and inter-racial marriage is a familiar phenomenon to be encountered in any society in any country in the world."[122]

The Ugandan Asian community decried the claims of economic sabotage as illegitimate. They argued that the 1969 Trade Licensing Act and the Immigration Act worked in favour of Ugandan Africans and created a near-virtual monopoly "for black Ugandans in cotton, coffee and tea processing, and marketing industries."[123] Historians Nicholas Van Hear and Thomas Melady and Margaret Melady argue that Amin's charges of economic sabotage were a self-fulfilling prophecy, as community members opted to send money abroad when they feared the loss of their economic position based on Obote's 60 percent ownership program and Amin's subsequent tightening of regulations related to Asian commercial practices.[124] However, as noted by Van Hear and Melady and Melady, only a few select members of the community possessed the means and ability to invest or save money abroad.[125] Ultimately, the meeting foreshadowed the expulsion decree, as Amin laid the foundations for his accusations and ignored the responses presented by the leaders of the Ugandan Asian community.

A host of factors contributed to the historical context surrounding the expulsion decree in 1972. The newly independent government in Uganda did not acknowledge the deep historical roots of the Asian community despite its significant contributions to developing several regions of the country. The three major groups of South Asian immigrants, who initially worked as indentured labourers, civil service workers, and shopkeepers, diversified their employment and eventually entered secondary professions and expanded their industrial enterprises.

Most importantly, Ugandan Asians were unable to escape the racial stereotypes initiated by the colonial government and, as some scholars have argued, self-imposed to a certain extent. The social exclusivity and privileged economic position perpetuated by the race and class hierarchy held devastating consequences for the Ugandan Asian community.

As mentioned throughout the chapter, there were many instances where Ugandan Asians attempted to counter the rigid race and class structures within society. Through political initiatives, philanthropy, personal relations, literature, and attachments to Uganda, many Ugandan Asians did not fit the mould of stereotypical "brown colonialists." Oral histories with Ugandan Asian refugees complicate the realities of Ugandan society throughout the twentieth century. On the one hand, there are recollections of economic sabotage and a failure to integrate socially with black Ugandans. On the other hand, there are examples of Ugandan Asians who invested their livelihoods in the country and were "diehard" citizens of Uganda.

During independence the intricate process of acquiring Ugandan citizenship left many Ugandan Asians in a difficult position. Their attempts to become citizens were fraught with speculation from Ugandan Africans, who viewed them as colonial collaborators or opportunists wishing to take advantage of the benefits of citizenship. Furthermore, the requirements for becoming a citizen were convoluted. The Ugandan government required proof that a person's British citizenship had been renounced, but the UK government only considered the revocation of a British passport legitimate after being presented with evidence of a person's Ugandan citizenship. Each of the newly independent countries of East Africa sought their own solutions to the "Asian problem." Tanzania embraced socialism, similar to Obote's Move to the Left campaign, and vigorously nationalized several industries. Kenya opted for nationalization under the guise of Africanization as a means of restoring control of the economy to black Kenyans. Uganda combined these methods, until Idi Amin staged a military coup and brought forward his own solution—expulsion.

Upon carrying out an updated census report on Asians living in Uganda and deploring the Asian community for their economic exploitation and social exclusion of Ugandan Africans, Amin issued a decree that fundamentally altered Ugandan society. On 4 August 1972, the president and military general declared that the country had no place "for the over 80,000 Asians holding British passports who were sabotaging Uganda's economy and encouraging corruption."[126] But he went further than that, ordering every person of Indian, Pakistani, or Bangladeshi descent, regardless of citizenship, to leave the country within ninety days. To further justify his decision, Amin claimed divine intervention had prompted him to expel the Asians: "I . . . had a dream that the Asian problem was becoming extremely explosive and that God was directing me to act immediately to save the situation."[127] The solution to the "Asian problem" in Uganda was attributed to a prophecy and created an international humanitarian crisis.

CHAPTER 2

DREAMS AND REALITY:
Amin's Expulsion Decree and the International Community's Response

When the expulsion was announced in August of that year—the same year, '72—I think that everybody laughed because you know, they thought, "This is a joke." How can you expel your own citizens? ... So anyways, we thought, "This is nonsense."

Errol Francis, 2015

None of us took it seriously at all. We thought this is a joke. How can you throw away eighty-thousand-plus Asians who had been second- or third-generation Africans? They have no connection with India, no connection with any other country. So nobody took it seriously. We ourselves were completely mocking it: 'Idi [Amin] is crazy.'

Jalal Jaffer, 2015

President Idi Amin's expulsion of Ugandan Asians sent shock waves throughout the international community. It was imperative for the Ugandan government to establish a legal framework to enforce the decree and limit the ability of expellees to export their assets out of the country. Legislation to support these measures was grounded in stereotypes of the Ugandan Asian community as "brown colonialists." Propaganda reinforced the president's accusations of economic sabotage and social exclusivity by Ugandan Asians. The Ugandan government's rhetoric in 1972 identified "true" Ugandans as the president's black brothers and sisters. Amin asserted that British passport holders were responsible for the country's social, economic, and political problems. Later, amid uncertainty about the situation of Asians with Ugandan citizenship, the government specified that only noncitizens would be forced to leave the country.

This was not the president's first major expulsion order. In March 1972 Amin had expelled all Israelis from the country. Israel had invested heavily in Uganda—through technical guidance in agriculture, industrial development, education, and military weapons and training—following its independence in the 1960s. As historian Arye Oded argues, it was a mutually beneficial relationship as the Israeli government gained an ally in a region that was close to hostile Arab countries, such as Egypt and Sudan, while Uganda secured expert military training and arms.[1] Israel was one of the first countries to open an embassy in Uganda and issued 150 scholarships to Ugandan students in the fields of agriculture and medicine.[2] Under President Obote, the partnership flourished, as the newly independent country was in need of foreign investment, military support, and technical guidance on economic development.

Relations deteriorated between Uganda and Israel in the fall of 1971 when President Amin made several requests of the Israeli government that were denied, including a loan of £10 million, recognition of Amin's regime (Israel recognized Uganda's new government but did not acknowledge Amin's military regime as a separate entity from the Ugandan government), phantom fighter jets (which were purchased by Israel from the United States), assistance in fighting Kenya and Tanzania, and cancellation of debts or reduced repayments for all the military weapons purchased from Israel.[3] Israel's refusal prompted Amin to send his Muslim education minister, Abubaker Mayanja, on a diplomatic mission to Egypt and Libya to create new partnerships. Egypt and Libya welcomed the extension of a diplomatic arm on the condition that Uganda cease all ties to Israel. Amin visited Libya in February 1972, and soon after, on 22 March 1972, the Ugandan government formally announced it would not renew its military agreements with Israel and that all Israeli personnel in Uganda must leave immediately. All 470 Israelis in Uganda returned home between 23 March and 8 April.[4]

The Ugandan Asian expulsion decree officially became effective on 9 August 1972, and the deadline for departure was midnight on 8 November 1972. Uncertainty about their citizenship left many Ugandan Asians in a state of disarray. The multifarious process for Ugandan Asians with British passports to obtain Ugandan citizenship, created in 1962 when the country became independent, had

created confusion about their citizenship status. These circumstances, along with changes in British immigration policies, led to one
in twenty-five Ugandan Asians migrating to Britain from 1962 to
1969.[5] Now, those affected by the decree had ninety days to leave
the country or else, President Amin declared, they would be "sitting
on fire."[6]

Also on 9 August 1972, the government of Uganda amended the
Immigration Act of 1969 to cancel every entry permit and certificate of residence for "any person who is of Asian origin, extraction
or descent and who is a subject or citizen" of the United Kingdom,
India, Pakistan, or Bangladesh.[7] Another amendment was made on
25 October 1972 to account for those who were stateless since their
Ugandan citizenship was revoked. The new provision cancelled the
entry permits of "any other person who is of Indian, Pakistani or
Bangladesh origin, extraction or descent"[8] to encompass virtually all
individuals of South Asian descent in the country, regardless of their
citizenship. There were to be no exceptions for those who remained
after the expulsion period, even though numerous exemption decrees
were announced and then repealed over the ninety days. The creation
of specific amendments to limit the rights of Ugandan Asian expellees became commonplace throughout the expulsion period.

To further complicate matters, the number of noncitizen Asians
alleged to be in the country—Amin said more than eighty thousand
alone held British passports—was incorrect. Thousands of Asians
had emigrated from Uganda since the 1969 census, which placed the
number of noncitizen Asians in the country at roughly seventy-four
thousand. Scholars argue that anti-Asian measures put in place by
former president Obote led to more than 24,000 Asians leaving the
country from 1969 to 1971.[9] According to a community-based Goan
magazine, 20 percent of the Goan community had left Uganda by
1970.[10] Oral history participants also provided examples of earlier
emigration. Nimira recalled, "A lot of these Hindus from our little
village, eight families out of fourteen families—when eight [Ugandan
Asian families] leave, you know, haha. So eight families had to leave
because they didn't, because they couldn't hold dual citizenship, so
they wanted their Indian or Pakistani rights so they couldn't give
those up to adopt the Ugandan ones."[11] Although Amin had ordered
his officials to confirm the exact number of Asians in the country

in 1971, these numbers were not formally registered. According to forced migration scholar Nicholas Van Hear, 36,000 Ugandan Asians held British passports, 9,000 were Indian citizens, 250 were Pakistani citizens, and 1,750 were Kenyan citizens. The remaining 26,650 Ugandan Asians were Ugandan citizens; however, this number included 12,000 individuals who were still waiting for their applications to be processed when the expulsion order was announced.[12] Amin's initial expulsion order excluded Asians who were Ugandan citizens, but this was reversed on 21 August 1972 when the president declared that "even Asians who hold Uganda citizenship will have to leave the country."[13] This created an international crisis, as those who were rendered stateless did not fall under the responsibility of any government.

With the expulsion decree coming into full effect on 9 August 1972, the Ugandan government realized that many public servants and professionals might be forced to leave the country, creating gaps in the fields of education, medicine, and civil service. Thus, Amin signed a new statutory law exempting specific categories of Asians, including "all employees of government and governmental bodies, teachers, lawyers, doctors, dentists, technical experts in industry, agriculture and commerce and certain other specialized categories."[14] He then granted the Ministry of Internal Affairs the power to extend exemptions to any individual whom the department deemed to be of vital importance to Ugandan society. However, this decision was repealed only a few days later, on 21 August 1972, when Amin declared, "I have taken a decision that there is to be no exemption of professional, technicians, etc, as was earlier announced."[15] It appeared that no Asian would be eligible to stay. A front-page headline in the national newspaper exclaiming that "All Asians Must Go" turned Amin's dream into reality for the Ugandan Asian community.[16]

The clarity was short-lived, however. On 23 August 1972, Uganda's representative to the United Nations, Elidad K. Wapenyi, assured the General Assembly that all citizens of Uganda would be permitted to stay "regardless of color, provided their papers were not forged."[17] Moreover, Amin informed the Sudanese foreign minister, Dr. Mansour Khalid, that "Asians who are Ugandan citizens will not be required to leave the country," but added he would "carefully check the citizenship of those claiming to be Ugandan Asians."[18] Not only was it unclear as to who would be allowed to remain in Uganda, it was also extremely difficult to provide valid documentation of Ugandan citizenship. Ugandan Asians were required to produce original copies of birth certificates, which was particularly difficult for older adults since an official birth registry program was not established in the country until 1930, and photocopies were deemed to be forged or invalid. The government also required all Ugandan Asians to verify their citizenship by 10 September 1972 or else they would "automatically lose their claims for Uganda citizenship and will henceforth be regarded as non-citizens of Uganda."[19] The arbitrary process of citizenship verification is exemplified by the case of Mr. Patel, which was described in a 1975 article examining the application of Ugandan citizenship laws. Patel had applied for citizenship after Ugandan independence. Initially unaware that he had to renounce his UK citizenship, he missed the deadline to do so by six months in 1963. In a letter to the Ugandan government, he explained, "[I was] registered as a citizen of Uganda on the seventh day of January, 1963, I was informed by you only on the first day of October, 1963, to renounce my British nationality within three months."[20] His subsequent appeals to the government were of no avail and he was expelled from Uganda as a noncitizen in November 1972.

John N., an oral history participant, described another common tactic used by government officials at this time:

> So here I'm verifying and all I had was this photocopy. And the guy was telling me that we can only take the original and …I said I can't find it. He says, "Okay, I'm gonna rip this." I said, "No, no, give me some time." So from the corner of my eye I notice that one of the guys verifying citizenship was one of my old school friends from Kisubi. So I immediately went to him, I left this guy and went to him, his name was Katabola. And he says, "Hey Nazareth, how are things?" And he pulls the things and stamp, stamp, and I was through.[21]

John N. was the only interviewee who was able to get through the arbitrary verification process. Others had their documents destroyed, confiscated, or called forgeries. *London Times* newspaper journalist Phillip Short noted how Ugandan Asians expressed to him that "immigration officers refused to accept duplicates of their renunciation certificates, even though they bore the official Home Office seal and were certified as authentic copies. Under President Amin's directive, no duplicates or photostats were admissible because of the danger of forgery."[22] Ugandan Asians tried to provide valid proof of their citizenship, which was often rejected under false pretences.

The fraught process of citizenship verification was described by many Ugandan Asian interviewees. This provides insight beyond existing scholarship, which does not engage with the question of how many Ugandan Asians believed they were citizens (such as Mr. Patel) and the ways they were stripped of their Ugandan citizenship. For example, Edmond recalled how his file was "misplaced": "When I got there and I gave my things in, they told me they couldn't find my file. I said, 'What?' And I know I did it legally. I could imagine if I didn't, there would be nothing there, it would just be somebody issuing a passport, but mine was all legal. I had given my papers and everything. They said that room had caught fire [laughs], the cabinet or something, you know? So they made me stateless."[23]

Other Ugandan Asians, such as interviewees Amin V. and Vasant, had their passports disposed of or seized. Amin V. described how an immigration officer turned down his family: "[Then the officer] said, 'Give me your passports,' and while we were watching him he threw them in the garbage. At that moment we walked out of the immigration office and we asked, 'What do we do next?'"[24] As Vasant recalled, "[I] went for verification and the officer said, 'Well you are not a citizen.' So I took out my birth certificate or my passport.... I said, 'Here is my passport.' He said, 'You are not a citizen.' So now he took my passport and chucked it with the others, so I became stateless."[25] Oral testimonies document various excuses that were made by officials to strip Ugandan Asians of their citizenship, such as the "misplacement" of files, and how sometimes documents were simply thrown in the trash. As argued by sociologist Meir Amor, the expulsion decree institutionalized the public robbery of Ugandan Asians, and the extent to which anti-Asian policies were applied indicated overall acceptance of these measures within Ugandan society.[26] Numerous legislative acts were put in place to limit the rights of Ugandan Asian expellees, leading to loss of property and restrictions on the amount of money each individual could possess when leaving Uganda.

Reinforcing Perceptions of "Brown Colonialists"

Within a week of the initial announcement of the expulsion decree, President Amin and the Ugandan government launched a coordinated effort to publicly antagonize Ugandan Asians. One of the first measures put in place encouraged government officials to begin selling shops that were owned by those who had been expelled. Amin argued that "our weakness in Africa is that we consider that the imperialists must continue to teach us, forgetting that they will never tell you that you are able to run your own affairs."[27] His rhetoric conveyed the idea of an economic war being waged in the country. Ordering the expulsion of Ugandan Asians was a central component of Amin's "Ugandanization" program, which aimed to restore control of the economy to those whom he considered to be Ugandans. For Amin, a Ugandan citizen was a black African. It was not a white European or a brown Asian. He made this clear when he responded to rumours that he would extend the expulsion deadline by saying, "I want the whole country completely black."[28] He reinforced his desire for a nation of black Ugandans by referring to black citizens as "his brothers and sisters."[29] Amin leveraged the idea of an economic war as a guise for the racial underpinnings of the expulsion decree. The president capitalized on and reinforced the notion that Ugandan Asians manipulated the local market and kept large sums of money abroad in offshore bank accounts.

All Ugandan Asian expellees were required to obtain a tax clearance form for presentation at the airport before they would be allowed to board any aircraft. The tax clearance forms were used to ensure that no debts were owed to the Ugandan government as well as to collect information on assets that would come under government ownership to be redistributed among Ugandan Africans. On 4 October 1972 Amin signed The Declaration of Assets (Non-Citizen Asians) Decree to restrict what expellees could take out of the country. This decree prohibited any departing Asian from mortgaging or transferring "any immovable property, bus company, farm, including livestock, or business to any other person." Those who owned a company could not "issue new shares; change the salaries or terms of employment of staff including terminal benefits; or appoint new directors or in any way vary the conditions, terms of service or remuneration payable to directors."[30] Those who violated the decree would face a fine of up to 50,000 Ugandan shillings and a maximum sentence of two years in jail. The declaration was applied retroactively to the date of the official announcement of the expulsion order.

The tax clearance forms were also used as a tool to prompt expellees to leave Uganda quickly once they had received a visa for another country. Members of the Ugandan Security Forces were instructed by the government that all those who had attained clearance from the Bank of Uganda had to depart within forty-eight hours.[31] The Ugandan government was unhappy with the slow pace of departures; even though it had the institutional capacity to "clear at least 1,500 out-going Asians per day . . . only a few of these people are coming forward for clearance."[32]

The Ugandan government spelled out what each expellee family could possess when boarding a flight out of the country. Ugandan Asian expellees were restricted to twenty kilograms of personal luggage and foreign currency to the value of £50, or roughly C$143, per head of household.[33] The Ugandan government wanted assurance that expellees were not able to circumvent the system or smuggle goods out of the country. A notice at Entebbe International Airport warned passengers that "not a single Ugandan shilling" should be taken out of the country and that departing expellees could possess only "one ring, two bangles, one necklace and one pair of earrings."[34] The Ugandan representative to the United Nations, J. Peter Okia, argued in the United Nations General Assembly that noncitizen Asians did not need to take money with them "because they have already put their money in British banks."[35] This reinforced the government rhetoric that accused Ugandan Asians of illegitimate economic practices.

Two major incidents during the ninety-day expulsion period featured prominently in local media outlets and further vilified Ugandan Asians as economic saboteurs. The first scandal, reported by the country's premier national newspaper, the *Uganda Argus*, involved a raid on 25 September 1972 at the main prayer hall of the Ismaili community in Kampala. Officers found what initially appeared to be packages of biscuits, which they discovered hid bills of five, twenty, and one hundred shillings. Security forces seized roughly 1.8 million Ugandan shillings in hard cash in what they called "Asian Sandwiches."[36] This led to the imprisonment of an Ismaili Ugandan Asian, Kassim Damji, in the dreaded Makindye prison, one of the leading torture and killing facilities under Amin's regime.[37] The funds had been collected from community members as donations for relocation costs and for general financial hardship. Not only did the incident make front-page news in bold print but also the article quoted an army officer saying "this is one of the many tricks the Asians are employing in exporting our money" while pointing to the confiscated bills.[38] Ugandan Asians were thus portrayed as conspirators against the Ugandanization program.

The other major incident involved an attempt by an expellee to sneak money out of the country through a border crossing on 19 October 1972 by hiding the cash in water pipes. Amin argued that his regime would not refrain from exposing corrupt Ugandan Asian expellees alongside their "dirty tricks" to smuggle money out of the country.[39] The apparent "trickery" of the community was emphasized in the *Uganda Argus*, which played a prominent role in reinforcing the stereotype of the exploitative Ugandan Asian and increasing support for the expulsion decree. A coordinated system of legislation, an arbitrary citizenship process, and anti-Asian propaganda had been implemented to disenfranchise the community. This would lead to a multitude of responses from international political leaders as they grappled with the expulsion decree.

International Responses to the Expulsion Decree

The British government was the first major party to denounce Amin's expulsion decree. Two days after the announcement, the United Kingdom contested Amin's claim that eighty thousand British passport holders were in Uganda, arguing that the number was between twenty-five thousand and forty thousand. On 7 August 1972, British Under-Secretary of State for the Home Office David Lane publicly announced that the United Kingdom would hold firm to its traditional annual admittance of thirty-five hundred immigrants from East Africa even for individuals who held British passports. Lane argued that Britain was already "a crowded island and immigration must and will remain strictly controlled."[40] Three days later, the British government formally created a contingency plan to resettle roughly twenty-five thousand Ugandan Asian expellees in case Amin stuck to his decision. Geoffrey Rippon, Britain's foreign minister, flew to Uganda to negotiate with Amin to extend the expulsion deadline, provide compensation for confiscated properties and businesses, and enlarge the number of people eligible for exemptions from the decree. However, Rippon was unsuccessful and was forced to announce that the United Kingdom would admit all those with British passports. The British government appealed to other Commonwealth countries for assistance but ultimately would resettle roughly twenty-nine thousand Ugandan Asians.[41]

Nativist sentiments ran high in the United Kingdom. Postwar migration from former colonies had already prompted the 1968 Commonwealth Immigration Act, which placed significant restrictions on further migration to the United Kingdom. Prime Minister Edward Richard George Heath had been elected in 1970 on an anti-immigration platform.[42] Ronald Bell, the member of parliament for Buckinghamshire South, argued that "these so-called British Asiatics are no more and no less British than any Indian in the bazaars of Bombay. They were either born in India or have retained close connections with India. They have no connection with Britain either by blood or residence."[43] Bell's statement ignored the historical roots of British colonialism in both the Indian subcontinent and East Africa, and effectively encapsulated fears of impending migrations from both regions. Other members of parliament were more aggressive in their opposition, such as Harold Soref of Ormskirk (Lancashire), who argued that "Britain is under no obligation to accept these people."[44] Many of those who openly protested the government's response to aid the Ugandan Asians, including Bell and Soref, were members of the governing Conservative party, demonstrating divisions on the issue. Some public figures, however, felt that the treatment of Ugandan Asians was unjust, including Lady Tweedsmuir, the former viceregal consort of Canada and a prolific writer, who said it was "inhumane to those concerned to suggest that people who have spent their lives in Uganda should suddenly be asked to uproot themselves."[45]

The politics of race relations in the United Kingdom required a delicate balance since immigrant communities had grown both in numerical terms and in political strength. In opposition to the rhetoric about limiting migration, some argued that failing to honour

British passports tarnished the United Kingdom's reputation in the international community. Beyond local and international political contexts, Britain was also concerned about its assets in Uganda. Amin announced within two days of the expulsion order that he would nationalize the British American Tobacco Company's processing factory, as it was a physical embodiment of how the British were sabotaging Uganda's economy. The economic threats and complex geopolitical context caused the UK government to tread carefully in its diplomatic response.

Instead, the British government purposefully portrayed the expulsion order as a global crisis. Historian Sara Cosemans argues that framing the expulsion as a refugee issue rather than an immigration issue allowed Britain to "successfully cut ties with its former colonial subjects."[46] The postcolonial challenge for the United Kingdom was that nearly six million South Asians resided in former British colonies in the 1960s. John Freeman, British High Commissioner to India, overestimated the size of the global Asian diaspora and created legitimate fears in Britain that all of these individuals would become eligible for citizenship.[47] Furthermore, the magnitude of Amin's expulsion order enabled the global community to shift their perception of Ugandan Asians from potential immigrants to refugees. This coincides with historian Laura Madokoro's view of how the term "refugee" is highly politicized.

The British government's reluctance to take in the Ugandan Asian expellees drew criticism from the international press, which emphasized the United Kingdom's responsibility to the expellees. The *Zambia Daily Mail* argued that protests and objections were "uncalled for" since "it was the British government that had encouraged these unfortunate people of Asian origin living in East Africa to take British citizenship."[48] Other international media sources argued that "the British have morally, if not legally promised the Asians a right to settle in Britain."[49]

The foreign minister for Uganda, Wanume Kibedi, accused the British government of "callousness to bar the door to its citizens because they are not white and then have the impudence to turn around and point an accusing finger at Uganda, a state which is doing no more than asking Britain to take care of her citizens."[50] He also criticized the British propaganda campaign targeted at smearing the reputation of Uganda. "It is Britain who is being racialist," he said. "Britain is refusing entry because they [Ugandan Asians] are not white. They are not kith and kin. That's the only test. Had they been white people, they would have not the slightest difficulty in getting in."[51] His charge underscored the hypocrisy of the British government and led to an increase in support among Ugandan Africans, who would later voice their approval of the government's decision to expel all people of South Asian descent. However, accusations of hypocrisy did not prevent the British government from trying to force Amin to repeal the expulsion decree. In an attempt to reverse his decision, the British government threatened to withhold all foreign aid and investment in Uganda. Kibedi responded by declaring, "Whether it is 4.5 million, 40 million or 400 million sterling . . . the Ugandan government is not going to sell the interests of the Ugandan people for a pittance from the British."[52] The Ugandan government remained firm in its decision to expel all Ugandan Asians from the country.

Despite some criticism of the expulsion by the governments of East Africa, they offered no refuge to the Ugandan Asians. President Julius Nyerere of Tanzania had strong words about Amin: "Every racialist in the world is an animal of some kind or another, and all are kinds which have no future. Eventually, they will all become extinct."[53] He also took issue with Britain for its poor extraction policy, claiming that "citizens must be accepted without discrimination."[54] However, his government did not offer to take in any of those affected by the expulsion decree. Tanzania's minister for home affairs, Saidi Maswanya, argued that "Uganda Asians are not our responsibility, and therefore allowing them to settle or giving them refuge was far from thought."[55] Kenyan president Jomo Kenyatta remained silent throughout the affair. However, his vice president and minister of home affairs, Daniel Arap Moi, announced that Kenya would close its borders to expelled migrants, arguing that "Kenya is not a dumping ground for citizens of other countries."[56] Moi sought to deter Ugandan Asians from entering Kenya and contended that those who had found their way into the country "had done so illegally and his or her presence in the country is undesirable."[57] Neither Tanzania nor Kenya was willing to accept an influx of Asians that would replace those who had already been successfully pressured to emigrate in the late 1960s and early 1970s. In Zambia, the president, Kenneth

Kaunda, described the decree as "terrible, horrible, abominable and shameful." He also stressed that the "seeds of trouble had been sown before Uganda's independence when the Asians were encouraged to become British citizens, but it is not right to commit another wrong because of Britain's treatment many years ago."[58] While attributing blame to both the British and Ugandan governments, he offered no aid any of the expellees.

Media sources on the continent also condemned the expulsion. The Nigerian newspaper *Renaissance* called for Amin to rescind his decision in the "interest of the Black race," as the loss of the business class and professionals would hinder Uganda's development.[59] India was criticized for its failure to provide assistance for people who had originally migrated from the subcontinent. Perhaps the most startling critique of Amin's expulsion decree came from the prime minister of apartheid South Africa, John Vorster, who condemned the removal of the Ugandan Asians as "the most immoral of acts."[60] Although the South African government did not offer safe haven to any expellees, Vorster clearly identified the hypocrisy behind Amin's order. The Ugandan government was one of the loudest critics of apartheid and regularly denounced South Africa's racialized policies, but now it was enacting its own piece of racially discriminatory legislation.

While Amin's expulsion order received international rebuke, many Ugandan Africans believed that ousting the "brown colonialists" would usher in an era of economic prosperity for the black population. Ugandans who expressed their opinions in the country's national newspaper—which received state funding—largely welcomed the expulsion. Several opinion pieces endorsed Amin's decree and encouraged him to remain firm on the ninety-day deadline or even reduce it to thirty days. For example, the Ugandan African sales manager of Simba Motors articulated in the *Uganda Argus* how he fully supported "the President's move, which I think is timely and, if not, overdue."[61] Many others were more aggressive in their denunciations of Ugandan Asians: "We don't hate Asians, but [despise] their selfish attitude and unbecoming attitude in trade with Africans."[62] This kind of sentiment aligned with the rhetoric of an economic war being waged in Uganda. Another piece in the *Uganda Argus* stated, "General Amin has shown in his typical humane way that he is only sorting the chaff from the wheat in ordering British Asians, Indian,

Pakistanis and Bangladesh nationals from Uganda's borders. . . .
Many Asians have devoted their lives to this country. . . . But there
are others who have sheltered under a foreign passport, working for
their own ends, picking the richest fruit and living in a cocoon; in a
world alien to Uganda and its culture."[63] The piece provides a more
nuanced understanding of the expulsion order, reflecting Amin's accusations against those Asians who did not become Ugandan citizens
while acknowledging the historical contributions of Ugandan Asians.

Other pieces acknowledged the roots of the expellees in Uganda
but highlighted the historical oppression of black Ugandans by
Ugandan Asians. Ugandan African Omugisha-Bukabbeha's letter
to the editor laid bare the deeply embedded resentment of Ugandan
Africans: "Looking back seventy years, one does not forget to realize
how enduring the period has been for both the Africans and Asian
alike, for Asians because they knew they were robbing people of their
own right, for Africans because they had never been thought to ex-
ist."[64] The colonial administration and the stratification of Ugandan
society had positioned the Asian community as agents of economic
and social oppression of African Ugandans. Although many Ugandan
Asians held strong affiliations to the country and contributed in many
ways to its development, they were routinely labelled as colonial
collaborators in the media, where many opinion articles, even from
those holding religious positions, continued to support the decree.
For example, Reverend Peter Ben Ocban expressed that "our Asian
friends have been in a deep sleep ever since they were shipped to
East Africa as coolies for the Mombasa to Kampala railway line.
During this sleep, they have had sweet dreams of East Africa being
an Asian paradise, I am glad that they are now having nightmares
for a change." Reverend Ocban ended his piece by bidding farewell
to those returning to Britain, wishing them a "long and very cold
winter."[65]

Dr. Mohan Kamarchand, the headmaster of a high school in
Soroti, instructed the expellees "to be calm and patient and realize
within their hearts that it was part of their disloyalty and dishonesty
when not all, but many of them in trade, commerce and industry
always concentrated upon oiling their wealth and exporting that to
other lands. Today when they are facing the results and fearing their
own safety [they] should very well know that this day could come."[66]

The notion that Ugandan Asians acquired their wealth through exploitation and hoarded it in offshore bank accounts matched the government's rhetoric. As mentioned earlier, scholars have challenged these allegations, arguing that only an elite section of the Ugandan Asian community had the means and ability to invest or save money abroad.[67]

The absence of dissenting opinions and articles critical of Amin and his administration is notable, but makes sense given that the *Uganda Argus* received state funding. Indeed, Amin nationalized the paper in 1972 and it was renamed the *Voice of Uganda*, after it allegedly published a false report of a sugar shortage in the country. Anyone who dared to challenge the government was undoubtedly endangering themselves and their families. Scholars have documented how opponents of Amin's regime disappeared, as the apparatus of terror left no room for self-expression or criticism.[68] The president made numerous public threats during his tenure, warning dissidents that they might end up "swimming in the Nile."[69] His administration closely monitored all forms of mass media to ensure that only positive reviews of his government's activities were published.

Four days after the expulsion decree was announced, an article in the national newspaper quoted two anonymous Ugandan Asian expellees who expressed their acceptance of the decree. The first individual wished African businessmen success, and the other declared, "We have given our service with a clean heart, and we think Ugandans will accept this. We have no quarrel with anybody and if it is the wish of the Government and the people of Uganda to see us leave, we are prepared to do so."[70] Government rhetoric surrounding the expulsion decree in conjunction with large-scale support from black Ugandans gave the impression that all Ugandan Africans were in favour of the decree. However, there were those who disagreed with the expulsion, and there were several cases, at the grassroots level, where Ugandan Africans aided expellees. For example, Thomas Melady, then US ambassador to Uganda, and his wife Margaret Malady assert that there were "stories of loyalty and unusual courage of some African friends, workers, and servants of Asians. Some Africans took great risks to protect their Asian friends and to help them to save some of their property. Several instances are known where Africans arranged to slip valuables across the border for the departing Asians."[71]

Although the authors provide little evidence to support this claim, oral history participants recalled several examples of how Ugandan Africans helped them. Mobina recounted how her husband was abducted by Amin's security forces, but instead of being taken to the notorious army barracks he was taken to the police station because of her father's influence: "If they had taken him [husband] to the army barracks [pause] I know I would have never seen him again. So thankfully they took him to the police station because this police officer had been educated by my father and absolutely insisted that they go to the police station."[72] Mobina's father had paid for the officer's education, and so the officer risked his personal well-being to avoid sending her husband to the army barracks. A similar instance occurred for Nellie and Sadru, who were warned of an impending raid by a Ugandan African who had received financial aid from the couple to attend high school. Nellie recalled, "He came to me and I said, 'Where have you been?' He said, 'I got a good job with Amin's office. I'm his personal secretary.' He said, 'Are you Ismaili?' I said yeah. He said, 'You know, we are going to raid your *jamatkhana* [Ismaili prayer hall]. We know there's money in your jamatkhana.'"[73] This helped the Ismaili community prepare for a visit from Amin's troops. At the Journey Into Hope commemorative event in Ottawa, Ugandan Asian refugee Zain Alarakhia explained how her father was protected by Ugandan Africans on two separate occasions: "The army came for my father twice and each time his friends, black Ugandans, themselves appalled by what was happening in the country, helped him evade the army or used their influence to protect him."[74] These examples demonstrate how Ugandan Africans offered warnings and advice to expellees to avoid further hardship.

Other black Ugandans openly protested the unfair treatment of Ugandan Asian expellees. John N. described an encounter between his brother-in-law and a Ugandan African:

> He was at the taxi stop and someone started needling him, saying "oh *muhindi*" [derogatory Swahili term for Ugandan Asians]. So my brother said to him in Swahili, "You wait, you are calling me *muhindi*, you wait when I become your Gombolola chief [Amin had threatened that Ugandan Asians would be moved to rural regions of the country to become leaders in remote villages known as Gombolola

chiefs],[75] I'll show you." So all the Africans there said, "Yeah, that's telling him. Who does he think he is speaking to you like that?" . . . Many months later after the expulsion when we went fishing somewhere [John N. stayed in Uganda after the decree], all the Africans were so happy to see us. They said "oh my god we thought all the Asians had left," so they were happy to see us.[76]

John N.'s testimony shows that not all Ugandan Africans favoured the removal of the Asian population, despite the well-publicized support for the expulsion decree.

Additionally, students at Uganda's leading university protested the expulsion within weeks of its announcement. The National Union of Students of Uganda at Makerere University in Kampala declared that Amin's decree was rooted in racism, as his initial rhetoric about the Ugandanization of the economy targeted only Asian businesses. The accusation was solidified when the government made clear that all Ugandans of South Asian descent, regardless of their citizenship status, would be expelled. In reaction, Amin attended a student rally at the university, arguing that the government was pursuing a policy that would create African capitalists. The students, however, criticized his motives and referred to these African capitalists as "a class of black Asians."[77] The National Union of Students was immediately outlawed, and the president sent armed paratroopers to the university to arrest all those who supported it. Amin claimed that the infiltration of the campus was part of a security operation to capture supporters of the Tanzanian government, after a Tanzanian-supported coup was attempted against Amin in September. These kinds of grassroots levels of resistance challenge the view that the expulsion decree reflected the desire of all Ugandan Africans.

Ugandan Asian Responses to the Decree

Oral history participants captured how unexpected the expulsion decree was and how farcical it seemed. Amin V. recalled, "When he [President Amin] announced, people thought it was a joke, nobody really anticipated that this is serious. And for the first few days nobody really paid attention."[78] The decree was a misinformed joke that people did not think would stand as a piece of legitimate legislation. "When the expulsion was announced in August of that year—the same year, '72—I think that everybody laughed because you know, they thought this is a joke," said Errol. "How can you expel your own citizens? . . . So anyways, we thought, 'This is nonsense.'"[79] Mobina recalled attending her sister's wedding, where "we all laughed, we didn't take it seriously. We were at the wedding in the evening and we all laughed, 'Ha ha ha, he wants us out, what next? Ha ha.' Honestly, we were laughing, truthfully."[80] Jalal reinforced how "none of us took it seriously at all. We thought this is a joke. How can you throw away eighty-thousand-plus Asians who had been second- or third-generation Africans? They have no connection with India, no connection with any other country. So nobody took it seriously. We ourselves were completely mocking it: 'Idi [Amin] is crazy.'"[81] Not only did Amin ignore the deep historical roots of South Asians in Uganda with his announcement, but Ugandan Asians did not believe it was feasible to expel eighty thousand individuals from the country.

President Amin justified his pronouncement based on divine premonition, leading many Ugandan Asians to question the mental well-being of Uganda's leader. Edmond explained, "We didn't take it seriously, you know. At that time, he was already going off his head or something, making all kinds of commands, talking about Asians milking the economy and, you know, making use of us as scapegoats."[82] Most interviewees called the decree unfathomable and unpredictable. Just one oral history participant noted that he had foreseen the expulsion and moved to Canada in 1971. Mossadiq explained, "When you have a small population that comes from a different background, i.e., Indian, and controls a significant part of the wealth of the country while the indigenous population con- stituting a majority . . . [has] power in terms of the control of the military and its weapons, this sets up an almost inevitable problem, especially if you have a mad man in power."[83] He was not alone in relocating to Canada before Amin issued his decree. An article in the *Calgary Herald* from 1972 describes two Ugandan Asian couples who arrived in the country during the expulsion period but argued that they "had already made plans to leave the country before the expulsion order came."[84]

Many interviewees identified a transition period during which the community came to terms with the reality of the expulsion decree. Jalal remembered that "it wasn't until two or four weeks in that people started galvanizing, and then different people had very different experiences."[85] The media continued to report on the decree and President Amin made further announcements regarding his plans to follow through on it. Amin V. recalled that "as time developed and you started seeing more, more situations where people started saying this is very serious. And then on top of that . . . two, three weeks after, he announced . . . 'anybody who is of non-black origin and who's got a Ugandan passport is stateless, I'm forfeiting them.' That's when I think paranoia came about."[86] Edmond and Maria also described the panic that set in over the transition period as the Ugandan government outlined the details of the expulsion:

> Edmond: Then three days later this guy [Amin] says, "By the Qur'an," he says, "Asians have to get out of this country within three months."
>
> Maria: Or they will be locked up.
>
> Edmond: They'll be locked up. People panicked when he made that announcement. We knew that he was serious about it. Then people had to make an effort to get out.[87]

Where were people to go? This is the principal issue that all Ugandan Asian expellees faced. Britain had reluctantly decided to admit its citizens but, given domestic debates about the levels of nonwhite immigration, it requested assistance from other Commonwealth countries. Canada would answer the call to help but not solely for the purpose of keeping the Commonwealth connection alive. Various memorandums to Prime Minister Pierre Elliott Trudeau's cabinet and other government documents illustrate that a delicate balance of humanitarianism and opportunism motivated Canada to participate in the resettlement initiative.

CHAPTER 3

"THANK YOU, PIERRE":
Canadian Immigration Policy in the 1970s and the Decision to Admit Ugandan Asian Expellees

Asian immigrants have already added to the cultural richness and variety of our country, and I am sure that those from Uganda will, by their abilities and industry, make an equally important contribution to society.

Prime Minister Pierre Elliott Trudeau, August 1972

These people are not destitute refugees, they are the most desirable type of immigrants. It's a windfall for us.

High Commissioner for Canada in Uganda Reginald Smith,
20 October 1972

After decades of statecraft devoted to keeping their people [South Asians] out, it would be a fitting act of retribution to waive our rules and let them in.

James Eayrs, *Toronto Star*,
21 August 1972

In the postwar economic boom, employers and major businesses advocated for a liberal immigration policy to supply workers. To reflect the prioritization of labour, the Liberal government created the Department of Manpower and Immigration in 1966. The department would be responsible for immigration and "take over placement and employment services, technical and vocational training and civilian rehabilitation."[1] Prime Minister Lester B. Pearson announced that "immigration policy must be administered in the interests of the country and of the immigrants themselves in a context that takes into account the entire position of employment, training, and placement in Canada."[2] It was deemed imperative that migrants be prepared to enter the Canadian labour force upon arrival, or at the very least be equipped with enough skills to be trained in Canada.

The immigration system underwent a transformation at the same time the country tried to forge a new national identity. Immigration policy shifted from a racialized and discriminatory approach to an evaluation of prospective migrants based on a mix of human and social capital through the implementation of Order-in-Council PC 1967-1616, more commonly known as the "points system." Before the introduction of the points system in 1967, immigration officers who evaluated the applications of migrants to Canada looked to admit those with at least eleven years of formal schooling. Meeting the educational requirement did not guarantee entry into the country though; the immigration officer was given final discretion to judge the candidate's personality and work experience in relation to Canada's labour needs.[3] The new points system assigned prospective immigrants a score based on the following categories: "age; education; training; occupational skills in demand; knowledge of English or French; a personal assessment made by an immigration officer; relatives in Canada; arranged employment; and employment opportunities in area of destination."[4] Those who received a passing grade of fifty points were permitted entrance into the country. There was no quota, so anyone who passed the assessment was supposed to be allowed in.

The points system created more diversity among source countries, supporting the migration of 2.25 million people between 1963 and 1976.[5] By 1973, Hong Kong, the Philippines, Jamaica, Trinidad, and India appeared among the top ten sources of Canadian immigrants.[6] Political scientists Christopher G. Anderson and Jerome H. Black argue that a "unity through diversity approach, legitimized by multiculturalism, provided the basis for turning immigrants into Canadians."[7] Despite the formal deracialization of Canada's immigration policy through the new points system, however, the emphasis on skills and education continued to discriminate against applicants from the developing world.[8] Since Canada did not have an official refugee policy until 1976, Ugandan Asians would be resettled under the immigration selection criteria, though with an additional provision to address their plight.

Canada in the 1970s

Formal Canadian multiculturalism policy was established under Pierre Elliott Trudeau's government in 1971. The policy indicated that Canada had no official national culture and was neither binational nor bicultural. Historian J.M. Bumsted argues that Canadians united under the banner of multiculturalism as a contrast to the melting pot model in the United States.[9] Although the Trudeau Liberal government largely promoted multiculturalism to negate French Canadian nationalism and provided little funding for ethnic communities, the concept gained significant support from the public, leading to the creation of the Canadian Charter of Rights and Freedoms in 1982.

Canada's multiculturalism policy emerged from significant changes in the preceding decade. During the 1960s and early 1970s, the country struggled to form a new sense of national identity.[10] The declining British connection and stronger North American identity, rising Quebec nationalism, and increased immigration altered traditional Canadian society during the 1960s. Throughout the same period, First Nations, Métis, and Inuit communities across Canada continued pushing for autonomy and the formal closure of Indian residential schools. Status Indians, as described under the Indian Act, finally gained the right to vote in the Canadian system in 1960 and witnessed the creation of the Department of Indian Affairs in 1966.[11] Based on the conclusions of the Hawthorne report in 1967, the Canadian government issued the 1969 White Paper under Prime Minister Trudeau and Minister for Indian Affairs Jean Chrétien, calling for a host of reforms including the abolition of the Indian Act, privatization of reserve lands, and integration. Indigenous communities across the country were outraged and argued that the White Paper and the Hawthorne report did not genuinely address their concerns and that forced assimilation would not create equity.[12]

A document called *Citizens Plus*, which became known as the Red Paper, was released by the Indian Chiefs of Alberta and cited land rights, upholding of promises made in previous treaties, and political organization as the keys to addressing marginalization. The Canadian government subsequently withdrew the White Paper in 1970. Throughout the rest of the decade, political organization among

Indigenous communities in Canada expanded. Under the National Indian Brotherhood and its leader George Manuel, First Nations secured federal funding for research into Indigenous land. The National Indian Brotherhood and its successor, the Assembly of First Nations, secured greater levels of autonomy throughout the 1970s and 1980s to administer funding for social work, childcare, and education, culminating in the recognition of Aboriginal rights in section 35 of the 1982 Constitution Act.[13]

The adoption of a new Canadian flag in 1965, the celebration of Canada's centennial in 1967, and the establishment of state corporations such as the Canadian Development Corporation in 1971 were some of the other major changes in Canadian culture and society at the time. Prime Minister Trudeau openly stated that the country was on the verge of formulating a new identity, and Canadians "must separate once and for all the concepts of the state and of nation and make Canada a truly pluralistic and polyethnic society."[14] The new nation-building program was built on "unity through diversity," as exemplified by the Liberal government's promotion of multiculturalism.

The march towards multiculturalism policy officially began in October 1971, when Trudeau told the House of Commons that "a policy of multiculturalism within a bilingual framework commends itself to the government as the most suitable means of assuring the cultural freedom of Canadians."[15] Trudeau's comments were a direct response to the public backlash against the Royal Commission on Bilingualism and Biculturalism's final report. Launched by the previous Liberal government, the royal commission concluded that Canada was bicultural and that bilingualism should be implemented across the country, but also noted that cultural dualism was not supported by many citizens since one in four Canadians were not members of either of the two charter communities (French and English). Thus, the idea of biculturalism left many ethnic groups outside the definition of Canadian identity. During the hearings of the royal commission, ethnic minorities—or noncharter groups—had lobbied to be included in Canadian society.[16] The term "multiculturalism" was actually a response to the royal commission's conclusion that Canada was "bicultural."[17] Trudeau argued that by "increasing cultural freedom—that is, by recognizing the equal legitimacy of all cultures in Canada—prejudice would be reduced."[18] Immigrants were encouraged to participate in Canadian society and also hold on to their own cultural practices and beliefs.

While multiculturalism policy was presented as a natural evolution of Canadian society as an inclusive space, it ignored Canada's long historical legacy of injustice towards Indigenous, Black, and immigrant communities. The head tax embodied in the 1885 Chinese Immigration Act, the 1914 *Komagata Maru* "incident," Japanese internment during WWII, the late repeal of the Chinese Immigration Act in 1947, and official deracialization of Canadian immigration policy in 1967 are but a few examples of how Canada implemented xenophobic and racist immigration policies. Considering how recent these official discriminatory regulations remained in effect, conceptions of formal multiculturalism policy were a veiled attempt to erase public awareness of Canada's exclusionary practices. The policy attempted to acknowledge a diverse and multicultural Canada in the 1970s but contradicted the realities of Canada's settler colonial past by creating a mythology of long-standing acceptance of all Canadian peoples living in harmony. It purposefully avoided acknowledging the historical roots of systematic discrimination levied against Indigenous, Black, and immigrant communities. Conceptions of a multicultural Canadian mosaic played a critical role in establishing a welcoming atmosphere for Ugandan Asian expellees; however, that welcome was tempered by a rise in unemployment levels.

Unemployment in the fall of 1972 reached slightly over 6 percent, contributing to growing anxiety among Canadians about the job market.[19] The impending arrival of Ugandan Asian expellees provoked fears that they would take jobs away from Canadians, which coincided with rhetoric among some parts of the public that "charity begins at home." However, historian Gerald Dirks's report to the government argued that "Canadians for the most part, seemed to accept the government's policy [to resettle Ugandan Asians] without much criticism, being otherwise engrossed in the developing general election campaign or the Canada-Russia hockey contests."[20] The federal election, scheduled for the end of October 1972, saw the Liberal government facing a strong challenge from the Progressive Conservative Party as Trudeau's popularity dwindled. The Summit Series, held in September 1972, attracted a huge television audience.

In terms of immigration, Canadians were concerned with the rising number of "immigrant visitors" who remained in the country without official documentation in the form of landed immigrant status or legitimate work permits.[21] With the first flight of expellees arriving at the end of September 1972, Canada prepared to receive Ugandan Asians while the majority of the population was concerned about rising unemployment, federal politics, and one of the most prominent sporting events in Canadian history.[22]

As the decision to admit Ugandan Asian expellees was made solely within Trudeau's cabinet, there was no major discussion surrounding the resettlement initiative in the House of Commons. Politicians acknowledged the special operation but did not engage in lengthy political debates, especially after Parliament adjourned on 1 September 1972 in advance of the federal election.[23] Parliamentarians focused on the logistics of the operation, including an avoidance of clustering expellees in major cities, and openly condemning the expulsion decree at the upcoming United Nations General Assembly. Publicly, the prime minister framed Canada's response as one that was rooted in humanitarianism and that reduced Britain's proclaimed burden of having to deal with a large number of expellees. Upon announcing that Canada would send an immigration team to Kampala, Trudeau had declared that his government was "prepared to offer an honourable place in Canadian life to those Ugandan Asians who come to Canada under this program."[24] It was imperative that Canadian officials reinforce the humanitarian considerations, as rising levels of unemployment played into the fears of Canadians that expellees would place an additional strain on the labour market. Bryce Mackasey, the minister for manpower and immigration, was well aware of this issue and stated that "there is always a backlash, and I'm prepared to live with it. These are people. I'm interested in people and so is the Liberal Government."[25]

While on the campaign trail, Trudeau was addressing a group of five hundred students at a high school in St. Catharines, Ontario, when a member of the audience suggested that Ugandan Asian expellees should not be permitted to resettle in Canada due to high unemployment. The prime minister responded that helping those in need only when it was easy to do so would mean "we don't have much merit as a government and Canadians don't have much heart if that is their attitude."[26] However, in the same address, Trudeau argued that expellees would not be given any favours in the job market. Ugandan Asian expellees would be taking "their chances like everyone else" and potentially end up working as fruit or tobacco pickers.[27] Canada's acting high commissioner for Uganda, Reginald Smith, publicly reinforced the government's rhetoric and declared that "these people are not destitute refugees, they are the most desirable type of immigrants. It's a windfall for us."[28] Officials understood the resettlement as an opportunity to provide asylum to a large group of well-educated, entrepreneurial, and highly skilled people and continually battled public anxiety about unemployment in the latter half of 1972.

Other agencies reiterated the low likelihood of expellees taking jobs away from Canadians. "Ugandan Asians pouring into Canada this month will have a negligible effect on the country's unemployment rate," outlined Robert Bell, research director of the Canadian Labour Congress. "Immigrants have historically picked up jobs rejected by other Canadians ... [and] an increase in the number of immigrants entering Canada at any time has usually resulted in a decline in the unemployment rate."[29] Bell's statement echoed the prime minister, who also said that Ugandan Asian expellees would most likely take positions within the economy that Canadians "are unwilling to accept."[30] Peter Stollery, director for the Canadian Institute on Public Affairs, added to these arguments by emphasizing that concerns over unemployment did not trump the plight of refugees.[31] While considerable efforts were made to calm public opinion regarding unemployment, other parties highlighted how underemployment might be the toughest barrier to integration for Ugandan Asian expellees. The lack of recognition of foreign credentials or work experience had posed major barriers for previous immigrants from the Indian subcontinent and East Africa. Though many immigrants had found work in Canada, the majority were working in positions that did not reflect their knowledge and occupational expertise, according to media coverage.[32] These concerns were not met with any official response and the government continued to focus on responding to negative reactions from the public.

In the first month of the resettlement initiative, the Canadian government received letters from the public that were "largely negative."[33] A radio talk show in Vancouver documented the results of an informal poll regarding the resettlement. Of those who participated, fifteen individuals were in favour, and twenty-four were against.[34] The majority of radio listeners based their criticisms on three principal arguments. First, they argued that charity should be targeted towards Canadian citizens who lived in poverty, or that taxpayer money should improve the livelihoods of Canadians before those of incoming noncitizens. Second, they maintained that Canada's social fabric was already being tested by struggles to create positive relations between French, English, and Indigenous communities. Third, they argued that expellees would burden the public health and unemployment insurance systems. A small minority of radio listeners thought that refugees living in Canada should be expelled, an influx of refugees would place additional strain on the labour market, expellees would invariably cluster into ethnic ghettos, and the Canadian government should focus on assimilating groups of immigrants already living in Canada. Other negative responses to the resettlement initiative appeared in newspapers. Though primarily focused on issues of unemployment, they also discussed assimilation. One commentator argued that Idi Amin's decree was "common sense" since Ugandan Asian expellees "were only interested in money and a comfortable living. They exploited the native population in every possible way . . . how is it possible for the [Canadian] government to turn completely around and bring in people who were expelled because they refused to support their own [Ugandan] government on the same principle?"[35] Although this author ignored the deep historical roots of the community in Uganda and their contributions to society, the critique of the government coincided with the Canadian public's concern over the allegiances and integration of Ugandan Asians.

The public's concerns focused on the importance of citizen rights as opposed to human rights, as some Canadians supported a restricted range of rights for noncitizens, demonstrating a liberal nationalist perspective. Nativists were concerned about the plight of Canadian citizens and the admission of a group of noncitizens that the state had no obligation to accept. In addition to reporting on anxieties relating to the Canadian labour market, media often cited the number of applications submitted to the immigration team in Kampala instead of the number of Ugandan Asians accepted into Canada. The *Globe and Mail* ran several articles that outlined how "unofficial estimates put the number of Ugandan Asians applying to settle in Canada at close to

15,000 and the number is growing by several thousand every day."[36] The application numbers added to public concerns and distorted the reality of the situation. The *Globe and Mail* eventually changed its reporting in mid-October to focus on the number of visas issued.

Overall, objection to the resettlement began to dwindle as operations in Uganda continued to unfold. With the arrival of the first flight of Ugandan Asians on 28 September, the volume of critical letters sent to various government departments had effectively "dropped off."[37] Leaders of major organizations including the YMCA, OXFAM, and the Canadian Council of Churches expressed their support for Canada's decision to accept Ugandan Asian refugees. The president of the YMCA, Mary Chadsey, urged the government to use the "utmost humanitarian criteria in granting entry permits even in cases where the necessary fifty merits would not be reached under normal immigration procedure. As a rich and developed nation, we should be able to extend a hand also to those who have been made most wretched by an arbitrary and cruel act."[38] OXFAM reiterated the need for a strong humanitarian approach. Chairman Derek Hayes stressed that asylum should be granted to "individuals who would not normally be acceptable . . . only by accepting such individuals can Canada truly demonstrate its compassion for the victims of the current situation in Uganda."[39] Large voluntary organizations continued to offer their assistance to the government while lobbying parliamentarians to exercise an altruistic policy when screening expellees. Moreover, Jewish Immigrant Aid Services and the Canadian Council of Churches communicated their full cooperation and support in facilitating the arrival and integration of Ugandan Asians.[40]

There were some positive opinion pieces in Canadian newspapers, even before the first Ugandan Asians arrived. Authors expressed their concern for the expellees by reiterating the importance of humanitarianism. Some argued that "Canada can do no less. There is a humanitarian duty to admit some of these unfortunate displaced people to the country—to prove that we are, as we so often boast, a tolerant open society."[41] Others said that many refugees "will take jobs which do not appeal to Canadians, others in the professions or with various forms of training and experience, should soon make places for themselves in our economy."[42] The *Vancouver Sun* went so far as to suggest that those who disapproved of the resettlement on "either economic or racial grounds only put themselves in a class with Mr. Amin."[43]

Some writers also noted that Canada had an obligation to accept Ugandan Asians given the country's previous discrimination against South Asian immigrants. University of Toronto professor James Eayrs argued that "after decades of statecraft devoted to keeping their people [South Asians] out, it would be a fitting act of retribution to waive our rules and let them in."[44] Professor Eayrs alluded to the infamous *Komagata Maru* affair in 1914, when Canada forced a ship carrying 356 migrants from the Indian subcontinent to turn back after a two-month standoff and Prime Minister Mackenzie King declared that "the Native of India is not a person suited to this country, accustomed as many of them are to the conditions of a tropical climate."[45] Others suggested that Canada should lead the charge in dismissing Uganda from the United Nations, arguing that "we ought not to pussyfoot with such demonic little tyrants as Amin . . . surely, the UN if it has any integrity at all, can see that Amin's expulsion order is the grossest violation of human rights."[46] Canadians also talked about the country's aid to refugees such as the Hungarians and Czechoslovaks in the postwar period, and beliefs that South Asians tend to avoid going on welfare because they are assisted by their own communities.

In sum, the public was torn between nativist concerns and humanitarianism, between citizen rights and universal human rights, between liberal nationalism and liberal internationalism.[47] But when Ugandan Asians expellees started to arrive at the Canadian Forces Base Longue-Pointe in Montreal, many Canadians believed that it was time to create "an honourable place" for these expellees in Canada.

Canada Responds to the Expulsion Decree

On 9 August 1972, in response to the issuance of the expulsion decree, Canadian Secretary of State for External Affairs Mitchell Sharp said that Canada "would consider taking 'positive action.'"[48] The Canadian government expressed its intent to provide some form of assistance to the Ugandan Asian expellees but added that it would cooperate in resettling expellees only "if Britain made a formal request."[49] Sharp explained that "we are hoping, indeed, that the government of Uganda will have second thoughts about this kind of operation. So this is one of the reasons why I don't think we should do anything until we are absolutely sure that the Government of Uganda is serious in wanting to throw out of their country people who have lived there for such a long time."[50]

Prime Minister Trudeau denounced the expulsion decree in an official statement: "It remains the hope of the Canadian Government that General Amin will consider the effects of his decrees not only on these long-time residents of his country but on the economy of Uganda and its development, to which Canada has made a contribution. I must also observe that General Amin's regrettable expulsion decisions, if implemented, would be contrary to his country's obligations under the United Nations Charter and Declaration of Human Rights as well as against the principles of the Commonwealth Declaration of 1971 in which member states reiterated their belief in human dignity and non-racialism."[51] Trudeau echoed the charges of racialism put forth by the leaders of several African countries and received written support from Tanzanian prime minister Julius Nyerere, who expressed his appreciation for Canada's rapid response. Trudeau also noted the economic impacts and numerous human rights violations entailed by Amin's decision. Unlike the British government, Trudeau had the liberty of taking an aggressive position when condemning the expulsion decree as the Canadian government did not have any legal obligation to admit Ugandan Asian expellees. However, after Trudeau had decided to take in expellees, Sharp cautioned against open criticism of the Ugandan government and argued that "if we hope to get the cooperation of the Ugandan government on the issuance of exit visas and otherwise helping in the transfer to Canada of those people who are being expelled, it would be well not to exacerbate relations between our two governments."[52] Thus, Trudeau and Sharp toned down reprimands of Amin and requests for the president to rescind his decision.

On 24 August 1972, Trudeau announced that a team of external affairs and immigration officials would be sent to Kampala to begin the necessary screening process prior to distributing entry visas. He explained that "this step will enable us to form a clearer impression of the numbers involved and of the extent to which exceptional measures may have to be taken to deal urgently with those who would not normally qualify for admission."[53] Part of the rationale behind sending the team to Uganda, however, was actually to assess whether the expellees could become integrated members of the Canadian community. Trudeau justified Canada's response by stating that "Asian immigrants have already added to the cultural richness and variety of our country, and I am sure that those from Uganda will, by their abilities and industry, make an equally important contribution to Canadian society."[54] Mackasey, the immigration minister, was also confident that the expellees would "make very good citizens once they are here."[55] Despite several significant factors behind Canada's decision to get involved, the government partly framed its response as adhering to a sense of brotherhood among Commonwealth countries. Newspaper headlines in the United Kingdom expressed gratitude for Canada's decision, even reading, "Thank you, Pierre."[56] A Foreign Office spokesperson in Britain described Trudeau's response as "genuinely humane and said he hoped the Canadian example would be followed by other Commonwealth governments."[57]

Once the Canadian government announced its decision to admit Ugandan Asians, the next major issue pertained to how many would be resettled. Trudeau initially avoided specifying a number, since the government did not have any official reports from Canadian officers in Kampala. "We know how much money we want to spend on it [the resettlement of Ugandan Asians], but I don't see any advantage in playing the numbers game," the prime minister explained when questioned by reporters. "It's the kind of answer that we have to find out before knowing numbers and involvement."[58] In contrast, one day after the formal announcement, Mackasey speculated that Canada could admit up to five thousand expellees and expressed that he "hoped all applicants would qualify under the immigration points system, but if necessary the system would be relaxed."[59]

The importance of adhering to the points system was emphasized by Trudeau and Mackasey to reassure the public that those admitted to Canada would not become dependent on income assistance. At the same time, Mackasey highlighted how the lives of Ugandan Asian expellees were under considerable threat based on the unpredictability of Amin's regime. He argued that "if a bunch of fanatics start a genocidal war against the Asians we'd have it on our consciences. We are very concerned that the situation in Uganda could rapidly deteriorate."[60] By emphasizing Canada's humanitarian impulse, admission of a significant group of individuals who would largely qualify under normal immigration criteria, and acceptance of the British request for assistance, the government effectively marketed the resettlement of Ugandan Asian expellees to the Canadian public as a worthwhile endeavour. As the prime minister aptly stated, "We would not have been Canadians if we had turned our backs on them."[61]

Several internal memorandums and reports to the Prime Minister's Office circulated before the public announcement articulated the benefits of responding to the expulsion decree. A memorandum to cabinet dated 22 August sought approval for the immigration of Ugandan Asian expellees from the prime minister in order to "demonstrate Canada's humanitarian concern for the expellees; provide orderly and timely processing and evacuation of those expelled; demonstrate to other countries, especially Britain, Canada's concern and sympathy for the very difficult position in which they have been placed by the Ugandan decision and to the degree possible within humanitarian requirements ensure that those expelled Asians who might best contribute positively to the Canadian economy and culture are admitted to Canada."[62] While highlighting the importance of humanitarian concerns and aiding the Commonwealth, the memorandum spelled out a preference for immigrants who would contribute to Canada.

An additional memorandum to the Prime Minister's Office from Deputy Minister for Manpower and Immigration J.M. Desroches, also submitted on 22 August, outlined that the Canadian government should get involved because it would "satisfy Canadian public interest without going so far as to invite a backlash because of employment problems, race relations, etc." and also "capitalize on [the] supply of entrepreneurs and professionals." The cabinet, as well as other government officials, were well aware that Ugandan Asian expellees tended to be well-educated, highly skilled, and savvy businesspersons. Desroches's report stated that "less than one percent of Uganda's population is comprised of Asians, but this small proportion virtually controls finance, commerce and the professions in the country."[63] Another report submitted to the Canadian government revealed pertinent statistics about the high levels of education among Ugandan Asians as well as their concentration in the fields of commerce, manufacturing, education, and medicine. According to the report, 50 percent of the Ugandan Asian population was enrolled in primary and secondary school in 1967. Furthermore, twenty thousand to twenty-five thousand Asians were employed in

Uganda by 1970, with 27.6 percent in manufacturing, 27.5 percent in commerce, and 16.5 percent in educational and medical services. The "high occupational and skill composition of Asians is reflected in their wages," argued the report, since "they earned an average wage of £EA 925 (East African shilling) in the private sector and £EA 1093 in the public sector compared to the Ugandan Africans who earned on average £EA 152 and £EA 199 respectively."[64]

A report received from the United Kingdom outlined the successful settlement of Kenyan Asian immigrants who had arrived in 1968. It highlighted their rapid labour market integration, stating, "The majority of those seeking jobs were placed in employment within a six-week period. In no case did the period of unemployment extend beyond six months."[65] This reinforced the Canadian government's position that Ugandan Asians would fare well in Canada as highly educated and skilled entrepreneurs who spoke English. The points system further ensured that Ugandan Asian applicants were screened for their potential to contribute to the economy.

The 22 August memorandum to cabinet specified that Canada should accept all applicants who meet the points system requirements and do not need special assistance up to a maximum of three thousand Ugandan Asian expellees. Using past immigration statistics from Uganda, which showed an acceptance rate of 40 percent of Ugandan Asian applicants, it was expected that only about twelve hundred Ugandan Asians would be admissible to Canada without any special assistance. The rest would receive additional aid in the form of "special transportation arrangements, including unrestricted Assisted Passage loans, and the provision of additional adjustment assistance in Canada," which would cost the government an estimated $5 million for three thousand Ugandan Asian expellees.[66] Both the memorandum to cabinet and the memorandum to the Prime Minister's Office mentioned the possibility of accepting more expellees if they met the normal requirements of the points system. This formed the basis for how Canada's chief immigration officer in Uganda, Roger St. Vincent, and his team evaluated expellees.

In his memoir, St. Vincent noted that on the same day that Trudeau publicly announced the screening of prospective immigrants, he received a telegram from G.M. Mitchell, the director of operations for the Foreign Service, to "proceed to Kampala and by whatever means undertake to process without numerical limitation those Asians who meet the immigration selection criteria bearing in mind their particular plight and facilitate their departure for Canada."[67] The immigration team in Kampala was expected to adhere to the points system. However, there was a policy provision that allowed the relaxation of selection criteria. Since Ugandans of South Asian descent were being targeted within their country of residence, and they made up only 1 percent of the population, they were considered to be an oppressed minority rather than refugees under the United Nations' 1951 Convention Relating to the Status of Refugees and the 1967 Protocol Relating to the Status of Refugees. According to the Canadian government, Ugandan Asian expellees were not considered refugees because "they will be citizens of other countries and could legally go to Britain, India, Pakistan, or Bangladesh."[68] As for those expellees who possessed Ugandan citizenship, those individuals must be "outside of the country of [their] nationality" to qualify as a refugee, according to the Refugee Convention and Protocol.[69]

Categorizing Ugandan Asians as expellees reflected the view of James Cross, acting assistant deputy minister for the Department of Manpower and Immigration. He argued that he "would recommend against treating these persons as refugees, or we may place ourselves in a position of having to react similarly in every country where the government wants to get rid of unpopular minorities by forcing them to migrate."[70] Consequently, the Canadian government used the terms "stateless" and "Uganda expellees" to describe Ugandan Asians during the period. It also exercised its oppressed minorities policy, which allowed officials to issue a one-time response and screen immigration applicants. The oppressed minorities policy had come into effect two years earlier, on 29 September 1970. It outlined that when oppressed minority applicants could not meet immigration requirements, "examining officers have discretion to admit such (members of oppressed minorities) when the information available indicates that there is sufficient private and/or government assistance available to ensure the applicants' successful establishment in Canada."[71] Thus, immigration officials had the flexibility to admit expellees on compassionate grounds but also had to make financial calculations in doing so.

However, feedback from St. Vincent's team within the first week of screening applicants in Uganda led to a significant shift in operations.

A new memorandum to cabinet from the Department of Manpower and Immigration on 13 September 1972 explained that more applicants passed the points system assessment than originally estimated: "Early processing results from Kampala now indicate that more than 3,000 applicants will meet normal requirements by the end of this month."[72] The memorandum outlined four possible courses of action for the government. Mackasey supported the fourth option, which allowed for an "unlimited number of unassisted applicants plus a limited number of fully assisted applicants."[73] This would remove the cap of three thousand expellees permitted entry under normal immigration requirements and allow for a maximum of one thousand expellees who did not qualify under the points system to be accepted under special circumstances. While there was no specified cap, the cabinet decision stated that "should it appear that the number of expellees coming to Canada will exceed 6,000 or that the cost will exceed $4.5 million, the Minister of Manpower and Immigration should report these developments immediately."[74] This appeased all parties involved. It demonstrated Canada's commitment to a humanitarian effort, met Britain's request to aid in the resettlement, and enabled the arrival of a highly skilled group of individuals who could easily integrate both socially and financially.

However, one fundamental element that influenced Canada's involvement was kept secret from the public. As the spiritual leader of Nizari Ismailis, the second-largest Shia Muslim group in the world, His Highness Prince Karim al-Husayni Aga Khan IV was deeply concerned about the expulsion decree because it affected a large number of Ismailis living in Uganda. During Ugandan independence in 1962, the Aga Khan had advised the Ismaili community to secure Ugandan citizenship to reduce tensions between the community and Ugandan Africans.[75] Unfortunately, this meant that many Ismailis had given up their British or Indian passports. Amin's decision to revoke the citizenship rights of all those of South Asian descent rendered a significant number of Ismaili Muslims stateless.

The Aga Khan was also a close personal friend of Trudeau's. Their friendship began in the 1960s and would continue to develop over the next decades through the exchange of numerous letters and shared family vacations, culminating in the Aga Khan appearing as an honorary pallbearer at Trudeau's funeral in 2000.[76] Upon hearing of the expulsion decree, the Aga Khan called Trudeau to ask if Canada could provide refuge for expellees.[77] While vacationing at the Aga Khan's private resort in Sardinia, during the summer of 1970, Trudeau and the Ismaili leader discussed the future of his community in East Africa. Under these circumstances, the prime minister and the Aga Khan worked closely to ensure the successful establishment of Ismaili Ugandan Asians in Canada. The government looked to earlier migrations for precedents. During the major nationalization programs that took place in Tanzania and Kenya in 1967 and 1969, respectively, Canada had accepted almost fifteen hundred Ismaili immigrants.[78] A background paper prepared for the government speculated that Ismaili Ugandan Asians would readily adapt to "the mainstream of Canadian life" as a "large number of them are professionals and entrepreneurs with available, often substantial, amounts of capital." The report aligned with the government's emphasis on adaptability to the Canadian labour market and the preference for highly skilled migrants under the points system. It also outlined that the past success of the Tanzanian Ismaili immigrants was due to the personal ingenuity of the community: "Well-qualified Ismaili candidates applied during the early stages to ensure the community started off on a stable basis, and there are credible reports that the Aga Khan established a special fund to assist in financing the resettlement."[79] The Aga Khan assured the Trudeau government in a letter that Ismaili Ugandan Asians settling in Canada would "do so in a methodical and orderly way" and that they would not "become a burden economically or a problem socially for Canada."[80]

The Aga Khan met with Canadian officials to coordinate the effort to aid the Ismaili community in Uganda. On 28 September 1972 the Aga Khan, his representative in Uganda and president of the Ismaili Council for East Africa Sir Eboo Pirbhai, and various Canadian government officials held a private meeting. The main issue at hand for the Aga Khan was what would happen to the Ismaili community after the November expulsion deadline. According to the meeting minutes, the Aga Khan stressed that after the deadline "no government would be responsible; Britain will not recognize them and will instead be concerned with her own nationals. There will be no shield to provide some security." To assist the Canadian government in resettling the Ismailis, he offered significant resources, including funding to support their flights to Canada, and guaranteed that they "would not take advantage of the situation." The Aga Khan also reminded the meeting attendees that "in practice, Uganda does not recognize them [Ugandan Asian Ismailis] and, as a result, they are *de facto* refugees." The majority of the meeting members agreed. However, Cross replied "that once out of the country, the stateless people definitely would be classified as such, but there is also a flexible policy for oppressed minorities which could be applied."[81] The Canadian government was sympathetic to the Ismailis in Uganda but also wanted to use existing immigration policies to admit them.

Government officials were concerned over possible criticisms of prioritizing "this particular group over the other applicants who represent the Hindu, Sikh, Christian religions as well as other Moslem elements."[82] During the meeting with the Aga Khan, the officials present agreed to keep the operation discreet. Pirbhai would provide a listing of Ugandan Ismailis to immigration officials via the Canadian High Commission office for the region, located in Kenya. As was the case in previous migrations of the Ismaili community in Canada for vulnerable individuals "a confidential list was passed to the government and as people [members of the Ismaili community] turned up they were checked off."[83] To avoid allegations of favouritism and backlash from the Canadian public and other bodies, officials decided to "instruct our team in Kampala to give priority in processing to all applicants who are stateless."[84] This enabled Canada to appease the public by showcasing its humanitarian efforts in regards to the plight of Ugandan Asians, answer Britain's call to the Commonwealth to support the resettlement, avoid using relaxed selection criteria for accepting refugees, honour the secret agreement with the Aga Khan and admit a large number of Ismaili Muslims, and dismiss accusations that the Canadian government was "skimming the cream off the total Ugandan movement."[85]

Officials justified the decision internally by agreeing it was the "Ismailis who had been hardest hit by the expulsion and citizenship measures" and who would be "given favourable treatment by virtue of our readiness to treat stateless persons on a priority basis."[86] This created a perplexing situation for St. Vincent and his team in Kampala since they did not know about this agreement. Their instructions were to accept anyone who was legitimately stateless, and they were puzzled by the consistent requests of Ismaili community leaders to accept more Ismailis. On 13 October 1972 local leaders in the Ismaili community requested to see St. Vincent. They handed him a list of 133 Ismailis who had not been called for an interview and demanded an explanation. St. Vincent responded that he would review the request over the weekend but that he was unable to provide preferential treatment to the Ismaili community. The local leaders threatened to turn to a higher power, which was undoubtedly Prince Sadruddin Aga Khan, who was the uncle of Aga Khan IV and the high commissioner for refugees at the time.[87]

In an oral history interview, St. Vincent recalled how he was asked to meet with Pirbhai in Nairobi to discuss the need to admit more Ismaili Ugandan Asian expellees. According to St. Vincent, the president of the Ismaili Council for East Africa

> was not happy, he was not pleased, he wished us to make a difference and see to the examination on exceptional basis of all the Ismaili citizens. And I said, "I cannot do that. . . . It is a universal immigration, it's based on universality, and universality means that the treatment is equal for all people. Already we are doing something different in selecting the stateless person, so the Ismailis. We cannot do more than that." He left me very unhappy, but I was not unhappy. I felt that I was doing what I was supposed to do. Look, after, if my government told me to select all the Asians stateless re-gardless of the others [regardless of their citizenship status], I would have done so but I never received such information, any such directive.[88]

Although St. Vincent was kept in the dark about the government's private agreement with the Aga Khan, he received specific orders from Ottawa on 31 October 1972 to reassess all the applications of those who claimed to be stateless before closing the Canadian immigration office. Those who had a legitimate claim were invited to be interviewed by the immigration team.[89]

The government refrained from specifying how many expellees would ultimately be admitted into Canada. As legend has it though, the final number of six thousand was determined by the September 1972 Summit Series. The Aga Khan's visit to Canada to meet with Canadian immigration officials coincided with game eight of the hockey competition between Canada and the Soviet Union. Because he merits head of state treatment, an honorary lunch was hosted for him at Rideau Hall.[90] Most high-level government officials, including the prime minister, the minister of manpower and immigration, and the minister of foreign affairs, had already met with him and could excuse themselves from the event, so it fell on Cross to attend. According to Michael Molloy, who was part of the immigration team in Kampala and was informed of this infamous luncheon by his Department of Manpower and Immigration colleagues, Cross's colleagues inquired if the maître d'hôtel could subtly communicate the score to the Canadian representatives during the lunch. Michael Molloy recalled in an oral history interview his description of what transpired at the luncheon from what he was told by others that once the game was tied at three goals apiece for Canada and the Soviet Union, the Aga Khan asked a very pertinent question:

> At a certain stage, with the score, the cumulative score, the Russians come up to six points. And Jo [Molloy's spouse] and I have gone through the game, and we've got it written down at what point that is when you've got a combined score that comes to six. . . . It was only there for a few minutes and . . . it's at that very minute that the Aga Khan says, . . . "So tell me, Mr. Cross. How many are you going to admit?" And it's at that minute that the maître d' flashes six fingers from the door. And Cross, as far as I can tell, puts six fingers down. . . . He's very excited and puts six fingers on that table and looks at his friends. And the Aga Khan looks at the fingers. And he said, "You mean six thousand? That's splendid."[91]

The events described in the "hockey story" coincided with a change in cabinet documents in September that specified the cap on expellees allowed entry into Canada was being increased to six thousand. St. Vincent provided a similar account of events at York University for the twenty-fifth anniversary celebration of the Ugandan Asian refugee resettlement in Canada.[92] There are no government documents or testimonies that verify the hockey story, but it has become a fundamental part of the resettlement narrative among the Ugandan Asian community in Canada.

Canada's response to the expulsion of Ugandan Asians ultimately reflects the dominance of the liberal internationalist approach to refugees and immigrants in the 1970s. Following the establishment of the points system, the resettlement of a significant number of Ugandan Asian expellees occurred within the emergence of a human rights discourse in Canada. The country affirmed its commitment to the United Nations by signing the Refugee Convention and Protocol in 1969, expressing its humanitarian impulses on the global political scene. Although the Liberal government announced the creation of multiculturalism policy in October 1971, no official records justified Canada's decision to admit Ugandan Asian expellees based on commitments to diversity. Immigration historians, including Gerald Dirks, Valerie Knowles, Ninette Kelley, and Michael Trebilcock have also not attributed Canada's mission in Kampala to the promotion of multiculturalism in Canada.

This chapter adds to the conclusions of Suha Diab, who argued that "Canada's swift humanitarian response to the Ugandan Asian crisis sought to affirm its loyalty and responsibility to Britain and the Commonwealth and secure the migration of a highly desirable group."[93] The push towards human rights, the Commonwealth connection, and the high education and skill levels of Ugandan Asians played a critical role in the government's decision to admit the expellees. Ultimately, the immigration team in Kampala implemented a universal admission policy that was both humanitarian and self-serving. It would set a precedent for how other major resettlements in the 1970s—of Chilean, Vietnamese, Cambodian, and Laotian refugees—would be carried out.

CHAPTER 4

"HIS DREAM BECAME MY NIGHTMARE":
Canadian Operations and Life in Uganda during the Ninety-Day Expulsion Period

His dream became the nightmare of 80,000 Ugandan Asians who were subsequently forced to leave the country.

Azim Motani, in Richard Saunders's *Journey into Hope*, 1994

He said, "I'm not going to leave this country, this is my home. . . . If I will die, I will die here."

Mumtaz, 2015

Initially what had happened was when the planes and stuff was coming into Uganda, nobody wanted to leave. People wanted to wait.

Errol Francis, 2015

Roger St. Vincent spearheaded operations in Kampala beginning on 31 August 1972. After meeting the rest of his team, he worked to establish a temporary Canadian immigration office. One of his chief contacts was A. Mevdghi, an Ismaili Ugandan Asian and manager of the Jubilee Insurance Company, who offered two desks, chairs, and the services of his secretary to help with the purchase of supplies from local shops. Prior to opening the office, St. Vincent consulted with British immigration officials who had already begun their application process. He noticed several differences between the British and Canadian procedures for issuing visas. According to St. Vincent's memoir, the British visa application process was completed within fifteen minutes. The British immigration officers had no "selection criteria, no medical section examination, x-ray, blood or 'stool' tests, no stage 'b' [security screening by the Royal Canadian

Military Police], no assisted passage, and no charter aircrafts."[1] It was also a largely paper process, where British officials asked few questions, as their primary objective was to identify if applicants were British subjects.

In contrast, Canadian immigration officials followed a strict procedure for granting visas to Ugandan Asian expellees. One of St. Vincent's greatest frustrations at the time was the mandatory medical examination required by the federal health department:

> The Ugandans were to have a blood test, urine test, stool test, which was incredible because they were healthy people that didn't require [medical tests]. I was never asked my opinion; otherwise, I would've said they didn't require any of those. Possibly the only thing I would've condoned was the x-ray, which was universal. . . . We had been going to East Africa for years, and during the years we were going there we selected people who were Asians, never requiring such documentation, such tests from them, because it was not required. They were healthy people and . . . an x-ray and a medical examination would suffice.[2]

The medical screening process slowed down the work of immigration officials and the distribution of visas. St. Vincent was perplexed by the requirement for medical tests in Kampala because immigrants from East Africa had not been required to have them in the past, and the Hungarian and Czechoslovak refugees that came to Canada in the 1950s and 1960s had their medical examinations completed upon arrival in the country.[3]

Documents from the health department provide insight as to why the government implemented these tests for the Ugandan Asian expellees. Regular immigration selection procedures included medical examinations, and the department said that "persons found inadmissible under the Immigration Act on health grounds are not being accepted."[4] Officials argued that Ugandan Asians needed to be screened for smallpox, cholera, yellow fever, tuberculosis, malaria, parasites, typhoid, and syphilis. There was discussion within the department about conducting the medical exams once the expellees had reached Canada, but this was "considered a very undesirable alternative," according to Dr. R.W. Robertson, the regional overseas director for the department.[5] Dr. Marcel Piché was the lead military doctor in Kampala and oversaw the Canadian medical team. According to Dr. Piché, 95 percent of the Ugandan Asian expellees who were screened had malaria at one point in their lives. However, this was the only major health concern. Medical officials on the ground screened almost two hundred expellees, all of whom were healthy, each day.[6]

Beyond medical screening, Canadian officials sought to ensure that expellees were not security threats. However, similar to the resettlement of Hungarian refugees, there was little security screening of the Ugandan Asians. Only one member of the Royal Canadian Military Police in Uganda accompanied the immigration team in Kampala, and that person was only in the country for seven days before returning to Canada. Government officials flirted with the idea of screening individuals once they arrived in Canada. Since President Idi Amin had dismissed seventeen of his top security men, it was effectively impossible for the Canadian military police to reliably screen expellees against local knowledge. However, intelligence reports by the officer in Kampala concluded that it was unlikely that Canada "will encounter any appreciable number of security problems with the Ugandans."[7] In the Cold War context of the 1970s, the expellees were considered a low security risk as they were fleeing an authoritarian regime and had no overt link to communism. The Canadian military police did give the immigration team in Kampala a list of known "undesirables" based on information received from Britain, and also provided an assessment that major protests by Canadians upon the arrival of Ugandan Asians were unlikely.

Beyond the medical and security concerns of the Canadian government, the final hurdle was transportation and the administration of the Assisted Passage Loans Scheme. Originally, the Canadian government's intention was to provide Ugandan Asian expellees with loans at 6 percent interest to cover the costs of their flights from Kampala to Montreal and subsequent travel to their final destination. Standard practice in Canadian immigration policy is for qualified immigrants to pay for their own voyage to Canada. But Ugandan authorities insisted that "if the airlift is in any way a commercial

Figure 2. Entebbe International Airport departure shed, 1972. Image credit: Literary estate of Roger St. Vincent.

venture with the immigrants being charged for their transportation, East African Airways must be involved with the operation."[8] East African Airways was the airline of Uganda, Kenya, and Tanzania. Since the Canadian government needed clearance from the Ugandan government to land charter planes, it could not circumvent the demand. Even if the Canadians were to use their own charter aircraft, the Ugandan government demanded that East African Airways receive a 50 percent share of the revenue regardless of whether the company carried any passengers. This placed the Canadian government in a difficult position. To appease the Ugandan government and get clearance to land, the Canadian government decided that the "operation was non-commercial in character, without cost to those transported."[9] The assisted passage loans were waived for the expellees' flights to Montreal but not for the second leg of their trip within Canada, which required repayment. In the end, the majority of those who were issued visas in Kampala received free transportation to Canada while 328 Ugandan Asians opted to personally fund their flights.[10]

When the Canadian immigration office officially opened on 6 September at 7:30 a.m., Ugandan Asian expellees had been waiting in line since 4:00 a.m. The immigration team followed a standard procedure in assessing candidates. First, the candidates received an application to be completed and returned as soon as possible for review by immigration officials. A list of eligible applicants was then posted in the local newspaper, the *Uganda Argus*. The next step was for candidates to undergo interviews. If they made it through, they were required to complete a medical examination including an x-ray and blood, urine, and stool tests. Only after passing every phase did an applicant receive a visa. Semin Kassam was the first expellee to receive a Canadian visa. Within the first week of operations, the immigration office distributed 3,736 applications to heads of families and individual applicants, which accounted for 11,208 expellees.[11]

As the team continued to process applicants, shifts occurred in the selection process to give immigration officers more flexibility in admitting expellees who did not meet the required fifty-point minimum. The 1952 Immigration Act granted "discretionary authority" to all immigration officials, authorizing them to add points in certain categories if applicants appeared "adaptable, had proved it and were ready and willing to go anywhere."[12] Officials also had discretion to allot an additional ten points under the "personal suitability" portion of the application form. Molloy, second in command in the immigration office, recalled, "We had ten points to give them on the basis of what was called 'personal suitability' and that meant evidence of adaptability, flexibility, you know, is the family hanging together? You know, that sort of thing. It was kind of quite subjective."[13] Another critical element of the selection process pertained to those who already had relatives living in Canada. Molloy noted:

> It was really amazing, by week two we were getting telegrams from people's aunties and uncles in Canada, or even friends, saying, you know, "My friend Mr. Ahmad, your number 443...." That quickly the numbers . . . went across to Canada and came back to us. And we got so many of those that we actually had to have a special system to keep track of them. Because it made a big difference when you opened that application and you look at their name and you open it up and right there is a telegram from somebody's auntie in Coquitlam, British Columbia, saying "this is my niece, nephew, my niece, my

friend, and if you let them in, we'll look after them." We just said that's as good as gold. That's one we don't have to worry about. So in those cases you would always use your discretionary authority, even if they didn't meet the points system.[14]

Thus, if Ugandan Asian expellees had a relative in Canada who was willing to support them, they were guaranteed admission to Canada, making previous migration to Canada of friends and family members a crucial asset to applicants during the expulsion period. St. Vincent recounted that some members of the Ugandan Asian community in Canada "had relatives which they left behind, and these relatives that were left behind, especially in Uganda, were given a priority because they had someone in Canada. That was one of the basic requirements for us, was to select on a priority basis those who would present no problem in resettling in Canada."[15] Having a relative in Canada was seen as protection against failing to adjust to Canadian society. One oral history participant recalled the significance of having a family member who had already immigrated to Canada: "Fortunately, my sister got married in 1970, and I don't know if this is destiny or something because . . . she decided she doesn't want to stay in Uganda and the place they chose was Canada. So in '71 they came to Canada. So they were here, they were just settling down in '72."[16]

Expellees were also required to demonstrate they would not become public charges or drains on the social system once they arrived in Canada. The bulk of applications for Canada were reviewed within the first week, and both Molloy and St. Vincent found that applicants were highly qualified under the points system, confirming the submissions to cabinet made in early September. Since applicants did not know what the selection criteria were, the officials concluded that applicants shared genuine information about their skills and expertise. "We had probably 60 to 80 percent of all the applications in the box before anybody out in the community had any idea what our criteria were," Molloy explained. "So what did that mean? That meant that we had enormous confidence in what we were seeing and the story of what we were being told reflected the reality. . . . If you're confident in the application you could have confidence in the people and you could sit back and relax and do your job."[17] Officials were still alert to attempts to circumvent the system though. As word spread throughout the Ugandan Asian community that Canada was admitting all those who were stateless, especially among the Ismaili community, individuals who were reluctant to go to Britain or the Indian subcontinent applied to Canada on the grounds that they were stateless. St. Vincent recalled in his memoir that he "had not invited all those claiming to be stateless for interviews and for good reason. At interviews, Ugandan Asian expellees would sometimes claim to be 'stateless.' When asked to produce a declaration form from the Uganda Passport Office stating that they had no claim to Ugandan nationality, most were reluctant. This suggested they were less than truthful."[18] Overall, government documents, St. Vincent's memoir, and oral testimonies from Molloy and St. Vincent describe how the immigration team in Kampala implemented an organized approach to the resettlement initiative. These sources refute arguments made by historians J.L Granatstein and Robert Bothwell that the lack of formal refugee policy in 1972 allowed immigration officials in Kampala to "invent one along the way."[19]

Oral history interviews document some instances where applicants were able to circumvent immigration procedures or where officials relaxed the selection criteria for applicants out of benevolence. Jalal recollected how squash games with an immigration official were considered to be his interview: "[I] didn't have to go through the hassle of lining up and getting the forms and getting an interview, which a lot of people went through a lot of difficulties [to do], and I felt badly that I was jumping the queue if you will. But it wasn't my doing: it was jump or my life."[20] Other applicants talked with immigration officials informally at local restaurants and bars during the expulsion period. Amin S. recalled that while waiting to hear about his application to Canada, he met an immigration officer at a bar:

> We became a little more friendlier. We had a drink together and then he asked me, "Do you have your application numbers?" I gave him my number, my other two brothers' numbers, and [that of] my brothers-in-law's family, my sister and her two children. . . . The next day he asked me to go there, and I went there in the afternoon at 2:30 p.m., and he had the files ready and he verified our identification and . . . then we got the numbers right away. We got a medical requisition, so we went and gave the medical. The very next

day when we gave the medical, as soon as they approved our
medical, they gave us CP air tickets.[21]

A friendly encounter at a local bar accelerated the application process
for Amin S. and his family, who were all able to resettle in Canada.
A similar process occurred for other interviewees, such as Karim. His
father's application was originally rejected for failing to meet the selection criteria. By chance he ended up at a dinner with several Canadian
immigration officials, and one of them inquired as to his immigration
status. Karim recounted how "my dad kind of inquisitively looked at
him and he says, 'I did [apply to Canada].' He says, 'Oh really? We
haven't seen your application come through.' He says, 'No, you're the
guy who failed me.' So when that was revealed . . . the person actually
reinvited dad to come in the next morning and he actually passed
him."[22]

There were some instances where Canadian officials aided Ugandan
Asian expellees in their application process to make sure they were
successful. Shamim remembered how, after her family's application
was initially rejected, an immigration official encouraged her to change
her date of birth on her passport to make her two years older: "He said
if I put '51 I can bring [my mother and two younger brothers] as my
dependants. . . . I was the adult. That's the only reason he asked me
to change it."[23] By applying as the head of the household who would
support the family, Shamim was able to pass the immigration process.
Using the oppressed minority policy and personal discretion, immigration officials assisted applicants in securing admission to Canada. As
scholars have argued, the flexibility of immigration officers in Kampala
reinforces the role that officials play as public and private gatekeepers.[24]

As the operation continued, it became clear that the number of
applicants who met the requirements under the points system exceeded
original estimates. The federal government predicted that three thousand people would meet the criteria by the end of September, filling
all spots allotted for Ugandan Asian immigrants. Officials in Kampala
were subsequently advised on 15 September to accept all those who
met the criteria and to accept up to a thousand Ugandan Asians who
required assistance.[25] The importance of adhering to the points system
was reiterated by the federal government, but as discussed, immigration
officials could make accommodations in a number of ways. By the end

of September, 6,335 applications had been received, 633 visas had been issued, and 2,500 persons were to be interviewed in the coming two weeks.[26] On the weekend of 7 October 1972, St. Vincent assembled a core group of the team to review all rejected applications and ensure that anyone who was legitimately stateless or who was admissible to Canada under more relaxed selection criteria was called for an interview. Upon revisiting 6,000 applications, officials invited 1,988 Ugandan Asians for an interview.[27] The goal of this exercise was to "yield a sufficient number of accepted persons to ensure that by 31 October, we would issue close to 6,000 visas," wrote St. Vincent in his memoir.[28] Whether the additional review was prompted by humanitarian considerations, the desire to admit highly skilled individuals, or the Aga Khan's meeting with Canadian officials on 28 September is up for debate. But it confirms the shift in the government's approach to admit all those who were genuinely stateless.

As the team began to conclude operations in Kampala near the end of October, a few issues remained. The first problem pertained to those who were stateless. Reports from the United Nations High Commissioner for Refugees (UNHCR), disclosed that more than 4,000 individuals had not received a visa as of 27 October 1972.[29] However, the immigration team in Kampala could identify only 1,200 stateless persons. Of this number, only 462 actually had visas in hand. During the last two weeks of October, 40 percent of those who had been called for interviews had not shown up, and 500 visas remained unclaimed.[30] St. Vincent outlined several reasons why he thought Ugandan Asians were reluctant to claim their visas. Despite visas being valid for entry to Canada within six months, some individuals had personal funds to finance their voyage to Canada and wished to travel to other destinations before arrival. Acceptance of a Canadian visa also prevented Ugandan Asians from visiting relatives in the United Kingdom or the Indian subcontinent before coming to Canada. Others sought to purchase first-class tickets for flights around the world to keep their money out of the hands of Ugandan authorities—after arriving in Canada, they would get a refund for the remaining portion their tickets, allowing them to get around the restrictions on taking money out of Uganda. Some expellees felt that the charter flights were akin to charity and they believed the Canadian government had already done enough. Finally, some opted to postpone their departure, including "dreamers, prepared to wait up to

Figure 3. Last chartered Canadian flight out of Entebbe International Airport, 1972. Image credit: Literary estate of Roger St. Vincent.

8 November in case the General changed his mind," as St. Vincent put it.[31] These factors made it difficult for immigration officials to confirm how many Ugandan Asian expellees would be coming to Canada.

Reports from Ottawa put the total number of visas issued by 8 November 1972 at 6,292, with 4,624 expellees officially in Canada leaving over 1,500 outstanding arrivals in Canada.[32] The visas were valid for six months, and Canadian authorities noted that "unfortunately, we have no way of knowing how many of these some 1,500 odd persons will eventually proceed to Canada."[33] Government officials in Ottawa argued that some of the expellees had already left Uganda by their own means, were able to secure visas to other countries or were granted an exemption to stay from the Ugandan government. According to St. Vincent, the overall operation was a success, leading to over 6,000 visas being issued. By the expulsion deadline of 8 November, 4,420 Ugandan Asian expellees had arrived on Canadian soil via chartered aircraft, 204 travelled independently and another 1,735 who wished to make their own travel arrangements had been granted visas.[34]

Figure 4. Canadian immigration team boards the last chartered Canadian flight out of Entebbe International Airport, 1972. Image credit: Literary estate of Roger St. Vincent.

International Organizations

International organizations played a crucial role in ensuring that every Ugandan Asian expellee was out of the country by the expulsion deadline. UNHCR partnered with the International Committee of the Red Cross and the Intergovernmental Committee for European Migration to coordinate the movement of Ugandan Asians who had nowhere to go. Their operations formally began on 26 October 1972—less than two weeks before the expulsion deadline. UNHCR officials arrived late in the expulsion period, having operated on the assumption that between the United Kingdom, India, Pakistan, and Canada, all stateless Ugandan Asian expellees were accounted for. UNHCR posted advertisements in local newspapers that identified the urgency of the situation and specified who was eligible for admission to refugee camps or transit centres in Europe. Refugee camps were short-term housing facilities in countries where Ugandan Asians would eventually resettle, whereas transit centres would accommodate Ugandans until they were resettled internationally.

UNHCR explained that it was in Kampala to "assist those members of the Asian Community who are of undetermined nationality and who are required to leave Uganda by 8 November. . . . All persons falling into the above-mentioned category, who do not have in their possession any valid travel document MUST report to the above address."[35] Local media sources estimated that the number of expellees who lacked any form of legal documentation was anywhere from four thousand to six thousand. A final report by UNHCR determined that there were roughly "5,900 Asians of undetermined nationality."[36] All those who required documentation were provided with the same Red Cross travel certificate that was issued to thousands of refugees upon the conclusion of the Second World War. Travel certificates were critical because the Ugandan government prohibited expellees without legal papers from purchasing airline tickets.

International agencies were prompted to action as the British and Canadian immigration teams concluded their processing of expellees. Britain was primarily concerned with anyone who possessed a British passport, and Canada had issued its quota of approximately six thousand visas. The remaining expellees became the responsibility of UNHCR. International organizations confirmed that they would fly four thousand Asians to various transit centres by 8 November 1972 through East African Airways at a reduced rate. UNHCR received $1.8 million USD in donations from the international community to support the relocation costs. Switzerland was the only country to finance the flights of all refugees who would be coming to refugee camps there. The Intergovernmental Committee for European Migration aimed to fly out up to 700 refugees per day, of which "2,300 will find temporary haven in Italy, 1,200 in Austria and 300 in Belgium. Austria will keep 250 and Belgium 150 permanently. Denmark has offered to take 40, Norway 200, Netherlands 300, the United States 1,000 and Argentina, Brazil and Colombia together [will accept] 300, also permanently."[37] The final effort by these international bodies ensured the relocation of a significant proportion of Ugandan Asian expellees who were ineligible or had missed the deadlines to apply to other countries.

A smaller number of expellees who had not been granted an exemption and were desperately in need of asylum remained in the country following the November deadline. Roughly eight hundred stateless Asians sought refuge in two Sikh temples and a Hindu community centre.[38] The stateless Asians were under direct UNHCR protection and needed to be evacuated within twenty-four hours based on agreements with the Ugandan government. Many of these stranded Ugandan Asians were flown to Malta, whose government had responded to UNHCR's request to provide temporary sanctuary for five hundred expellees on the condition the United Nations would provide funds for their subsistence and they would not be able to work while awaiting international resettlement. By mid-November almost every expellee who was not granted an exemption to remain in Uganda had left. Temporary transit centres alongside refugee camps were established across Europe and adhered to conditions similar to those imposed by the Maltese government.[39]

Ugandan Asian refugees were housed in a variety of facilities, including hotels, refugee camps, youth hostels, holiday centres, and military barracks. Rome provides an example of standard procedures for those sent to transit centres. Refugees were put in hotels, such as La Villa, just outside of the city, as they awaited relocation to more permanent refugee camps in places such as Oslo and Bergen in Norway. In upper Austria refugees were provided accommodation in hotels along the Danube River, since the spring and summer tourist seasons had concluded. Other Ugandan Asians were stationed in refugee camps, such as the Centro Canzanella refugee camp in Naples, Italy, where 386 stateless Ugandan Asians awaited permanent resettlement. Austria's main camp was in Traiskirchen, thirty kilometres from Vienna, and it provided sanctuary for not only seven hundred Ugandan Asian refugees but also nine hundred Eastern European refugees fleeing oppression under the Eastern bloc.[40] It was common practice to house refugees temporarily in central transit centres before moving them to smaller regions of the country. In Sweden expellees were flown to Stockholm and then relocated to cities in the southern part of the country, such as Alvesta, where 140 refugees were permanently resettled.[41]

Once expellees had safely left Uganda, the primary issue for UNHCR, the International Committee of the Red Cross, and the Intergovernmental Committee for European Migration was finding permanent settlement locations for them. UNHCR's special fund to aid in the initiative would be exhausted by February 1973. The crisis for the United Nations was twofold, since two thousand Ugandan Asians still required permanent resettlement and countries such as Austria, Italy, Malta, Morocco, Spain, Belgium, and Greece reluctantly faced the possibility of caring for stateless individuals for a prolonged period. Another obstacle for the international agencies was the unwillingness of specific countries to accept refugees generally. It was imperative that the international community provide asylum without being selective and refusing to admit "hardcore" refugee cases—those where individuals would need significant government assistance to resettle due to physical or mental health issues, lack of language skills or lower levels of education. The UNHCR representative in Austria articulated the issue: "The Austrians did not select when it was a question of saving life. Countries coming forward to help must not pick and choose, but should simply take people by numbers. Otherwise, Austria will be left with duds. It has happened before." However, the Austrian representative also noted how "in twenty years I have never met a better crowd of refugees."[42] The discourse employed by the Austrian representative coincided with the idea that humanitarianism is the foundation of refugee resettlement.

In early 1973 Canada would play a critical role in helping resettle stateless Ugandan Asian refugees located in transit centres as well as supporting reunification for families that had been separated during the expulsion period. Upon the conclusion of the ninety-day deadline to leave, Ugandan Asians who were ineligible to remain in Uganda had for the most part been resettled elsewhere on a permanent or temporary basis. By that point, they had navigated many perils, including harassment from Ugandan military and government officials, while also having to deal with the bureaucratic hoops of securing admission to Canada.

Ninety-Day Expulsion Period Through the Eyes of Ugandan Asians

Oral histories with Ugandan Asian expellees recapture the realities of the ninety-day expulsion period and provide historical insights into the lived experiences of community members as they prepared to leave their homeland. President Amin, along with his government, made it abundantly clear that Ugandan Asians were not to remain within the country unless they had been granted an exemption. Some expellees stayed until the final days, hoping that the decree would be lifted. Laila described how her father, a second-generation Ugandan, "didn't believe until the end that he would have to leave."[43] Laila and her family needed extra time to organize their personal affairs such as managing how they would gift their possessions or leave them with trusted Ugandan Africans. Others felt rooted in the country and defied the expulsion order. Unlike the rest of the family, Azim's uncle refused to apply for a visa. Azim recalled that his uncle said, "I'm a Ugandan citizen. . . . I'm not going to move. You guys are crazy to be applying elsewhere."[44]

Like Laila's father, many expellees were reluctant to leave out of pride and love for their homeland. Mumtaz recounted her grandfather's decision to remain in Uganda: "He decided that he was not gonna leave. He was old, and his wife passed away there, and his home was there. He said, 'I'm not going to leave this country. This is my home. . . . If I will die, I will die here."[45] For many older Ugandan Asians, leaving was too much to bear. It was also difficult for older adults to travel the long distance from villages to Kampala or to endure the long flights to their final destinations. Nimira recounted that her grandmother was 102 years old at the time and couldn't "travel even seven miles. How are we going to get her to any mode of transportation or even leave the country? So, we found somebody in Uganda, in Bududa. . . . She would be more comfortable with them. So what we did was we asked these people if they would take care of my grandmother and we left them everything we owned in Bududa."[46]

As the expulsion period progressed, government and military harassment of Ugandan Asians increased. An August 1972 telex from the Canadian High Commission in Kenya documented numerous closures of Asian shops in Uganda and that "Asians [are] still under surprise of shock. No panic noticed but all very anxious." However, the same telex reported mounting violence: "Good sources inform us that two Asians [were] taken away by army officers and shot dead near Jinja. Newsmen here report rumours of Asians being beaten and Asian women raped in [the] past two days."[47]

Amin's regime promoted and condoned widespread violence against Ugandan Asian expellees. Scholars have noted five principal categories of antagonism from government and military officials. The first was the inconvenience. Expellees were forced to adhere to a strict curfew and subjected to extremely long queues at passport offices. Property loss was another issue. Expellees' property was confiscated by officials, looted, or given up as a bribe for safe passage at various checkpoints. The third form of antagonism was personal harassment through unwarranted arrests and searches of homes and businesses. The fourth and fifth were rape and murder, committed by the military as well as members of the public. Though these occurred less often than the other forms of antagonism, they nonetheless struck fear in the community.

The extent of physical and sexual violence against Ugandan Asians during the expulsion period is debated amongst scholars and oral history participants. Sociologists Bert N. Adams and Mike Bristow contend that "physical violence was much less frequent than people thought it was, with beatings by the army involving about one family in twenty, and killing and rape occurring in less than one of every 300 families expelled. Rumours were rampant in the Asian communities, focusing especially on physical violence."[48] Adams and Bristow attribute widespread reports of violence to attempts by the British media to garner support for the reception of expellees, as well as exaggeration and rumours circulating throughout the Ugandan Asian community. Oral testimonies from Jalal and Munira support the arguments presented by Adams and Bristow. As Jalal argued, "Within the Indian community, if one person is robbed, the whole community goes ballistic. If one person is beaten up it's like, whoa, what's happening? If one woman is raped it's like the most despicable thing you could ever hear of, right? So the emotions rise because we'd never been exposed to that [sexual harassment from Ugandan authorities]."[49] Munira described how news spread quickly within the community: "Because we are so tight-knit, when somebody is kidnapped or someone is being tortured you hear of it first-hand. Because news travels like dominoes, right?"[50]

In contrast, other scholars and the majority of oral history participants have documented many instances of violence and harassment. Anthropologist Anneeth Kaur Hundle and geographer Joanna Herbert record varying gendered experiences of violence during the expulsion period in their research. Hundle argues that there was a particular interest in the Ugandan Asian community to keep women safe alongside fears of sexual harassment and further that the expulsion decree signified the emasculation of South Asian men. In her interviews with male Ugandan Asian refugees, they spent large portions discussing the need to protect female Ugandan Asians and felt the need to keep their wives and daughters confined to various private spaces for safety. Men already acted as the primary intermediaries between African society and the private South Asian household, and they placed further restrictions on women as anti-Asian sentiment increased throughout Uganda. Male anxieties were strongly linked to historical gender constructs and concerns surrounding the purity of women's bodies, their *izzat* or honour, based on religious and cultural norms in the East African Asian community. These were exacerbated by embedded ideologies and stereotypes that labelled Ugandan African males as hypersexual and aggressive.[51]

Oral histories from male Ugandan Asians in Herbert's study relay specific instances where they needed to protect women from the violence of Ugandan officials. One man described how an official "even had the guts to ask my wife to remove her golden ring out of her finger . . . and also tried to force, I would use the word snatching, the bracelet out of her neck."[52] Herbert agrees that Ugandan Asian men's emphasis on shielding women from security forces during the expulsion period conveys a sense of duty based on historical constructions of race and gender. However, her study problematizes male anxieties about the prevalence of sexual harassment. One female interviewee stated that "the army was not cruel like you've heard in some countries where there is a coup. The people are raped and looted and this and that. It didn't happen and we were very, very lucky in that respect."[53] The challenge with distinguishing rumours from reality is noted by Adams and Bristow. Interviewees may exaggerate stories of violence based on community gossip.

Oral history participants that I interviewed described several instances where women were the targets of sexual harassment. Sikandar reflected on a particularly harrowing experience while en route to Kampala with his two younger sisters. As they reached a checkpoint, soldiers ordered their car to stop:

> Then the soldiers grabbed my sister by her shawl. Before that they said to the driver, "You can go. We are going to marry them." So my sisters are pretty much in tears, in shock. They were younger than me, so they were only fifteen. . . . So finally, he [the driver] talks to them [the soldiers] and they come

and grab my sister by her shoulder and the necklace, and it says "Allah." So he grabs it and says, "Allah." He could read Arabic because he was [one of] Idi Amin's Muslims. So he says to my sister, "You are my Muslim sister. How can I do that to you? You can go." They took the money and if there was no necklace, what would have happened? Who knows?[54]

The threat of sexual violence features prominently in several of my oral interviews.[55] Nellie described how she began helping women leave the country. As Amin's soldiers were given free reign, she was concerned that drunken soldiers were "going to start raping them [female Ugandan Asians]" and she used her job at British Airways to get as many Ugandan Asian women as possible out of the country.[56] Ugandan Asian novelists have also conveyed the threat to the safety of female members of the community during the expulsion period. As the protagonist in Shenaaz Nanji's *Child of Dandelions* attempts to verify her Ugandan citizenship and is refused, she pleads with the government officer that her father will build him a house as large as her own. He responds, "I'm going to get your house anyhow, but right now the warmth of a pretty girl like you will make me happy."[57] This interaction personifies the gendered experiences of Ugandan Asian expellees.

Concerns for the well-being of female expellees were fuelled by restrictions President Amin placed on their attire. Nimira recounted, "He [Amin] got up one morning and he said Asians were teaching the Africans to wear miniskirts.... So he said nothing above the knee. So if you were caught with even one inch above the knee they hurt you bad. Sometimes they would cut you, sometimes they would beat you up, just put you in jail things like that."[58] An article in the *Uganda Argus* reported on two expellees who were fined for wearing "mini-dresses": "Two Asian girls were fined in Kampala court yesterday after admitting to being idle and disorderly persons. The girls who pleaded guilty ... were Shajda Nasrullah and Gulzar Nasrullah, all residents of Rubaga Road Kampala.... Inspector Oryema said that S. Nasrullah's dress was 3.5 inches above her knee line and that of G. Nasrullah 3.3 inches. Mr. Kantini fined each girl 50 [East African shillings]."[59] The hefty fines made it apparent that this law would be seriously enforced. By targeting females specifically, the Ugandan government exacerbated the anxieties of the Ugandan Asian community, who feared for the safety of their female members. As scholars debate the prevalence and gendered aspects of violence during the expulsion period, oral histories, government reports, and media sources complicate the historical record.

Ugandan Asian expellees became increasingly apprehensive as tensions rose over the expulsion period. The failed Tanzanian-supported coup attempt in September 1972, along with the imprisonment and kidnappings of various prominent Ugandan Asian expellees, led to an increasingly desperate situation for expellees. Reports from the High Commission of Canada revealed incidents of violence being carried out against noncitizens, particularly during the failed Tanzanian invasion of Kampala in late September. The Canadian High Commission in Kenya reported to the authorities in Ottawa that "there are continuing reports of arbitrary detentions and harassment and molestations of whites by undisciplined soldiers, near breakdown of law and order plus tensions engendered by Tanzanian/Uganda dispute continue to contribute to apprehensions of non-Ugandans."[60] Amin's military personnel created an atmosphere of wanton harassment where anyone was susceptible to interrogation, imprisonment, and verbal or physical abuse. The arrest of Manubhai Madhvani on 5 September 1972 sent shock waves through the community, showing that one of the most powerful Ugandan Asian families was not immune from government harassment. Nor was the other famous industrialist family, the Mehtas—an old family friend was dragged from his car and imprisoned for several days in the "notorious Makindye military barracks."[61] The youth was later released from the prison and reunited with his family, but his detention sent a powerful message.

Oral testimonies from expellees alongside research from other scholars nuance the claims of Adams and Bristow that rumours inflated claims about the incidence of harassment. Raids on the businesses of Ugandan Asians as well as impromptu searches of their homes were widely documented by oral history participants. Aziz and his wife, Fatima, recounted how Aziz's brother continued to run their family business during the expulsion period; since Amin's decree was amended on a frequent basis, he thought he could stay in Uganda:

> Aziz: He knew that things are changing from day to day, maybe he'll stick around. So he was running the business

and I think six weeks to two months later there was an army colonel and a general, they just walked into the store with a gun and said, "Okay, you've got two minutes to get out."

Fatima: "Take your papers and go."

Aziz: So his hands were shaking and he was just hoping that he'd find his passport, you know. He's searching and at the last second he found his passport and he left. So, you know, he just left everything, lock and key.[62]

This became a common occurrence for expellees who owned businesses, especially larger commercial enterprises. Edmond and Maria recalled how the manager of Dunlop's central tire factory in Jinja became one of Amin's "marked men." Edmond said his close friend "was marked by these soldiers. I don't know why they were after him. I don't know if you heard sometimes they would come and check some Indians and take them to the prison, barracks, and all that. And they were after him and he was so worried."[63] Fortunately, he avoided being captured and was able to flee the country within a few days of becoming aware that he was a target. Those who did not obey commands from military officials suffered the consequences. Errol remembered how a family friend refused to turn over the keys to his rental car company: "He was resisting it, which was silly. I told him, 'Just give them [military officials] the keys. It's worth nothing anyways.' And this was in the midst of the problem. But he didn't, so they picked him up and they actually killed him."[64]

Physical violence and confrontations between business owners and army officials also extended into residential areas. Several interviewees described raids that took place in their neighbourhoods, particularly during September and October of 1972. Amin V. recalled that the community was becoming increasingly anxious: "People were, towards the September–October months, were starting to get very nervous. Military people were going into different homes, they knew people were leaving, raping women ... stealing their luggage."[65] Officials raided Nimira's home: "They took my brother and my father to some place and out of sheer luck my brother happened to notice somebody else who was driving by and asked for help and they snuck away into that car. But otherwise, god knows what they would have done. We were hearing all kinds of things about what they were doing because they had guns, they had nobody to ask them what they were doing, nobody to question their power."[66] Nimira's testimony makes clear that Amin's government had generated an atmosphere of widespread violence where soldiers were not held accountable for their actions. Another instance of abduction was mentioned by Mobina: "Before we left, the army picked up my husband, which wasn't a very pleasant experience. We suffered a lot. But happily because of my father and those with influence they didn't take him to the army barracks, because just the day before we lost one Ismaili and we never heard from him again, from Fort Portal. And if they had taken him [husband] to the army barracks [pause] I know I would have never seen him again. . . . It wasn't pleasant, it was very unpleasant what happened there, but still he did come home."[67] Her father's influence, derived from his philanthropic work helping Ugandan Africans with their education costs, prevented her husband from being sent to the army barracks—a place from which many individuals never returned. Although her husband sustained severe injuries from the kidnapping, he was returned to the family and successfully sought refuge in Britain.

The mistreatment of expellees stretched beyond their homes and businesses to include various roadblocks and random checkpoints throughout the country, especially along the airport road from Kampala to Entebbe. According to historian Nicholas Van Hear, Ugandan Asians "were robbed on the way to the airport by rank and file soldiers, who realized, rightly, that it would be the higher ranking officers and officials who would be the beneficiaries in the officially sanctioned carve-up of Asian assets later on."[68] Travelling to the airport became a harrowing experience for many expellees. British media described the road as "an obstacle course with 10 roadblocks manned by trigger happy soldiers."[69] Upon arriving at Entebbe International Airport, expellees were subjected to another round of inspections. East African media sources reported that Ugandan soldiers were looting baggage and delivering verbal and physical abuse. Physical confrontations could be more extreme. The Mombasa Red Cross reported that a person named Ajit Singh needed medical treatment after being severally beaten by soldiers while en route to Kenya from Uganda.[70] St. Vincent argued in his memoir that expellees "genuinely feared for their lives."[71]

Several Ugandan Asians had to travel great distances from their hometowns to apply for visas to Canada, making their way through a

vast series of military checkpoints where many were robbed, harassed
verbally and sexually, and subjected to long delays because of prolonged
and unwarranted searches. Iqbal, an oral history participant quoted under a pseudonym, was responsible for travelling to and from his family
home to have documents verified in Kampala and recalled the numerous
roadblocks set up between Jinja and the capital city: "Every day travelling, two to three times travelling, from Jinja to Kampala. Then nine
roadblocks, army roadblocks. And they tell you in Swahili, 'Muhindi,'
with a gun like this, holding onto your face, '*toka chini*,' get down. . . .
You're supposed to get down there every time. There were about nine
roadblocks in fifty miles of road."[72] Azim remembered that his mother's necklace was taken from her at one of the roadblocks as they were
travelling to Kampala: "[The soldiers] stopped her. The necklace was
hidden. They of course saw it, took the necklace, and you know hit her
with the butt of the gun. And she was lucky she didn't get killed."[73]
Each checkpoint aroused fear and anxiety for Ugandan Asians, as they
did not know what to expect. This was particularly traumatic for Zul,
who vividly remembered the "seven checkpoints where they searched
everything. Okay? So I was only able to bring my one bag and maybe
one picture of my wedding. . . . Idi Amin . . . his friends were, one of
them was a friend of mine in the army, and it's amazing that they shot
an Ismaili neighbour of mine. . . . He shot him right in front of me."[74]

The road to the airport became so dangerous that Canadian immigration officials provided escorted buses draped with large Canadian
flags to transport visa holders from Kampala to Entebbe. Even these
buses were not impervious to random stops by the Ugandan army. Azim
described his family's journey to the airport as follows: "The Canadian
High Commissioner had a bus set up for a safe transportation because
people were being hassled and looted and beat up when they were
travelling from their homes to come to the airport. . . . [But still] you've
gone through umpteen army stops, people [soldiers] have come on the
bus. . . . They couldn't have been barred from the buses."[75] Those who
took private journeys to the airport were subjected to harsher treatment
by armed guards, since they did not travel under the protection of any
government. Zabina recalled how the trip to Entebbe was "another
fearful drive I should say because at every point there was a stop. There
were a lot of stops on our way. It wasn't just a direct drive, and each stop
had the army, so of course they were asking us where are you going, what

are you doing. . . . The army wanted us to bribe them in order for them to let us go."[76] Bribery had become fairly common at the roadblocks, as poorly paid soldiers sought to line their own pockets.

After the journey to the airport, expellees were met with another round of checks and searches of their personal belongings. Mohamed and Almas chronicled the thorough searches conducted at the airport as well as the importance of not trying to hide valuables from airport security:

> Mohamed: They were checking everything. Now, my only concern was my occupation listed on my passport said I was a civil servant. So I kept praying. . . . If they notice that, they might start questioning and then I'm in trouble. So fortunately they didn't look at the occupation on the passport.

> Almas: The way we left we couldn't take anything with us of course, just one bag of clothes and that's all we were allowed to. Nothing, no jewellery, no money, no nothing. Twenty dollars . . . [in] shillings, Uganda shillings, in his [Mohamed's] pocket. . . . They let the suitcase go through but they searched us and they took that twenty dollars from him at the airport.[77]

As noted in Chapter 2, there were tight restrictions on what expellees could and could not take out of the country. These restrictions were strictly enforced at the airport, and anyone could be searched. Oral history participants documented vigorous strip searches conducted by airport security and soldiers. Munira described how her entire family was thoroughly searched, including her youngest sister who was only a few months old:

> Then we had to go and individually be hand-searched, right? So here my grandmother went in first, got searched. They came out with her hand luggage on the side and gave it to one of the officers and my grandmother . . . didn't say much but she had tears that were just dribbling down her face and my dad knew that whatever valuables she had in there were being possessed. Now it's our turn, Mum and the three of us. So Mum gets frisked, the baby gets frisked, even through her crotch, right? . . . My turn, my sister's turn, and here goes

the hand luggage. My mother was just shaking like a leaf, she could barely hold my baby sister, but we managed to get out of that little inspection room.[78]

Airport security and military officials worked to ensure that very few expellees were able to smuggle valuables out of the country. As argued by Van Hear, security personnel were well aware that the higher value possessions, including businesses and properties, would be distributed among high-ranking officials. Thus, they used opportunities in residential neighbourhoods, at road checkpoints, and at the airport to reap their own rewards.

In some instances, expellees were able to hide jewellery or other valuable items in secret compartments of their luggage.[79] Ugandan Asian novelist Yasmin Alibhai-Brown describes another technique in *The Settler's Cookbook*. As an older expellee explains to the novel's protagonist that one must be clever, she pulls out a container of bhajias (spicy deep fried potatoes) and opens one "carefully with her bent and brittle fingers. Inside are a couple of diamond rings. 'Many more in here, you have to be clever. Fifty-five diamonds and some gold—I fried the whole afternoon.'"[80] She had baked her wedding jewellery inside deep-fried snacks.

Some Ugandan Asians attempted to circumvent the restrictions on transferring funds abroad and taking physical money out of the country by purchasing first-class around-the-world tickets. Expellees who did so would complete the first leg of their journey, then get a refund for the remaining portion of their tickets. By doing so, they kept the money out of Amin's hands. Nellie, who worked for British Airways, described how this was a common but dangerous practice in the initial days of the expulsion period. She recalled how she was "helping people to issue tickets. Our assets were all frozen. So what do we do with our money, all the salaries that we get? We were just buying watches and this and that . . . and they were buying around-the-world ticket."[81] Selling around-the-world tickets was particularly dangerous for Nellie. She encouraged expellees to buy multiple airline tickets instead of a single one to avoid drawing attention to what they were doing: "Buy one ticket, one person went to Nairobi, one from Nairobi elsewhere. Don't buy one ticket. Get multiple. They didn't listen to me. . . . They [Ugandan officials] came, they found out that

I had helped them issue the [around-the-world] tickets, so I had to leave the country the same day."[82] In response to this practice, Amin prohibited the purchase of around-the-world tickets in addition to implementing the mandatory tax clearance forms and bank account restrictions as noted in Chapter 2.

Harassment was manifested in varying degrees, including in personal inconvenience, property loss, verbal harassment, sexual harassment, and physical abuse. Oral history participants identified concrete examples of violence and how these experiences varied based on gender. These examples complicate the conclusions drawn by scholars who argued that harassment was overrepresented in the media or based on community gossip. While oral histories need to be nuanced given the prominence of rumours and possibly exaggerated memories of trauma, oral historians contend that local knowledge and experiences, and the inclusion of the voices of marginalized communities, complicate and enrich our understanding of the past.[83] The oral histories of Ugandan Asian expellees are supported by reports from various Canadian officials who described the deteriorating conditions in Uganda and the severity of the expulsion decree. As the expulsion deadline expired, Uganda's social and economic climate was quickly transformed.

By the end of the expulsion period, 4,624 Ugandan Asian expellees had arrived in Canada.[84] In the coming winter months, these refugees began to adjust to Canadian society. They were resettled in Canada amid high levels of unemployment and mixed reactions among Canadians regarding the operation in Kampala. The context in which the Liberal government had announced its plan to aid in the resettlement process of the Ugandan Asians included the recently established multiculturalism policy, the Canada–Soviet Summit Series, and an impending federal election in October.

CHAPTER 5

"AN HONOURABLE PLACE":
Establishing New Roots in Canada and Evaluating the Resettlement Initiative

For our part we are prepared to offer an honourable place in Canadian life to those Uganda Asians who come to Canada under this program. Asian immigrants have already added to the cultural richness and variety of our country, and I am sure that those from Uganda will, by their abilities and industry, make an equally important contribution to Canadian society.

Prime Minister Pierre Elliott Trudeau, August 1972

You know I cried when I saw the Indian curry, chicken curry, and pilau being cooked for us. I said, "There are people, and then there are people."

Ishad Razack, in Richard Saunders's *Journey into Hope*, 1994

What is Canadian experience? I mean if you're a lawyer or a secretary or whatever, you have experience. So it was tough to get a job. But the more devastating thing for me was they wouldn't accept my qualifications.

Jalal Jaffer, 2015

Once Ugandan Asians arrived on Canadian soil, the lengthy processes of adaptation, adjustment, and integration began. They were immediately labelled as refugees by the media. Volunteers and members of the Manpower and Immigration office greeted the refugees who came via chartered flights, which landed at the Canadian Forces Base Longue-Pointe in Montreal. Collaborative efforts between the various levels of government and the voluntary sector at the Longue-Pointe military base were supplemented by the twelve Uganda Asian

Figure 5. Reception of Ugandan Asian Refugees at Longue-Pointe, Canadian Forces Base. Library and Archives Canada, Department of National Defence fonds, e011052358.

Figure 6. People getting food and refreshments. Library and Archives Canada, Department of National Defence fonds, e011052360.

Committees set up by the federal government across Canada. Their primary objective was to provide knowledge about the job market, housing, and social support to incoming refugees. Committee facilities served as a central location for encouraging open dialogue and interactions between Canadians and newcomers. These combined efforts from the government, voluntary sector, and the public were critical to the success of the resettlement. They quelled public anxieties about the integration of Ugandan Asians and provided an inclusive and welcoming environment for the newly arrived refugees.

The chartered flights flew directly from Entebbe to Montreal with a refuelling stop in Accra, Ghana, or Addis Ababa, Ethiopia. Longue-Pointe served as the principal reception centre for refugees, who required a short rest after their eighteen-hour journey.[1] Operations at the Canadian Forces Base commenced on 22 September 1972. Six buildings on the base provided lodging for families and individuals, while other buildings housed the reception area, dining quarters, emergency health services, nursery, clothing outlet, recreational space, and offices for the relevant government departments. Longue-Pointe received 4,448 Ugandan Asians during Operation UGX, named after the code for Entebbe's airport.[2] Ten to twelve volunteers arrived daily to care for the children while their parents attended to administrative affairs. These volunteers came from various church groups, the Salvation Army, or were private citizens. Volunteers also offered their services at refreshment tables and provided more general assistance to families. Miracle Mart, a grocery store in Montreal, donated winter clothing and provided food and beverage to the reception centre.[3]

Upon arrival at Montréal–Dorval International Airport, refugees met with officials from the Department of Manpower and Immigration and boarded school buses headed to the military base. Once at Longue-Pointe, they were welcomed by the base commander, Major D.O. Tinklin, and the head of the Manpower and Immigration office in Montreal, René Lefèbvre, as well as other dignitaries. Then they were assigned to their rooms at the base. Registration was accompanied by refreshments and any necessary medical attention. Bryce Mackasey, the immigration minister, was present to greet new arrivals from the first flight, and distributed small plastic Mountie dolls to children.[4] Flights arrived in the earliest hours of the day, around 2:00 a.m. to 3:00 a.m., so the vast majority

Figure 7. Family greeted by soldier. Library and Archives Canada, Department of National Defence fonds, e011052346.

of Ugandan Asians promptly retired to their quarters after a short meal. After being served breakfast the following day, they returned to the reception centre to undergo more stringent documentation procedures, including agricultural and immigration clearances and interviews with Manpower counsellors (one from each region of the country). They also received allowances and pocket money, if needed, and winter clothing. Most refugees who came to Longue-Pointe were able to depart for their final destination within twenty-four hours.[5] Quick turnaround times were implemented at the base because "it was felt to be psychologically encouraging for the Uganda Asians to get to their final destination quickly [and] also to avoid establishing anything like a refugee camp however temporary," according to government records.[6]

Meetings with Manpower counsellors were crucial for refugees to learn what Canada had to offer and where they were most likely to find employment based on their occupational skills. There was a desk for each of the Manpower regions (Atlantic, Quebec, Ontario, Prairies, and the Pacific) in the drill hall. These consultations elicited information necessary to reconnect refugees with family members or friends who

Figure 8. Couple speaking with soldier at accommodation centre. Library and Archives Canada, Department of National Defence fonds, e011052354.

had previously migrated to Canada, or who had arrived on an earlier flight. Azim recalled how his family was able to reunite with his sister in St. Albert, just west of Edmonton in Alberta: "They were asking where we should go, where we wanted to go. And my sister was in a little town in St. Albert. . . . If you had family, or if you had the means, then the government would say, 'Okay, we will get you there and then you are on your own.'"[7] The Canadian government wanted refugees to reunite with family members so they would not need further financial support.

Refugees incurred all travel costs from the military base to their final destination through assisted passage loans. There was some confusion among the Ugandan Asian refugees about these loans. For example, volunteers with Regina's Uganda Asian Committee gave inaccurate information to refugees, telling them that assisted passage loans did not need to be repaid.[8] A small number of families who resettled in Regina were "very upset" to receive a letter from the government prompting them to repay their respective loans, as they were not "yet successfully re-established" and "claimed they had no knowledge they would be charged with this debt."[9] However, the Canadian government

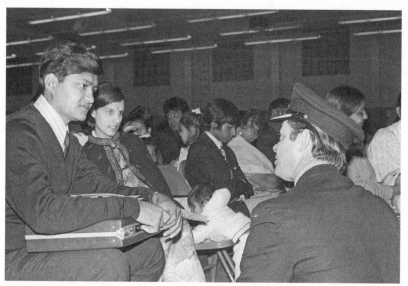

Figure 9. Couple talking with soldier. Library and Archives Canada, Department of National Defence fonds, e011052357.

enforced repayment only when individuals were "financially able to do so."[10] James Cross, a director at the Department of Manpower and Immigration, argued that the loans should not be forgiven because the repayment had already been significantly delayed to grant refugees more time to achieve financial stability and because the refugees "were fully aware of the conditions attached to them [loans]."[11] Although the government had agreed to cover the cost of chartered flights to Canada because of the conditions imposed by Idi Amin, transportation within the country would not be absorbed by Canadian taxpayers.

Manpower counsellors were also responsible for ensuring that Ugandan Asian refugees did not cluster in major Canadian cities in order to avoid the creation of ethnic ghettos and to match local demands for labour. Oral histories with Ugandan Asian refugees provide insight on the realities of their permanent resettlement across Canada and the role Manpower counsellors played in assuring that they were evenly dispersed. Umedali explained that even though his sister lived in Toronto, he was instructed to go elsewhere: "They said, 'No, you can't go to Toronto or Vancouver because lots of people are going to

Vancouver and Toronto.' So I said, 'Okay, send me wherever you want but somewhere around Toronto.' So they sent us ... to Wallaceburg [a town in Ontario about 300 kilometres from Toronto]."[12] Edmond was also directed away from Ontario's largest city: "I told him, 'I want to go to Toronto.' 'Oh you can't go there' and all this stuff. Then he said, 'I'll send you to British Columbia.' ... See, they didn't want us in major cities."[13] In some instances, assignments to Canadian cities occurred in a haphazard manner, particularly for those who did not have any friends or family in the country. One interviewee was placed in a smaller Canadian city because their surname rhymed with the city, according to the counsellor.[14] Others received guidance from Manpower counsellors about where to settle based on their previous work experience and Canadian labour needs. Of the 5,611 refugees who flew to Canada on either chartered flights or independently by 5 December 1972, 237 were resettled in the Atlantic provinces, 638 in Quebec, 1,956 in Ontario, 501 in the Prairies, and 2,279 in British Columbia.[15]

Both the media and the Ugandan Asian refugees applauded exemplary service at Longue-Pointe. Vic Wilczur, information officer for Manpower and Immigration, reported that the first week of reception activities were "an unqualified success in every respect." Wilczur emphasized how the reception story, which coincided with the final match in the Summit Series, "sold itself" and the second flight was promoted on "the angle that all the kinks and bugs had been eliminated as a result of the trial run. We told the media what we learned from our mistakes, listed them, and said what would be avoided on future arrivals." The Canadian government continued to provide members of the press with exclusive access to news stories and treated them favourably as a means of garnering positive reviews of the resettlement. For example, Wilczur granted CTV News the opportunity to be the only television station to cover a birthday party held for a refugee who arrived on one of the first flights and celebrated her eighteenth birthday in Canada. In a report to his superiors in late October, Wilczur asked whether it was best to continue "planting and pushing stories or do we let it die a quiet death." He also noted that although media interest had dwindled after the arrival of the second flight of refugees, it would pick up again as the expulsion deadline approached, since that "will result in really heartbreaking stories."[16] Wilczur purposefully gave stories to the media to create positive coverage of resettlement operations in Montreal. He

Figure 10. People being served hot food. Library and Archives Canada, Department of National Defence fonds, e011052347.

argued that the "base is chock full of feature stories for tv, radio, news agencies, magazines, daily papers and the army has given me a blank check to release anything I want."[17]

One of the most prominent features of the reception centre was the food served in the dining quarters, which were operational twenty-four hours a day and accommodated the dietary restrictions of the refugees. A local Indian restaurant owner trained the army and civilian cooks, and officials working at Longue-Pointe paid particular attention to religious prohibitions on certain foods. "We certainly did not want to offend the refugees right on the first day by giving them food they are not allowed to eat because of their religious beliefs," said a spokesperson for the armed forces.[18] Refugees had a sense of being truly welcomed by Canadians. One Ugandan Asian who was quoted in a newspaper article at the time described the food as authentic and even "better than what I can cook at home. They thought of absolutely everything."[19] Edmond recounted how "there was food and everything.... I mean they [soldiers at Longue-Pointe] were quite polite and all that."[20] Others described the reception they received at the base as being indicative of the Canadian spirit of humanitarianism. Rossbina remembered:

Figure 11. Soldier filling plate for woman carrying child. Library and Archives Canada, Department of National Defence fonds, e011052348.

[I felt] proud of coming to Canada. I felt like I was a chosen one, you know. It felt really, really good. And my teachers [at a Calgary school], my students [classmates], they all respected me so much and they wanted to help me a lot, you know. They didn't want to trip you, or come in your way, and that was such a different feeling, I'll never forget that. Especially upon arrival, when we first arrived at the airport it was October, winter, 1972. It was a freaking blizzard there and I think we landed in Montreal. . . . We were taken into this army barracks . . . but we were taken into this humongous warehouse, which was filled with winter clothing. With coats and boots and whatever and we were asked to select our winter clothing because we landed at the airport in our summer tropical clothes right? Wearing this summer dress with these *champals* [sandals] on my feet.[21]

The reception centre in Montreal made a genuine attempt to welcome refugees to Canada and was well received by the Ugandan Asian community. Nazir described the first experiences of Canadian hospitality in Montreal as "incredible. They had food that was good . . . food that at least we could eat. You could move around the barracks, not a problem."[22] Longue-Pointe provided crucial and beneficial services to refugees, though in some instances Ugandan Asians were not allowed to settle in their city of choice.

A letter addressed to the prime minister from Reverend A.I. Avery of St. John's United Church in Quebec indicated how the teams in Kampala and in Montreal had carried out their duties with professionalism and the spirit of humanitarianism:

> In the past month my congregation and I have been greatly involved with the hosting of Ugandan Asians to Canada. This has been one of the most rewarding experiences of my life. These wounded people are the essence of charm and gratitude. They speak so highly of the warmth and thoughtful treatment given to them in Uganda by the Canadian officials. The Canadians that went to Uganda for this occasion must have been superior people. They were able to treat the Asians with such empathy—a smile, a cheery hello and a chair, these

Figure 12. Couple receiving drinks from canteen worker. Library and Archives Canada, Department of National Defence fonds, e011052353.

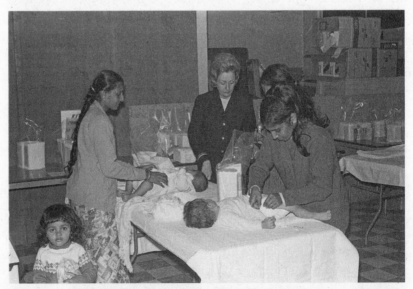

Figure 13. Women changing babies' diapers. Library and Archives Canada, Department of National Defence fonds, e011052359.

Figure 14. Circle of children eating apples and sandwiches. Library and Archives Canada, Department of National Defence fonds, e011052361.

have been mentioned so often. Facilities at Longue Pointe Barracks have truly done justice to Canada. The warmth of the reception, the personal touch, the carefully prepared meals, the clothing store, Immigration and Manpower— each one has made its unique and valuable contribution. The Asians have been overwhelmed. The tribute for opening the door and escorting these people through is especially attributable to you, Mr. Prime Minister, and to Mr. Mackasey, for carrying through your humanitarian wishes. I am proud to be Canadian.[23]

For Reverend Avery, the reception centre was emblematic of the entire resettlement initiative. It demonstrated the continued empathy of Canadians, from those who were on the ground in Kampala to others helping with resettlement efforts back home. Ugandan Asian refugees told the reverend about their sincere gratitude to the Canadian government and military on several occasions. They also made public statements in the media to thank the Canadian government. Maurice

Pinto was quoted in the *Toronto Star* extending his "sincere appreciation
to the Canadian people for their hospitality . . . from our departure
in Kampala to our destination here, everything was carried out with
perfect coordination by so many of the various organizations and we
hope to be citizens of credit to the Canadian nation."[24] The success
of the reception centre encouraged the establishment of welcome
committees across the country to aid Ugandan Asian refugees in the
integration process.

Uganda Asian Committees and Canada Manpower Centres

The federal government set up twelve committees across the country
with an approved budget of $73,000 for all of the centres. The com-
mittees were found in the following cities: Halifax, Montreal, Ottawa,
Toronto, Hamilton, Windsor, Sarnia, Winnipeg, Regina, Edmonton,
Calgary, and Vancouver.[25] Their mandate was to "assist in every possible way the satisfactory settlement and adjustment of the Uganda
Asians in the Canadian community."[26] These committees, officially
called Uganda Asian Committees in government documentation, were
composed of a diverse group of individuals. They incorporated members of local voluntary organizations, all three levels of government,
local religious communities, and ethnic communities. For example,
Regina's team consisted of Dr. H. Gupta, the president of the East India
Association of Saskatchewan; Merle Kennedy, a consumer consultant
with the Department of Consumer and Corporate Affairs; Eleanor
Bujea and L.A. Petry, the president and a member of the Regina Folk
Arts and Cultural Council, respectively; G.F. Bruce, a representative
from the Imperial Order Daughters of the Empire; R.M. Paiement,
the social animator with Cultural Association of Franco-Canadians
of Saskatchewan; A.L. Lamontagne, a member of Canadian Women's
Club; Klaus Burmeister, a member of Can-German Harmony Club;
A.H. Nogue, social development officer for the Citizenship Branch;
Leo Courville, a member of the provincial Planning and Research
Council; and Murray Whitmore and Betha Kohli, Canada Manpower
Centre representatives.[27] Collaboration between all these organizations
was fundamental to addressing the immediate needs of Ugandan Asian
refugees while promoting an inclusive approach to integration.

Bernard Ostry, the assistant undersecretary of state (citizenship),
built on the mandate of the committee: "We hope that, through the

work of these Committees . . . we may be able to encourage what has evidently been a rather inner-oriented community to participate as fully as
possible in Canadian life; and by creating a very positive role for voluntary organizations in the settlement process we hope to encourage their
acceptance in the Canadian community in this difficult period of high
unemployment."[28] Ostry outlined two primary motivations behind the
establishment of the committees. First, the committee would shift the
focus of the allegedly "inner-oriented" community of Ugandan Asians
so they could become full members of Canadian society. Ostry echoed
comments made in opinion pieces about Ugandan Asians self-segregat-
ing in Uganda and the possibility they would duplicate these practices
in Canada. Chapter 1 examined how accusations of Ugandan Asian
social exclusivity were complicated based on the colonial hierarchy in
Uganda and generalizations made about the community.

Second, the committees would reduce animosity in local communities in terms of labour competition. Since the committees collaborated
with local Canada Manpower Centres, it was implied that they would
facilitate improved employment prospects for refugees and a reduced
"degree of general public criticism of the decision to accept the
Asians."[29] The committees were a means of reducing misconceptions
about the employment of refugees and establishing a physical site where
Canadians and refugees could interact with one another. The creation
of the Uganda Asian Committees aligns with theories that underscore
the importance of integration being a two-way process. The memo to
deputy minister for Manpower and Immigration, J.M Desroches, from
assistant deputy minister Robert M. Adams revealed the government's
acknowledgement of the issues raised by the Canadian public. By creating committees with high levels of civic engagement, the Canadian
government sought to facilitate the resettlement of Ugandan Asian
refugees while combatting negative criticism pertaining to high unemployment rates and concerns over integration. These committees were
based on the past success of reception centres established in 1956 to
facilitate the integration of Hungarian refugees into Canadian society.[30]

The three major tasks of the committees were to provide refugees
with access to the job market, assist in locating suitable housing, and
organize orientation activities. To do so, it was imperative for the committees to have a visible central location for reception and information
services for at least one year, establish a housing registry, and develop

an orientation program with specific programming for older adults, women, and children. The committees were instructed to facilitate any program that might be beneficial to the integration of the Ugandan Asians. The committees embodied the concept of social integration as an interdependent process that involves the adaptation of immigrants to their receiving society in conjunction with the host society embracing newcomer communities.[31] Encouraged to look beyond the immediate basic needs of the refugees, the committees actively engaged in grassroots-level interactions with Ugandan Asians, facilitating some of the more intangible components of integration. This reflects Dirk Hoerder's theory on the importance of everyday casual interactions between Canadians and newcomers in defining inclusive pathways to belonging.[32]

Before embarking from Longue-Pointe, all Ugandan Asians received a copy of *Your First Few Months in Canada*, composed by the Citizenship Branch to help introduce the refugees to Canadian society. The pamphlet outlined the organizational framework of the Uganda Asian Committees and provided extensive information on them. It also included information about provincial citizenship programs, community organizations, telephone service (how to place long distance calls and how to use the Yellow Pages), telegrams, emergency contact procedures, long- and short-distance travel (air, bus, and train), shopping, buying on credit, consumer protection, banking, housing, education, medical care, public libraries, and the weather. Information ranged from specific details such as "long distance calls can be made on a public telephone by dialing '0'" to general advice such as "do not hesitate to ask for information, it is available without charge." Similar to the underlying intentions of the committees, the pamphlet reinforced the social aspects of citizenship, encouraging the refugees to ask a police officer, or to "ask anyone," for assistance if they were lost. The leaflet also detailed that the committees would host information sessions on Canadian society and "be arranging social activities in which you can participate." This demonstrated the ways in which the government reiterated its commitment to making Canada a permanent home for the refugees.

Several sections of *Your First Few Months in Canada* offered guidance on Canadian society. For example, the pamphlet included instructions on how to conduct credit purchases in Canada. In Uganda many Ugandan Asians had made purchases on credit on an informal basis with local dukawallahs and other businesspersons, but these often did not include interest payments. The pamphlet advised, "Great care should be taken when buying on credit. If you cannot maintain regular payments, do not buy. You should also be aware that you are paying interest on items bought on credit." Although the pamphlet took a paternalistic tone at times, such as when giving advice on budgeting and housing, most of the content provided crucial guidance on the particularities of life in Canada.

The most pertinent piece of information for Ugandan Asians concerned the Canadian climate. To aid refugees in adjusting to the weather, the pamphlet explained that central heating is universal in public spaces and homes, provided advice on how to dress appropriately for the winter, and ended on a positive note asserting that "most Canadians enjoy their cold but sunny winters very much, partly because of the delightful opportunities it offers for winter sports and vacations." The leaflet concluded with a positive message: "We hope the few suggestions offered in this pamphlet will be of some assistance to you as you begin life in Canada. We hope your adjustment will be easy and your life in Canada a happy one."[33] Again, the message was that Canada was the new permanent home of the refugees.

Numerous local organizations were also mobilized to provide assistance to the Uganda Asian Committees. For example, the Toronto Transit Commission extended service of the Bay Street bus route to allow refugees to reach the new Ugandan Asian Centre, established by the Ontario government, on weekends and after 6:00 p.m. on weekdays. The government collaborated with the *Indian Times*, a bimonthly journal, to "produce a special issue of their journal for us which will contain a message of welcome, practical advice and help for the Uganda Asians and useful background material."[34] Uganda Asian Committees across the country used the same strategy of cooperation among a variety of groups to host social activities that promoted inclusivity and created a welcoming environment for refugees. For example, in Toronto and Edmonton the East Africa Asian Association and the Hindu Association invited all Ugandan Asian refugees to participate in their social gatherings. The local YMCA and YWCA in Montreal, Hamilton, and Vancouver offered free memberships for refugees from six weeks to three months as a means of promoting healthy lifestyles in Canada.

Monthly reports to the Department of Manpower and Immigration
on the committees' activities emphasized the social events organized for
the refugees, including tours of the city, theatre evenings, dances, teas,
and dinners. For example, Montreal averaged three social activities per
week and many other committees reported that their facilities evolved
into drop-in centres. The physical centres provided a source of comfort
and a one-stop shop for the Ugandan Asians. The "welcome house became the Ugandan Asians' second home," argued Diana F. Eaton, the
former coordinator of the Ontario Welcome House Settlement Project.
"A place where people reunited, where they inquired about family
and friends they had been separated from."[35] Centres also facilitated
voluntary efforts by private individuals and other immigrant-serving
agencies. The Vancouver Immigrant Reception Service worked out of
the Vancouver office to aid in the appraisal and assessment of Ugandan
credentials. Members of the British Columbia Medical Association,
Bar, and Chartered Accountants Association volunteered to assist in
the process. According to the monthly reports, refugees made extensive
use of these services offered in Vancouver. Smaller centres developed
more structured orientation programs as well as mentorship programs.
Volunteers assisted refugees on a one-to-one basis in areas such as
Edmonton, Sarnia, Winnipeg, and Windsor, and two refugee families
were provided with private accommodations by a Canadian and a South
Asian family.[36] In the larger centres, initial housing support was not a
prominent feature, although attempts were made by Anand Chopra,
the secretary of the Toronto Uganda Asian Committee, who expressed
that "we are looking for families—Canadian or Asian—who would
be willing to take a refugee family into their home until they can get
settled in more permanent accommodation."[37]

One of the most distinct findings from the smaller committees
pertained to the dietary habits of Ugandan Asians. The Sarnia Food
Sub-Committee reported in the monthly newsletter that circulated
among all Uganda Asian Committees that "the first and most important fact to keep in mind is that the majority of the Uganda Asians
are vegetarians. Some will eat meat, some will also eat fish or eggs. Of
those who will eat meat, Hindus can eat no beef, Moslems no pork."[38]
Beyond compiling a detailed report about respecting religious dietary
restrictions, the committee also noted a few particularities that were
distinct from standard Canadian meals such as the heavy use of plain

yogurt, boiled rice, and the consumption of rice pudding during the main course. Furthermore, it outlined that Ugandan Asian refugees recognized Christmas and "share in celebrating it. Should you invite a Uganda Asian family to Christmas dinner, those who are vegetarian would enjoy all but the meat dish, and you could substitute an omelet for them. Include rice in the menu as well. In their own celebrations they serve lots of sweets."[39] Sarnia may have received a small number of Christian Ugandan Asian refugees based on their observations that Christmas is a recognized holiday.

Several committees embraced the suggestions from Sarnia, including the one in Edmonton. More than two hundred Ugandan Asian refugees and Edmontonians attended a Christmas party and dinner sponsored by the Uganda Asian Committee of Edmonton and the Catholic, United, Anglican, and Unitarian churches. Children received presents ranging from small stockings filled with candies and oranges to gift certificates for a free pair of ice skates from Woodward's department store.[40] Donna Archibald, the head of the Gold Bar Neighbour voluntary agency, coordinated with sponsors to provide ninety meals for the attendees, and said that the intent of the dinner was "to provide an opportunity for Edmontonians to meet the Ugandans and we hope they will establish friendships. We're also trying to stress to the Ugandans that different religions can work together."[41] Not only did the event adhere to the advice of Sarnia's committee but it also included other religious and voluntary agencies in the celebrations. Archibald's comments epitomize the efforts of numerous Canadians who participated in the resettlement initiative. The committees created inclusive environments for Ugandan Asian refugees to participate in celebrating a major Christian holiday, and several committees also hosted other religious festivals in the month of December. Celebrations for Diwali and Eid were held across Canada, reflecting two major celebrations in the Hindu and Muslim religions, respectively. The "very elaborate party" for both religious communities in Toronto was well attended with over 250 participants.[42] Community-based programming continued as refugees sought to secure employment and integrate into Canadian society.

As months passed, several committees shared observations on the adaptation of Ugandan Asian refugees to life in Canada. The Toronto committee argued that refugees were reluctant to meet with others in their homes to socialize since "they are not very happy about showing the drabness of their homes to people whom they have known in their better days."[43] The observation offers a possible explanation for the hesitancy of refugees to provide temporary accommodations to others and for the popularity of the Ugandan Asian Centre as a central social hub. The Edmonton committee reported success in connecting refugees to employment: "Job opportunities in Edmonton attracted Ugandans from other cities, too (and we were able to find jobs for them also), e.g., from Calgary, Vancouver, and Saskatoon. There is a trend for more Ugandans to come to this city than to leave it."[44]

The final progress reports conducted by Canada Manpower counsellors concluded that the committees were largely successful. As a whole, the reports revealed that the social and cultural aspects of the committee were critical in establishing a welcoming atmosphere for refugees. J. Paproski, a Manpower official based in Hamilton, argued that "it is the unanimous opinion of our counsellors who dealt with Ugandan Expellees, that the Uganda Asian Committee was a most effective asset."[45] J.W. Edmonds, Manpower and Immigration's director general for the prairie region, said the Uganda Asian Committees' "greatest contribution lies in the area of social and cultural orientation," but added that "the responsibilities of accommodation, job finding, and financial assistance can best be dealt with through our Department."[46] Collaborative efforts among committee members and the local community provided an unintended but tangible economic benefit to the federal government. K.D. Allen, a Manpower counsellor in Toronto, "estimated that approximately 100 to 200 man days and approximately $15,000 to $25,000 were saved by the activities of the Committee."[47]

Employment, one of the central responsibilities of the committees, was one of the primary measures the government used to claim that the local resettlement committees were a success. By 9 March 1973, the Uganda Asian Committees along with Canada Manpower Centres had found employment for 2,041 refugees who were issued visas in Kampala while 453 were still seeking employment, 308 were participating in a Canada Manpower training program, and 44 were waiting to enter the program.[48] This was considered "extremely encouraging," according to the Citizenship Branch of the Department of the Secretary of State.[49] For most regions of Canada, the Uganda Asian Committees were considered a success based on their facilitation of economic and social integration.

However, British Columbia, and Vancouver in particular, faced significant employment issues. A formal complaint was filed by a member of parliament in British Columbia alleging that Ugandan Asians in the Pacific region were abusing the assistance program offered in Vancouver. The member of parliament, who is not named in the archival records, accused refugees of taking advantage of the Canadian government's offer of two years of financial aid if needed. As of 29 June 1973, Vancouver had the largest number of unemployed Ugandan Asian refugees with nearly 60 percent of those who received visas in Kampala still receiving financial assistance from the government. This translated to nearly 365 Ugandan Asian refugees being supported by the Canadian government.[50] "It now seems clear that it was a bad judgement call in permitting so many expellees to proceed to the Pacific Region," said the acting chief of the procedures branch of Manpower and Immigration. "Worse still, they have now been there a long time and if they do not become self-sustaining within the next few months, the picture becomes very bleak indeed."[51] Although Vancouver received a large group of Ugandan Asians, including 545 refugees in the first month of the program, government documents underline issues that contributed to the higher levels of assistance needed for refugees in the region.[52]

Miscommunication between Manpower counsellors and local volunteers at the Howe Street Centre in Vancouver led to overpayments of adjustment assistance. The auditor's report concluded that overpayments were made for the following reasons: "(A) Adjustment assistance was not terminated when applicants found permanent employment. (B) Payments were made to refugees without adequate investigation of personal funds on arrival or of funds subsequently transferred. (C) Payments were made for accommodation, furniture and clothing when refugees were no longer indigent. (D) Adjustment assistance was paid in addition to Canada Manpower Training Program allowances. (E) Payments continued in respect of refugees for whom responsibility had been transferred to another Centre in Vancouver, resulting in duplicate payments."[53] Further, local volunteers assisted Ugandan Asians in finding employment opportunities; thus, "the quality of placement was not always the highest as, generally, the volunteers are not experienced in employment placement and were more concerned at the time with obtaining a job for the immigrant rather than whether the immigrant was actually qualified for the job. The number of immigrants who failed to retain their jobs appears to support this opinion."[54] The auditor's report showed that excess expenditures in Vancouver were not due to abuse of the system. In addition, other documents record that the city received a large proportion of refugees suffering from shock and fatigue who required costly "medical attention on arrival."[55] The reports that indicated a large number of Ugandan Asian refugees in Vancouver were unemployed and still receiving assistance months after resettling may have been exaggerated, according to the auditor general's report filed in January 1975, because $35,984.18 of adjustment assistance was actually overpaid to 332 refugees who did not "properly disclose their status with regard to work and/or financial position."[56] This obscured the real number of Ugandan Asian refugees who were unemployed and in need of financial assistance.

The committees played a significant role in garnering public support for the resettlement initiative across the country—even in Vancouver, where the Manpower counsellor noted the favourable public reaction to the committee given its coordination of several community groups and organizations that wanted to assist in the resettlement. Committees in Ontario noted that only a small number of individuals continued to express negative views of the resettlement program. The government noted that in Quebec the committee "has been welcomed and accepted by the public at large, who demonstrated their interest and its help in making available clothes and used furniture. The radio, television, and press praised the committee for its active participation in this project and they, without a doubt, contributed largely to the favourable reaction of public opinion concerning this subject."[57] Beyond providing a collaborative effort for the resettlement of refugees, the committees offered avenues for any Canadian to participate in the initiative. Formal membership in the committee was not required to contribute in some way.

The committees ended their formal activities in March of 1973 "in order to avoid any feeling that the Uganda Asians were having prolonged special treatment in a period of high unemployment."[58] However, some of the committees continued their efforts informally or established permanent centres for welcoming refugees and immigrants from other regions around the world. For example, the Immigrant Services Society of BC supported the integration of eight hundred Ugandan Asians in 1972 and continues to offer dedicated services to newcomers today.

Canadians Lending a Helping Hand

In addition to the Uganda Asian Committees, other groups were formed across the country to help in the resettlement initiative. Examples include the Interfaith Immigrant Reception Committee based in Cambridge, Ontario, which provided assistance during the 1968 Czechoslovak refugee resettlement and continued to collaborate with Canada Manpower Centres to assist the Ugandan Asian refugees. A similar committee was created in Guelph, Ontario, based on the previous successful efforts in resettling Hungarian and Czechoslovak refugees. Friends of Ugandan Refugees (FOUR), established by three faculty members at the University of Waterloo, coordinated with the Canada Manpower Centre to provide assistance to the refugees in the Waterloo-Kitchener area. Shiraz, an oral history participant, recalled, "As soon as I landed, there was a Manpower guy who came to receive me and he told us about this FOUR. And he says, 'Your arrangement has already been made. You are going to stay with one of the professors. He has invited you to his house and he is going to take care of you and get you on your feet, basically.' That was amazing that they would do this."[59]

Many people offered temporary accommodations to Ugandan Asian refugees, giving the committees and refugees time to search for permanent residences. Local resettlement committees requested that people "open their homes to Asian refugees from Uganda to help them settle in the city."[60] Canadians responded generously to these requests; within three weeks in Toronto, for example, two hundred families had made offers to temporarily house Ugandan Asian refugees.[61] Terrence, an oral history participant, remembered how a couple in Thornhill, Ontario, opened up their home to his family of four: "They took us to the basement and it was all done up, and he said, 'Listen, you are here as our guests. This house is your house, this is where you can sleep, you can go anywhere in the house you want and what we have is yours.' . . . They were just unbelievably wonderful people."[62]

Offers of employment were made to Ugandan Asians as well. Tejpal Thind, president of the India-Canada Association, said that by the time the first flight of refugees arrived in Canada, forty-two jobs were already waiting for them in Montreal. "Most of the offers were for skilled technical help," according to Thind, and the first ones came from the Hungarian community.[63] This trend continued in Toronto, where 250 employment opportunities were submitted to the Uganda Asian Committee by mid-October 1972. The private sector, in conjunction with the Canadian public, coordinated a notable response to the government's call for assistance with the resettlement effort.

One area in which the Canadian government did not want to provide support for the Ugandan Asian refugees was education. In Kampala, visa officers admitted Ugandan Asians on the grounds that they would enter the Canadian labour market as soon as possible. A representative for the Department of Manpower and Immigration argued that "Ugandan Asians were selected in their home country for admission to Canada as landed immigrants. They were given entry visas on the understanding that they would join the work force on arrival in Canada. None were admitted as students."[64] Manpower and Immigration reinforced to all Uganda Asian Committees that "no financial support for tuition would be provided by this department."[65]

Evidently, part of Canada's response to the expulsion decree was motivated by economic considerations. The government had extended financial support for tuition fees to Czechoslovaks who arrived in 1968, but Manpower officials argued that "the Czechs [and Slovaks] were true refugees in that they fled their homeland to seek asylum in other countries."[66] Since Ugandan Asians were officially classified as an oppressed minority rather than refugees, the government was not obligated to provide additional financial assistance. James Cross did suggest that the federal government should provide further funding to Ugandan Asian refugee students. He referenced how the "Ontario Department of Health made arrangements with this Department [Manpower and Immigration] and the Department of National Defence for sixteen Czech [and Slovak] dentists to attend a ten-month course designed to qualify them for practice in Ontario. Ontario provided $160,000 to finance the course and this Department paid subsistence and travel costs for the dentists and their families."[67] However, the government still refused to fund education for the Ugandan Asians. It was estimated that roughly a hundred refugees would be forced to withdraw from Canadian universities due to a lack of funding.[68]

However, this did not prevent individual institutions from providing grants, scholarships, and bursaries. The London Academy of Medicine issued funding for five Ugandan Asian refugees to attend medical school at the University of Western Ontario. It also supported a refugee enrolled in chemistry.[69] The Manitoba government offered bursaries to four refugees to attend the University of Manitoba's medical school, while in Sarnia, Ontario, two students received $500 bursaries from the Sarnia Municipal Regent of the Interested, Organized, Determined, and Energized charity organization to attend local colleges. In Vancouver, "a special eight-month professional re-orientation course for five Ugandan expellee teachers who had had up to twenty years of teaching experience in their former country of residence" was hosted and fully funded by Simon Fraser University.[70] Several universities supported refugees by issuing individual forms of financial assistance or waiving tuition fees for recertification courses.

Many Ugandan Asians continue to hold fond memories of average Canadians extending a helping hand. "Dinner invitations, periodic phone calls, or just tea and chit-chat," as requested by the chair of Edmonton's Uganda Asian Committee, Dr. Ram Gupta, helped ease refugees' transition into Canadian society.[71] Oral history participants discussed numerous examples of friendly neighbours and others who made personal efforts to introduce refugees to Canadian society. Edmond and Maria recalled how they happened to meet a friendly man who was very welcoming:

> Edmond: [He] would come every Saturday and pick us up and take us out. That was a wonderful thing he did, you know.... For Christmas day he called all of us to his place for dinner.
>
> Maria: Seven [in one family] and five [in the other]—twelve of us he would call. Even on Sunday evenings he would have a simple meal, you know, mashed potatoes and something. But he would call twelve of us, would you believe it? It was amazing.... In Uganda we had two cars and we used to take the children out for drives. They loved the car. They missed it. But this man....
>
> Edmond: Leo.
>
> Maria: Leo. Yeah, he would come and take the children for a drive.... Oh, that meant a lot to us, you know.[72]

Recalling her family's first few weeks in Smiths Falls, Ontario, Zabina observed it was "a very small but warm community, so people came over and they brought us things because now we found a home, but we need to furnish it and everything. So they brought us furniture and whatever else they could. They brought us welcome baskets with food and all kinds of goodies."[73] In Montreal, Errol and Delphine attended their first National Hockey League game within days of their arrival in Canada:

> Errol: We came on October 5, and the first weekend was Thanksgiving, so. . . even we got tickets to the Montreal hockey game.
>
> Delphine: That's why he's a staunch Montreal Canadiens fan.
>
> Errol: At that time, we didn't know much about ice hockey so we watched it on TV a bit and we saw these people chasing the black little thing all over the place. So when they offered us the tickets, actually nobody wanted the tickets, and then two months later we were hooked on the game.[74]

Canadians opened up their homes as temporary accommodations, offered employment, made physical donations, and provided less tangible assistance in the form of social support. Especially considering the harassment and trauma experienced by some Ugandan Asian refugees, these gestures were instrumental in creating a receptive atmosphere. The government argued that the resettlement was a success for two principal reasons: first, the "massive participation of the Canadian people in the resettlement and integration of the Asians," and second, "the initiative and adaptability of the Asians themselves."[75] The efforts of Canadians and Ugandan Asians themselves dramatically shaped the refugees' first few months in the country as they put down roots in Canada.

Early Days in Canada

Upon their arrival in Canada, Ugandan Asian refugees quickly embraced the challenges of establishing themselves in a new country. Various media outlets reported on how relieved refugees were to be in Canada. For instance, in the *Calgary Herald*, a refugee couple named Zul and Yasmin expressed how happy they were to be in a country that "really wanted to help us."[76] Another refugee, Tom de Souza, explained to the *Toronto Star* that he and his family "really like it here . . . what has really pleased me is the friendliness of Canadians," who "just don't seem to know the meaning of bigotry." His partner, Lucy de Souza, said her children "could sense the tension and they were afraid. Now they see how happy my husband Tom and I are to be here in Toronto and they can't help but feel happy too."[77] Ugandan Asian refugees even noted the generosity of Canadians within a few days of arriving. T.N. Noormohamed remarked how the Ugandan Asian community was "getting used to this place very quickly. . . . I am very surprised. People are kind."[78] Others were filled with a renewed sense of hope, including Hamil Nagla, who described how "nobody in Canada is going to rob me of my work and my country the way President Amin has."[79] Refugees were hopeful about their futures, according to a government survey, due to the "security of life, personal liberty and the public services offered in Canada."[80] Many refugees felt reassured about the opportunities to settle their families in Canada. However, they were not unaware that some public resistance to the resettlement initiative existed. "We are willing to do all kinds of jobs," explained one refugee in response to concerns about unemployment. "I see that the Prime Minister of Canada said that some of us might work on farms picking fruit. There's nothing wrong with that."[81]

Since the Ugandan Asians were admitted to Canada as landed immigrants, the government's primary concern was securing employment for them. This was also the greatest concern for refugees once they had safely arrived in their cities of resettlement. "Let the winter come," one refugee told a local newspaper. "At the moment all I'm worried about is finding a job."[82] Some refugees found employment upon arrival. Avril De Souza, for example, started working at the University of Saskatchewan within just three days of landing in Canada.[83] Her experience not only represents the desire of many refugees to begin contributing to the economy and rebuilding their lives in Canada but also underscores their employability as highly skilled and well-educated workers. A quote from T.N. Noormohamed captures the attitude of many refugees towards employment: "There's always something if you are ready to work hard. . . . If I can't get a job as a hairdresser I can work on a farm, drive a tractor, pick fruit—anything."[84] On 5 December 1972, nearly 50 percent of those who applied as heads of families and single

persons to come to Canada were employed. This increased to almost 90
percent within the first six months of arrival, according to a government
study.[85] These high levels of employment mirrored the 1956 Hungarian
refugee resettlement, where 86 percent of Hungarian refugees secured
jobs within their first three months in Canada.[86] Officials attributed the
rapidity of Ugandan Asians integration into the labour market to "their
initiative and skills ... a number of new arrivals were highly successful
entrepreneurs and businessmen in Uganda."[87]

However, these statistics do not capture the forms of employment
discrimination levied against Ugandan Asian refugees or the number
of refugees who had jobs but were underemployed. Government reports noted that many refugees were willing to "accept employment
below their accustomed level," citing the example of one Ugandan
Asian engineer "who worked locally as a farm labourer until he
found more suitable employment."[88] Credentialization, the process
of recognizing foreign degrees, certificates, or work experience, is a
common feature of global migration and is particularly problematic
in North America.[89] A survey of 1,839 Ugandan Asians found that
the refugees "disliked the requirement for Canadian experience
in order to obtain employment and they indicated some racial
discrimination."[90] The lack of Canadian experience as a barrier to
employment was a common theme among oral history participants.
Sudha struggled to find employment with two young children and
"no Canadian work experience."[91] Sikandar wanted to continue his
career in agriculture, but his "Ugandan qualification was not recognized in Canada." The University of Calgary did offer to reduce the
length of his undergraduate program by one year; however, he could
not justify spending three years in school while his family was facing
financial hardship.[92] Jalal faced the same issue of lacking Canadian
work experience and having his credentials ignored. "Coming here
was not a pleasant experience because first, as you know, to come
here to get any kind of job you need Canadian experience," he said.
"What is Canadian experience? I mean, if you're a lawyer or a secretary or whatever, you have experience. So it was tough to get a job.
But the more devastating thing for me was they wouldn't accept my
qualifications."[93] Jalal felt betrayed by the Canadian system, which
failed to acknowledge his educational qualifications and experience
as a practising lawyer in Uganda.

Other Ugandan Asian refugees were offered jobs or given work that did not reflect the positions they had applied for. Vinnay applied for an engineering position at Canadian Pacific Railway and was called in for an interview, where he was told, "We've got a new car shop opening up here in Ogden. We have a position of labourer." The job interviewer acknowledged that Vinnay had applied for a different position, but said, "You can apply for the CEO position, but I have a job that is a labourer job. You told me a story so I called you. If you want it, take it. If you don't want it, I've got somebody else on the list."[94] Aziz found himself in a similar position after he applied for a sales position at a furniture store. "I have experience in sales," he explained. "Back home I was selling, doing the sales.... This guy, he hired me, he says, 'Meanwhile, I want you to work in the warehouse.'"[95] While in Uganda, Terrence had held a senior position at Trans World Airlines. He recounted his struggle to resume work in the airline industry and his need to advocate to be hired into an entry-level position:

> I went into the interview with this guy and he looked at my resume and said, "You know, we have a job for a person loading bags onto an airplane, but that's the only job we have." He says, "You're overqualified for it and you don't have any Canadian experience." I said, "I'm confused. I thought I had just come to a democracy after living in a third world country. I thought the system of democracy worked. You tell me what you have and I'll tell you what I want. Don't say you can't give me a job because you don't think I'll take it. Ask me first. Secondly, I told you I landed here four days ago and you're looking for Canadian experience, so I'm under the belief that it's something I can get in four days?" ... It was just the way he was acting, and then he said, "Okay, I can offer you a job as a baggage agent with the airline. It pays $400 a month or something." And I said, "I'll take it."[96]

Structural barriers to employment were reinforced by misleading job advertisements. Iqbal recalled applying to an advertisement for "management trainees" in Sarnia:

> I took up a job in the gas station that says ... management trainees so I thought I would become a manager of a gas

station.... This was a job pumping gas. They said, "You have
to start like this here. You can't get management trainees like
that. We'll give you a gas station but later." So I worked there
only for a week. I didn't—I was a boss there [in Uganda]
running a business. I had a watchmaker, two African watch-
makers working at a shop... and here we had to pump gas.
I felt so small myself that I'm a servant now. I had to run
when someone comes into the aisle, and when there's no one
in the aisle I have to sweep the aisle. I felt so bad, and I had
to learn to fix tires and all that, manual job, labour job, and
doing sweeping the floor and all that.[97]

Iqbal's story captures one way that certain companies restricted
opportunities. The personal narratives of Iqbal and Terrence also indicate the loss of sense of self that some Ugandan Asians experienced.
Refugees began to adjust to the reality of the Canadian job market by
accepting jobs that were not reflective of their abilities. Employment
discrimination against individuals with a South Asian background was
confirmed in a study conducted in Montreal by historian K.U. Chandra
in 1973. Chandra found that when identical resumes were distributed
to employers, the resumes with Anglo-Saxon names received calls for
an interview thirteen times out of twenty-four, but those with South
Asian names were called only two times out of twenty-four.[98]

The struggles described by oral history participants reflect the findings of a government study on Ugandan Asian refugees' first twelve
months in Canada. Immigration historian Freda Hawkins surveyed
seventeen hundred Ugandan Asian refugees and found 60 percent of respondents were unable to secure employment in their field of expertise.
Lack of Canadian experience along with an absence of opportunities
in their field were the principal barriers encountered by refugees.
Nonrecognition of foreign qualifications by Canadian employers and
educational institutions was cited as another limiting factor by 23 percent of survey respondents. Low levels of English-language proficiency
were listed as an issue for only a handful of refugees.[99] Language was
not a significant barrier to employment since many Ugandan Asians
were accepted into Canada on the basis of being conversant in one of
the country's official languages. During an interview with *Globe and
Mail* editor-in-chief John Stackhouse, the Aga Khan commented

that one of the principal reasons the Ugandan Asian community was able to successfully integrate into Canadian society was their fluency in English.[100] Sociologist Cecil Pereira also found in a study with 369 Ugandan Asian refugees that language was not an issue for most. "Over sixty percent indicated they had experienced no problem" communicating with Canadians, reported Pereira. "Only ten percent of the sample were not content with the type of communication they had with Canadians."[101] The research study by Hawkins indicated that over time some conditions did improve as two-thirds of those surveyed were satisfied with their earnings within the first year of resettlement.[102] However, this does not mean that refugees were employed in their fields of expertise, nor does it reflect the realities of the deskilling process that occurred for many Ugandan Asians.

A critical element of adapting to life in Canada for many Ugandan Asians pertained to the employment of female refugees, which often happened quickly. Many Ugandan Asian women sought employment, which aligned with the overall trend of rising employment levels for women in Canada.[103] Within one year of resettlement, 50 percent of Ugandan women were employed; of the jobs they found, 40 percent involved clerical work or sales. They earned an average of $390 per month, which was considerably below the overall average salary for Ugandan Asian refugees of $581.[104] Among married women, their primary dislikes of Canadian life were low pay and poor working conditions. In many of the oral history interviews, women described obtaining rapid employment. Shamim and Delphine, for example, were employed within a matter of days.[105] Almas described how her job at Wood Gundy, an investment firm in Toronto, served as the primary source of income for her household while her husband was unable to find employment during their first six months in Canada.[106] High levels of employment for women refugees were influenced by the push for female empowerment within the South Asian community in Uganda dating back to the 1900s. Both Aga Khan IV and his grandfather openly encouraged female emancipation within and outside of their religious community. Sir Sultan Muhammad Shah, Aga Khan III, argued that "no progressive thinker of today will challenge the claim that the social advancement and general well-being of communities are greatest where women are least debarred, by artificial barriers and narrow prejudice, from taking their full position as citizens."[107]

Many female refugees sought employment as a means of providing supplemental income for their families. Rossbina described the importance of immediate employment to contribute to overall family earnings: "McDonald's was my first job, so you won't believe it, it was 90 cents an hour at that time in 1972.... It was not that 'oh now I'm able to earn because now I can invest in this or I can do this.' No, it was just earning it and paying back into the family pot and just supporting the family."[108] The centrality of contributing to the family's overall income defined women's acceptance of almost any job. Farida recalled her first job in Canada, in Kamloops, British Columbia: "My first job was as a dishwasher, which I'm not ashamed of saying [laughs]. Because I could get any job because we wanted to support our family and stuff, right? So I did that work for almost a year, then I went and worked for the leather factory in Kamloops."[109] Although being granted landed immigrant status in Canada required Ugandan Asians to seek immediate employment, female refugees did not indicate this requirement was a primary motive for working in Canada.

Seeking employment as a means of supporting one's family was a dominant theme in interviews with men as well, even for those who were not household heads. Sikandar explained he was unable to complete his postsecondary education in Canada because his older brother asked him, "How can you go to school when your parents are sleeping on carpet?"[110] Agreeing with this brother's sentiments, he acquired a manual labour position at a local factory. Accepting underemployment was not only a response to structural employment barriers but was also motivated by the need to support one's parents. Refugees who were in their early teens were expected to contribute to household earnings. Amin V. recalled:

> From the minute we landed, even when we were at the Waldorf Astoria, the motel, I started working. I remember making my first quarter at the age of thirteen. There was a baker's milk store and the guy would tell me 'please go do this for me, go do that for me' so he would give me a quarter or fifty cents. My brother Azim was working in the hotel, cleaning floors downstairs. So they were paying him and he was what, seventeen, eighteen, at that time. And when we came to Mississauga, right away within hours, within a day

we were all working. I worked ever since I was thirteen, all my life, all my life, and so I started working delivering, you know, those flyers back then.[111]

Earnings for Ugandan Asian refugees were an amalgamation of funds collected by all members of the household. Nimira detailed how she and her nine siblings worked as a single unit performing odd jobs to provide additional income for their family. She remembers her siblings who worked in the evening delivering "newspapers, going and mowing somebody's lawn, plowing and shovelling somebody's driveway, anything so that we could help. So, at least, even if we couldn't provide for the rest of the family, we could at least depend on them to support our ... school money. So that's how we did for a good ten years."[112]

Some refugees sought immediate employment regardless of its suitability to avoid taking advantage of the Canadian government and becoming a public charge. Karim explained how his father, who had worked in accounting, accepted his first job within a week of resettling in Canada: "It wasn't in accounting. My dad, in fact, had never picked up a hammer in his life. But he became a display fixturer [sic] for Sears, and the only reason was simply that he had three kids to feed. He didn't want to stay on Manpower because that was not the right thing to do."[113] For Karim's father, it was unethical to continue receiving social assistance from the government of Canada. Similarly, Vinnay explained, "The minute I got a job, I went back [to the Manpower counsellor] and I said, 'I found a job, so I don't need the money anymore.' Because we were not used to welfare or somebody giving us money. It would be not right to take money, in fact. . . . Since then, I have never gone on unemployment insurance."[114] Nimira also remembered how "in those days, relying on the government to supply you, for us, it was not ethical. . . . All of us were striving to support ourselves. We wanted to get off the government as quickly as we could."[115] The impulse to avoid government subsidies was a prominent feature of oral history interviews. Many oral history participants mentioned how they repaid initial government loans or avoided claiming unemployment insurance.[116]

Beyond finding work, refugees also focused on adapting to the norms of Canadian life. The most considerable obstacle was the climate. In her survey of Ugandan Asian refugees for the government, Hawkins concluded that "many of the expellees found the variety of climate

in Canada difficult to become accustomed to."[117] Bhanumati Patel, a
Ugandan Asian refugee, was quoted in a December 1972 newspaper
article as saying, "We came here with the intention of starting from the
beginning. If we can just get used to the climate we'll be all right."[118]
Considering the equatorial climate of Uganda, arriving in Canada just
before the formal start of the winter season was a significant change for
the refugees. Oral history interviews capture the shock and excitement
of encountering the Canadian climate. Amin S.'s personal narrative
about his and his wife's first winter epitomized the experience of many
refugees:

> Coming from Uganda you probably mostly have khaki pants
> and cotton shirts but luckily we were given warm clothes in
> Montreal and we had some warm clothes.... [But] we had
> these shoes from Uganda, and in the month of November
> coming into Kamloops, it starts snowing and here you've got
> light clothes on. So it was freezing. It was freezing. It was the
> first time I saw snow in Canada, in my life. I had never seen
> snow and it did get very cold.... Weather-wise of course we
> [had] to get used to it. It was cold. It was very, very cold.[119]

Refugees were stunned by the below zero temperatures. Munira recalled: "Holy crap, what an experience it was coming to Toronto! Or
rather coming to Canada, landing in Toronto to now realize what it is
to have minus temperatures."[120] For some refugees the first few winters
in Canada were particularly harsh as they struggled to adjust to the
bitter temperatures. Diamond remembered how winter was "terrible,
lots of snow to the knee. Like now is nothing, to the ankle and that's
it. Oh the snow was terrible."[121]

Others, particularly those who were in their youth, recalled their
initial excitement about their first snowfall. Just a few days after their
arrival in 1972, the children of the de Souza family were already looking forward to snow. "It's all they talk about, their first snowman,"
recalled mother Lucy de Souza.[122] Edmond remembered when "we
saw the snowflakes and everyone ran out. Snow! Snow! So excited to
see the snow, everyone was trying to catch the snowflakes in our hand
and then it used to melt. Then we saw the snow on the ground and ...
everyone was so excited. The first time in our lives we saw snow."[123]

Shiraz recalled asking someone on the street. 'What's this white stuff?' He was shocked. 'You don't know? This is snow!' They were flurries, but this was my first time experiencing snow, and I had no idea how snow fell. . . . I had seen it on the ground in pictures when I was back home . . . so that was my first experience with snow. . . . Boy, forty years of snow, I've had enough [laughs]."[124] Others were more hesitant to rush out with other refugees to observe their first snowfall. Sikandar recounted how "all the Ugandan Asians, there were seven, eight of us working, they run out like crazy . . . and I was embarrassed, so I stayed inside. So didn't want to go out and I thought I would make myself look like a fool in front of these white guys, you know, so I stayed inside."[125]

The early experiences of Ugandan Asian refugees reinforced the government's conclusion about the overall success of the resettlement initiative being attributable to both the Canadian effort and the resiliency of the refugee community. The government's initial review of the program was based on the major study conducted by Hawkins on Ugandan Asian refugees' first twelve months in Canada. With 94 percent of the seventeen hundred surveyed Ugandan Asian refugees expressing a desire to remain in Canada, the preliminary report provided a positive review of the resettlement. Further, over 70 percent of respondents were "satisfied with their opportunity to meet Canadians," and after a year in Canada, "nine out of ten of the Ugandan households surveyed believed they were accepted in the community in which they lived."[126] Hawkins argued that "to the extent that Ugandans did not experience long periods of unemployment, an inordinately low level of income, or feelings of social isolation, it may be concluded that they adapted without serious difficulty to their new life, at least at the outset."[127]

The conclusions from the government study are complicated by the employment discrimination that many refugees faced alongside their experience of the harsh Canadian climate. Regardless of these barriers, however, refugees made conscious attempts to adapt and appreciated the efforts of the government and the public in offering them an "honourable place" in Canadian society. These collaborative efforts encouraged Ugandan Asian refugees to quickly integrate into Canadian society. At the same time, the foremost concern for many refugees was to reunite with family members who held passports for other countries, such as

Britain, India, or Pakistan, or who were temporarily sent to United Nations transit camps in Europe.

Family Reunification

At the end of the expulsion period, forty-two hundred Ugandan Asians remained in transit camps across Europe. Additionally, four hundred to five hundred expellees sought temporary refuge in Kenya before the expulsion deadline. The Canadian high commissioner in Kenya, William Oliver, noted that the "in transit" status of these expellees amid the political and cultural climate in East Africa created "a veritable 'time-bomb,'" as President Kenyatta requested the removal of refugees.[128] Under these circumstances, Ugandan Asian refugees sought to reunite with family members who had migrated to Canada. They may have been rendered inadmissible to Canada based on a failure to meet immigration selection criteria or because they held British, Indian, or Pakistani passports. Family reunification became particularly complex for the Canadian government due to miscommunication with UNHCR based on different understandings of Canada's role in the resettlement initiative.

After the expulsion deadline passed, UNHCR continued to advocate for the permanent resettlement of refugees being held in transit centres and encouraged the Canadian government to participate. In January 1973 UNHCR representatives reminded global leaders of the urgency of resettling refugees to avoid the "demoralization and frustration that camp life invariably causes. This group with their high professional qualifications and will to succeed should be contributing positively to a country of resettlement. Moreover, the reunion of families which became separated through the exodus is becoming increasingly more urgent."[129] The Canadian government was perplexed about UNHCR's request for further assistance. G.M. Mitchell, who had become the director of programs and procedures for the Department of Manpower and Immigration, argued that Canada had "already done more both in terms of financial outlay and of the number accepted for resettlement than all other countries combined, excluding Great Britain."[130] The Canadian government was also hesitant to commit to any major extension of the resettlement initiative because it would require cabinet approval and further funding.

Fifty to seventy-five Ugandan Asian refugees continued to arrive each week related to the fifteen hundred visas that were left outstanding as of 7 November 1972. To further complicate the request from UNHCR, the Canadian government did not know how or when those fifteen hundred refugees might eventually travel to Canada. Since visas were valid for six months, government officials reasoned that refugees might visit relatives abroad or seek entry to other countries such as the United Kingdom, the United States, India, or Pakistan. United Nations officials presumed that Canada would accept a number of refugees from transit camps equivalent to the number of outstanding visas, which had risen to 1,600 by the end of November. The discrepancy between the two sets of outstanding visas is based on whether government officials composing internal government documents outlining the number of visas issued by November 7th (6,292) or November 23rd (6,400). The Canadian response to this supposition was definitive. Robert M. Adams, under-secretary of state for External Affairs, firmly expressed that although "some 1,600 of the people issued visas in Kampala have not arrived in Canada [it] has no bearing whatsoever on Ugandan Asians in temporary transit in Italy, Austria, Belgium and Spain."[131] Immigration authorities in Ottawa expected that a significant portion of those who had not travelled to Canada by charter aircraft would arrive before the expiration of their visas.[132]

Once the Canadian government had clarified its position on the issue surrounding outstanding visas, the central problem of how to apply for entry to Canada remained. Mitchell emphasized that those who sought to come from transit centres or from countries in which they had been granted asylum would be required to meet regular immigration selection criteria. An exemption was permitted for Ugandan Asian refugees who had family in Canada. They were instructed to apply as sponsored dependents. In addition, stateless individuals who received asylum in the United Kingdom were eligible to apply under relaxed selection criteria. Canadian embassies in Britain and other regions of Europe received hundreds of requests to migrate to Canada but applications were to be strictly evaluated under regular selection criteria unless they were sponsored by a relative living in Canada or if they were a stateless individual who had received asylum in the United Kingdom.[133] Since stateless Ugandan

Asians were outside their country of origin and were applying for asylum from transit centres, they were to be evaluated as refugees as opposed to immigrants. Of particular importance in extending visas to those who did not meet regular selection requirements was the availability of "sufficient private and/or government assistance available to ensure the applicant's successful establishment in Canada."[134] Family members who were applying as refugees, especially those who did not meet the outlined criteria, could seek special admission under the oppressed minorities policy within the 1952 Immigration Act. They were considered to be "unresettled refugees" if their prospective sponsors did not possess the necessary finances to nominate them. Thus, officials in Ottawa stressed that a "lenient approach" should be used when "the member in Canada has not yet established satisfactory settlement arrangements to have a nominated application approved."[135]

The Canadian government eventually accepted UNHCR's request to admit more refugees who were in transit camps and did not have relatives living in Canada. It agreed to take in 200 to 350 of these refugees, noting in a report that they would be "less qualified than earlier arrivals, possibly even what are usually referred to as 'hard-core cases.' If so, their establishment will be more difficult."[136] The same report argued that it would be within the government's interest to delay the admission of these individuals until the spring when the Canadian labour market and weather would improve. Further, an annual renewal of federal funding would provide $150,000 for financial assistance to incoming refugees as of 1 April 1973.[137] According to government documents, stateless refugees who did not meet regular admission requirements were supposed to be accepted under the "same conditions of selection and settlement assistance as prevailed for the main movement, including free transportation if required."[138] However, free transportation was not provided to refugees. They were granted loans of C$120 to C$135, which were to be repaid to UNHCR and the Intergovernmental Committee for European Migration six months after arrival. Ugandan Asian refugees in Canada who wanted to sponsor family members applying for "remigration" from Britain, India, or Pakistan had to prove they possessed the financial means to do so. If family members were in transit centres in Europe or in Kenya, they would be admitted under relaxed criteria and did not require settlement funds from family.

Ugandan Asians in Canada were given detailed information on how to locate family and friends who were in the United Kingdom or in transit centres. To find people in transit centres, they were asked to contact the International Committee of the Red Cross. To request information on relatives in the United Kingdom, they had to contact the Immigration and Nationality Department of the British Home Office. Ugandan Asians who wished to nominate their relatives for resettlement were required to provide examining officers with relevant information, which was forwarded to the appropriate visa office abroad. Visa officers were encouraged to "use their discretion where the relative is a refugee, is in one of the transit camps in Europe, and has some reasonable prospect of eventual successful establishment in Canada. Relatives accepted for immigration in this way would be eligible for all normal settlement assistance from the Department, having been dealt with as independent applicants."[139] Refugees wishing to reunite with their families needed to demonstrate adequate financial resources, whether provided by the government, a private institution, or the sponsoring family, were available. Assisted passage loans were also distributed when UNHCR or the Intergovernmental Committee for European Migration was unable to assist with travel costs.[140]

As major operations continued in 1973, government officials began to screen and process applications from both Europe and Kenya. On 22 January 1973 there remained 1,937 stateless refugees in European transit centres in need of permanent resettlement.[141] When Canada's annual budget to resettle refugees reset in April, more assistance became available for stateless refugees from transit centres. With the continuing arrivals of those who were initially issued visas in Kampala, new applicants, and sponsored individuals, 6,137 Ugandan Asians were officially resettled in Canada by 11 May 1973. This number included 465 people who were issued visas abroad.[142]

Canada also needed to respond to the "time-bomb" of Ugandan Asian refugees in neighbouring East African countries. Kenyan authorities were under pressure to relocate refugees quickly as animosity towards African Asians continued to rise in the region. The

Kenyan government also did not want to risk "antagonizing Amin by harbouring imaginary enemies of the general."[143] A range of refugees had filtered into Kenya. Some had travelled there irregularly after being targeted by Amin's military regime. Others had been refused entry to Canada due "to a lack of qualifications in Kampala," which principally included "hardcore cases."[144] Ugandan Asian refugees in Kenya and Tanzania submitted 500 and 150 applications, respectively, for asylum to UNHCR.[145] UNHCR's representative in East Africa, Dr. J. J. Kadosa, requested Canadian assistance for these individuals, who were outside their country of origin and thus officially considered refugees based on the United Nations Refugee Convention and Protocol. Kadosa estimated that nearly two-thirds of these individuals were "genuinely stateless."[146] Initially, the Canadian government responded to this request by clarifying that UNHCR should not "expect that even *bona fide* Ugandan refugees in Kenya would be considered for the type of special assistance provided to expellees in Kampala."[147] St. Vincent, leader of Canada's immigration team in Kampala, echoed these recommendations and outlined that "all applications [should] be assessed under normal criteria stage B as per 7.18. We [Manpower and Immigration] concur that you should continue to follow this instruction in dealing with Ismaeli [*sic*] families in Kenya or elsewhere."[148] His advice was to continue following the same protocol used in Uganda, enabling visa officers to apply their own discretion when dealing with refugees in Kenya and Tanzania. Correspondence between Prime Minister Pierre Elliott Trudeau and the Aga Khan IV regarding Ismaili applicants demonstrated how St. Vincent was left in the dark regarding requests from the Ismaili community.

Many refugees in Kenya remained "in transit" until April 1974. In a letter to the Aga Khan, Trudeau explained that UNHCR had informed his dignitaries that "some 300 Ugandan Asians, mainly Ismailis, are regarded by the government of Kenya as persons 'in transit.' At present these people are able to obtain extensions to their residence permits in Kenya."[149] The prime minister informed the Aga Khan that most refugees were not under any immediate duress and could safely remain in Kenya, according to immigration officers on the ground. Refugees continued to apply for asylum in Canada following the standard protocol outlined by St. Vincent, and the prime minster clarified to the Aga Khan that these procedures did not include information gathering on the religious background of applicants. However, Trudeau told the Aga Khan:

> You may be interested to know that during 1973 our Nairobi office received applications representing 1,619 persons in Kenya and issued 1,181 visas. During January of this year the number of visas issued exceeded the number of applications received. It is our estimate that well over one half of this movement of persons represented members of the Ismaili community—in excess of 800 people. I have instructed the Canadian immigration officer in Nairobi to get in touch with the leader of the Ismaili community in Kenya in order to be assured that all cases of duress or distress be communicated to him without delay and thus permit the priority process mentioned above to be instituted.[150]

The letter noted the difficulties of determining which individuals were stateless refugees from Uganda or independent applicants from the entire region of East Africa who applied for various immigration pathways to Canada. Nairobi served as the sole visa office in the region and accepted applications from Uganda, Tanzania, Rwanda, and Kenya.

The Aga Khan replied that he appreciated the efforts made by the Canadian government but also expressed his concern for those who were still considered to be "in transit." He underscored the reality of the situation for those without a place to resettle:

> The reason I raised the matter with you was because I know that for internal reasons, as well as because of the delicate nature of their contact with the Ugandan Government, the Kenyan Government cannot extend the "in transit" status indefinitely. I have discussed the problem at the highest level with the Kenyans, and while I am satisfied that the present Kenyan Government intends to treat the issue as humanely as possible, it is the Government's serious wish that a definitive home for the Ugandan Asians should be found as quickly as possible. I am therefore extremely grateful that you should have instructed the Canadian Immigration Officer in Nairobi to get in touch with Sir Eboo Pirbhai, so that when

the problem becomes immediate, the appropriate priority
process will be instituted.[151]

Government documents reiterated the Aga Khan's concern and detailed
that "it is not unlikely that the increasing pressure being exerted on
the Asian community to emigrate will produce charges that Canadian
immigration requirements are too stringent, and that Canada should do
more to assist Asians wishing to leave Kenya."[152] Immigration officials
continued to admit refugees who fit within Canadian immigration policy but were cautious when accepting applications. Internal documents
reinforced that "the Prime Minister, in his letter to the Aga Khan dated
21 March 1974, promised nothing beyond giving priority to Ismaili
applicants who were subject to duress or distress (oppressed persons).
On this basis any Ismaili who is not an oppressed person or refugee will
be treated like any other applicant."[153] Ultimately, documents outlined
that there was direct contact between the prime minister and the leader
of the Ismaili community but the application of immigration policy was
universal. Canada accepted all those who were stateless and fit within
the oppressed minority policy on a priority basis, especially after the
expiry of the ninety-day deadline.

However, Ugandan Asian refugees around the world continued to
seek permanent resettlement and family reunification in Canada. The
first group of arrivals pressured the government to facilitate the sponsorship of their family members and accept additional refugees. Many
sent letters and aggressively petitioned for expellees to be assessed less
stringently as they were genuine refugees. For example, representatives
from the Ismaili community argued that the Canadian government
"be requested on humanitarian grounds and sufferings to waive the
condition of sponsorship and even consider our applications on reduced
selection criteria and reunite our separated families."[154] The leaders of
the Ismaili community sent lists of Ismaili Ugandan Asian refugees
who were in transit centres in Belgium and Spain. A collaborative effort
between the Ismaili community in Toronto and the National Interfaith
Immigrant Community raised $1.3 million to support the sponsorship
of Ugandan Asian refugees in Canada.[155]

James Cross of the Department of Manpower and Immigration responded firmly to appeals from the Ugandan Asian refugee community
in Canada: "Under normal circumstances we would not accept such a

blanket guarantee for unnamed refugees, and our visa officer in Brussels has quite properly refused to take action on it without clearance from Ottawa . . . they have been given no encouragement . . . to believe their proposal will be accepted."[156] Building on the community's request, UNHCR also pressured the Canadian government to facilitate family reunification cases from European transit centres. Immigration officials outlined that it was impossible to create an additional special assistance program since the sponsorship of 540 Ugandan Asian refugees in European transit camps required "Cabinet approval and a further financial commitment."[157] Officials in Ottawa reiterated that sponsorship of family members continued to be assessed on compassionate grounds. Many oral history participants documented how sponsorship was ongoing from 1973 to 1974.

Sponsoring family members to Canada was not a straightforward process. Diamond articulated the struggle of postponing recertification to have his university credentials recognized in order to reunite with his family: "Immigration said, 'No no, you work and you sponsor these guys [family].' So I said, 'Okay, I'll go next year.' And getting people here from there takes years. I had a mother who has diabetes so in that she has problems. One person was mentally challenged. It took two years to get them here but I got everybody here. So I had to work for two or three years."[158] Many refugees began working immediately in order to sponsor family members who were abroad. Nimira's testimony about trying to come to Canada encapsulates the complexities of family reunification as her three siblings in Canada coordinated with the six others in Sweden to raise the required funds:

> After getting in touch with the other brothers and sisters [in Canada], we decided that this is the best time to go to Canada, try for Canada. But by that time, you have to remember a lot of refugees were already here so they [Canada] started to get picky at this point. They wanted to reunite families but there were conditions, like they were making it not so easy. . . . They were saying, 'No, no, no, you are not in any danger where you are. You just want to be reunited with your family, but you are fine in the place that you are.' . . . So my other three brothers and sisters [in Canada], they had to show like something like $10,000 in the bank plus pay for all

of our tickets in order for us to come and all of our medicals
and this and that. So these were new. Even though they had
graduated from university and all that, you can't come right
away. They had no Canadian experience, so you can't find
decent jobs, university-level, their level jobs, so they had to
do like any job. One of my brothers worked at a grocery store
at a $1.80 per hour and this was considered good pay . . .
were doing like three shifts. First double shifts on an everyday basis and then they used to do one weekend shift in
order to get as much money together as they could. Plus us
too, whatever they were giving us in the form of allowances
for learning Swedish [while in a European transit centre] or
whatever, we were trying everything. Strawberry plucking,
this, that, anything we could lay our hands on for money
and we had the advantage of numbers, eight to ten [family]
members there, so we got together as much as we could so
that we could put it in the bank and show the ten or twenty
thousand dollars because whoever was left in Sweden out
of [the entire family] that only two, my oldest brother and
another one after him, were like working age.[159]

Nimira's entire family endeavoured to participate in multiple forms
of labour to amass capital collectively in order to prove to Canadian
authorities that their family indeed possessed "sufficient private assistance." As government priorities shifted away from the immediate
perils of the expulsion deadline, officials in Ottawa were not as hard-
pressed to admit Ugandan Asian refugees. Authorities believed that
refugees had a durable solution in Europe. For Nimira's family, it was
crucial that they have the required finances as well as proof of adequate
housing waiting for them in Canada. For a family of fourteen, this was
a significant challenge. However, appeals made to local religious institutions in Canada facilitated their eventual resettlement in Montreal
by the end of 1974.[160] A similar experience was described by Sikandar,
whose transportation costs from Malta to Edmonton were funded by
the Catholic Church of Canada.[161]

Resettling larger families required coordinated efforts that in some
cases were facilitated by Canadian authorities. Khaerun and Aziz

recounted the leniency provided to their family who were also sponsored by family members from the refugee camp in Malta:

> Aziz: It took almost one year for everybody to join the family
> in England and in Canada mostly, in America, you know. So
> like for us, for my family, we were lucky that, you know, my
> two sisters they were in Montreal already, you know, like in
> Canada. So Zarine the elder sister and my younger sister.
>
> Khaerun: Yeah, I came with my sister Zarine. And we were the
> two ones who, we were lucky that we found jobs very quickly
> and we had both done secretarial studies in Nairobi. . . .
> We could sponsor them if we had a good, you know, income
> coming in as well, right? Because how can we support these
> nine people with nothing, no jobs, you know? So anyways,
> after as soon as we found the jobs then we applied with the
> immigration thing that we want to call our families, so one
> by one they started coming.
>
> Aziz: Okay, so Zarine sponsored five of them. My parents,
> my two brothers, and one sister. So five of them she man-
> aged to sponsor at once. And then my Khaerun, my sister
> Khaerun, she sponsored me. So, six of us we were sponsored
> from Malta to Canada. So we came. We ended up as refugees
> in Malta but we ended up in Canada by landed immigrant . . .
> because Canada has already closed the door at that time. . . .
> But still Canada was quite helpful for bringing in. So when
> you go to the immigration that I want to bring my family
> from the refugee camp, they will do everything possible to
> help.[162]

Similar to Nimira's family, Khaerun and Aziz discussed the importance of rapid employment as a means of collecting financial resources
to expedite family reunification in Canada. Although government
documents emphasized universal treatment and leniency for those applying in the sponsored dependent category, they failed to address the
realities of the sponsorship process for Ugandan Asian refugees. Rapid
employment was not only a response to barriers within the Canadian
labour market, but it was also a conscious decision taken by refugees
whose priorities were to be reunited with their loved ones. The agency of

refugees is embodied by oral histories that outlined various motivations regarding employment and appeals to the Canadian government to accelerate the resettlement of stateless Ugandan Asians. These efforts, combined with the greater calls from international organizations such as UNHCR, the Intergovernmental Committee for European Migration, and major religious leaders and institutions, effectively motivated the Canadian government to accept more than the officially mandated six thousand Ugandan Asian refugees.

Ultimately, the Canadian government accepted 645 refugees from camps in Europe based on the requests of Ugandan Asians in Canada as well as UNHCR's general request for the country to admit stateless refugees. Of those who arrived from Europe, 69 were privately sponsored, 278 were nominated by recently arrived friends and family in Canada, and 298 were independent applicants who met the selection criteria. An indeterminate number of refugees were sponsored from Britain, India, and Pakistan due to "Canada's liberal sponsorship and nomination provisions" in reference to the changes under the introduction of the points system and the 1976 Immigration Act.[163] As operations came to a formal conclusion at the end of 1974, government officials again deemed the initiative an overwhelming success. Reports indicated that Canada's response to the expulsion decree was "lauded by the Asians themselves, the UNHCR and the press throughout the world."[164] Praise from the international community fulfilled the Canadian government's desire to come to Britain's aid, assert itself on the international political scene, respond to the Aga Khan's appeal for help, and provide humanitarian assistance to a group of individuals who desperately needed asylum. The response echoed the prevailing dominance of liberal internationalism and Canada's transition to an international champion of human rights in the 1970s.

A Mission of Mercy or Selecting the Cream of the Crop?

Some Ugandan Asians were admitted to Canada on purely humanitarian grounds, but the majority exceeded the points required for standard independent immigrants. In a personal memoir, Michael Molloy confirms that "those who qualified under the point system were accepted regardless of whether they held British, Indian, Pakistani, or Ugandan citizenship, or whether they were stateless or not."[165] This led to charges from scholars and the press that Canada took the strongest members of the Ugandan Asian community and was not on a "mission of mercy." Evaluation reports from immigration officials in Kampala, and a series of internal studies produced by scholars for the Canadian government, provide a basis for understanding criticisms that the government was "bidding for the cream of the crop, the most attractive potential immigrants in skills and education, [and] those who it may be predicted will offer Canada the most."[166]

Gerry Campbell had only been working in the field for six weeks in London, England, when he was selected by Molloy to join the immigration team being sent to Uganda. Of particular confusion for the young visa officer was how lenient to be in regards to the selection criteria and the oppressed minorities policy. He wrote in a report that there was "constant uncertainty over the degree of liberality to be used in applying the selection criteria" and "this problem did result in a degree of inconsistency of selection."[167] As discussed earlier, visa officers could use discretionary authority to assign additional points to Ugandan Asian refugees who appeared "adaptable, had proved it [their ability to establish themselves in Canada] and were ready and willing to go anywhere."[168] It was up to them to decide how flexible to be.

An additional source of complexity involved the priority of resettling stateless Ugandan Asians. Campbell explained, "Where immigrants appeared to be stateless, travel documents were issued on the spot if the claim to statelessness could be substantiated. This substantiation was difficult to obtain and a liberal issuance of these documents doubtless resulted in many unwarranted persons obtaining them." Under the circumstances of the resettlement initiative, he admitted, "little could be done to avoid this problem." Campbell spelled out another issue related to a lack of clear directives from the Canadian government: "individual cases meriting humanitarian consideration but requiring special assistance," where "referral to Ottawa before approval resulted in delay and uncertainty." He said that "the arrangement of prior provincial approval for a given number of tuberculosis cases would be particularly useful in this respect. Also, previous indications of the degree of assistance which will be available for potential long term financial liabilities and/ or hard-core unemployed." Complex cases ranged from ones where applicants were epileptic or pregnant to ones where specific questions needed answering, such as whether stepchildren were considered to be the dependents of the principal applicant. Having to seek approval from department officials based in Ottawa hindered the processing of Ugandan Asian expellees, especially under the strict deadline, leading to frustration on the part of immigration officers. Campbell wrote that "an advance indication of Ottawa's attitude towards acceptance of these more dubious cases would facilitate selection decisions and obviate the necessity of constant referral back to headquarters."[169]

The government also did not provide clear guidance on how to approach the separation of families who applied for asylum in Canada. Campbell sought clarification: "[Should visa officers] approve two brothers and refuse the third if he does not comply? What about parents who were independent in their country of residence but will have poor prospects of employment in the Canadian labour market and become either dependents of their children or public charges?"[170] Ugandan Asian expellees were also required to certify that "I [name of applicant], hereby declare that if my admission to Canada is authorized, it could result in a permanent separation from my dependents."[171] The government of Canada was aware that some families would be separated, which brings into question the scope of the humanitarian motivation to admit Ugandan Asian expellees. Campbell also pointed out that letters and telegrams sent by relatives in Canada to the Department of Manpower and Immigration offering assistance and accommodation for applicants were not substantiated to see if they really had sufficient financial means or adequate housing. These letters of support increased an applicant's chances of being accepted into Canada. Molloy's personal memoir confirms that those who "had a relative or offer of assistance from someone in Canada" were called back for interviews even if they had British, Indian, or Pakistani citizenship.[172]

Finally, Campbell critiqued the apparent favouritism expressed by leaders of the Ismaili community in Uganda that they were to be admitted to Canada. He outlined that "above all else our selection of expellees/refugees must be done on a purely individual basis ... even the entertainment of verbal representations from members of one segment of the community will leave our department open to unfounded charges of discrimination and threaten to negate much of the positive publicity attached to Canada for its role in an emergency operation."[173] The universality of the resettlement initiative remained of utmost importance to visa officers on the ground. Molloy and St. Vincent, in oral history interviews and in their published works on operations in Uganda, have reiterated Canada's commitment to accepting all those who met the selection criteria and those who were genuinely stateless.[174] Although there were communications between the prime minister and the Aga Khan, Ismailis did not receive special treatment from immigration officials on the ground. Their admission to Canada was facilitated by specific legislation that was applicable to all Ugandan Asians.

Campbell's reflections on the resettlement initiative informed the work of scholars who debated the altruistic nature of Canada's decision to admit nearly eight thousand Ugandan Asian refugees from 1972 to 1974. The first academic assessment of the resettlement was conducted in 1973 by Gerald E. Dirks, who was commissioned by the Canadian government to compare the three most recent movements of refugees to Canada. These included the Hungarians who arrived in the 1950s and the Czechoslovaks who arrived in the late 1960s. Dirks concluded that Ugandan Asian refugees were not welcomed as warmly as the Hungarians in 1956 due to concerns over employment but that these anxieties dissipated as they integrated into the Canadian labour market. Considering the per capita expenditure, the Ugandan Asian resettlement was the cheapest refugee assistance scheme since the resettlement of displaced persons following the Second World War, in 1947 and 1948. Dirks pointed out that decisions about funding and the admittance of refugees from Hungary, Czechoslovakia, and Uganda all derived from the cabinet. However, one significant caveat to this is that both the Hungarian and the Ugandan Asian resettlements were carried out by cabinet members "where no strenuous opposition to the movements seems to have existed," which also "demonstrated the confidence in the correctness of their decision often associated with policy-making bodies which have enjoyed responsibility for considerable periods." Dirks highlighted Canada's geography as a factor that limited the number of asylum seekers. Since Canada "is not a state of first asylum," the government could "continue to carefully select those refugees from throughout the world who show promise of quickly and quietly integrating into the society." Historically, Canada had the advantage of choosing desirable refugees, which had "become almost routine owing to the existence of facilities and programmes suited to bringing about their prompt and smooth integration into Canadian society."[175] Cabinet members had immediately reviewed the potential of Ugandan

Asian refugees to become contributing members of Canadian society and thus commenced the resettlement process as noted in Chapter 2.

The notion that the government knowingly selecting those who were considered "desirable" is reiterated by other scholars. Freda Hawkins chaired a longitudinal study on various refugee movements in the postwar era and argued that "with few exceptions the Ugandan Asians were admitted as normal immigrants to Canada. Most were processed as independent applicants."[176] Both Dirks and Hawkins outlined the realities of how immigration policy was applied on the ground in Kampala: many Ugandan Asian expellees were evaluated according to the regular selection criteria and admitted to Canada because they had amassed the required number of points. Their conclusions supported the idea that Canada had received a disproportionate number of young, highly skilled, and well-educated Ugandan Asian refugees.

Two sociologists from the University of Wisconsin, Bert N. Adams and Victor Jesudason conducted a major study covering 400 heads of Ugandan Asian households in Canada and India as well as 490 heads of Ugandan Asian households in Britain. They drew strong conclusions about the skills and qualifications of the refugees who were resettled in each of these countries. Adams argued that "Canada utilized its own immigration criteria in accepting the stateless, with the result that those entering Canada were likely to have good English skills, to have a sponsor or a job waiting for them, to be young, and to be of reasonable economic means. Canada was not on a 'mission of mercy' so much as on a search for possible contributors to the Canadian economy."[177] The two sociologists also found that "only four percent of the Ugandan Asians coming to Canada were over fifty years of age while thirty-five percent of those going to Britain were and thirty percent of those going to India were over fifty" and that "only ten percent of those coming to Canada" had a primary level of education or less.[178] These statistics coincided with Dirks's report that more than 50 percent of refugees who were offered visas in Kampala possessed a minimum of fourteen years of formal schooling.[179] Political scientist Reginald Whitaker also argued that Canada chose the most educated and desirable migrants.[180] Adams and Jesudason concluded that Canada received a disproportionate number of "professional and managerial class members while the less skilled workers and operators of small retail stores tended to go to Britain and India."[181] An official from the Department of Manpower and Immigration reiterated that there was "no doubt about it—we've got the cream of the crop."[182]

Scholars, outside observers, and even some government officials accused the federal government of hand-picking the best qualified Ugandan Asian refugees by strictly applying immigration selection criteria to the majority of applicants. As these allegations erupted in the late 1970s, the Canadian government and the public defended the resettlement initiative by accentuating the humanitarian motives behind it. Although researchers used raw data to support their findings, government officials argued that there had also been a sufficient intake of dependents and relatives who would not have been eligible to enter Canada under the regular selection criteria. A memorandum to Prime Minister Trudeau from the immigration department outlined that "while most of the heads of families selected in Uganda were those whom we considered would settle successfully in Canada, we also accepted a large number of dependents and relatives who met virtually no criteria, because we felt they could become successfully established here with the assistance of other family members."[183] Newspapers also responded to allegations of Canadian opportunism. As one writer stated, "Yes, we did pick young, healthy, well-educated heads of families … but we also included the sick, the old and the frail members of their families." The same writer also addressed the reality that many Ugandan Asians were underemployed, saying they "had to take their chances with the rest of us in weathering hard times. We aren't auditioning for the role of angels, but looking back, we sure did a bang-up job on behalf of the Ugandan refugees. What's more we're glad, because they sure made fine citizens for Canada."[184] Again, officials and the public conceded that Ugandan Asian refugees were particularly well educated and highly skilled and making strong contributions to Canada, although they faced barriers to employment; however, they also highlighted instances of perceived benevolence in letting refugees in. Ultimately, the Canadian government did receive disproportionate numbers of highly qualified refugees but argued that it had focused on those who were stateless. Stateless refugees happened to be particularly young, well educated, and skilled workers.

However, the push to accept those who were stateless led to criticisms that Canada had done so to let in more Ismaili Muslims. At a press briefing in London, UK, hosted by a the group of sociologists and researchers who conducted the major report, an Indian journalist argued that the Canadian government accepted a large proportion of Ismailis because the high commissioner for refugees was Prince Sadruddin—the Aga Khan's uncle. The journalist exclaimed that the high commissioner wanted to secure the "best possible homeland for his co-religionists [and] pulled strings to get them into Canada," and as noted by journalist Ross Henderson "perhaps the most significant thing is not whether that accusation is true, but that Indian journalists think it is true and write as if it is."[185] However, sociologist Mike Bristow, who attended the press conference, said that under Canada's resettlement policy, a large number of Muslims just happened to be accepted by Canadian visa officers. According to Bristow, "the Hindus and others had retained these [British passports] ... but the Moslem, urbanized professionals in Uganda had believed that they would be accepted into Ugandan society, and had renounced their British passports and adopted Ugandan citizenship. Then, when the Ugandans expelled all types of Asians, the Moslems were stateless ... but Canada had agreed to take in the stateless—and these just happened to also be the most urbanized, educated, youngest and occupationally advanced."[186] Bristow's analysis reiterated Canada's focus on admitting those who were stateless and supported the universality of Canadian immigration policy. Also of note is that visa officers in Kampala had reported to Ottawa in 1972 that "earlier estimates that most Ismailis were stateless are not being borne out. Neither is the belief that most stateless are Ismailis. Accordingly, the decision to give priority to the stateless group will not necessarily mean that a sizeable portion of the Ismailis will come to Canada as originally expected."[187]

It is unknown how many of the 7,550 Ugandan Asian refugees that came to Canada were Ismaili. Visa officers did not require information on religious affiliation from those in transit centres who were sponsored by a family member and those who applied as an independent class immigrant from the United Kingdom, India, or Pakistan.[188] The only reliable statistics on religious background pertain to those who were issued visas in Kampala and had arrived in Canada by 8 November 1972: 2,862 were Ismaili Muslims, 649 were Hindus, 466 were Christians, 382 belonged to other denominations of Islam, and 61 were Sikh.[189] Thus, the majority of Ugandan Asians that arrived in Canada by the end of the expulsion period were Ismailis; however, they represented under 70 percent of the overall Ugandan Asian refugee population. Most importantly, drawing any strong conclusions about the religious affiliations of the entire group of 7,550 refugees is impossible. Further, the Canadian government was aware of the high qualifications of Ugandan Asians before it formally announced its intention to admit expellees to Canada, but it did not purposefully select the "cream of the crop." The large proportion of professionals and managers who fell within the stateless category resulted from Uganda's push towards Africanization after independence, when Ugandan citizenship became required to conduct business in the country. Additionally, anyone who worked for the Ugandan civil service was required to hold citizenship to remain employed. This led to a large number of Goan Christians also being rendered stateless when Amin issued his expulsion decree. Evaluations, reports, and academic studies of the Ugandan Asian resettlement clearly demonstrate the qualifications of Ugandan Asian refugees but also confirm Canada's application of a universal immigration policy. Although the resettlement initiative was not entirely altruistic, the Canadian government acted humanely to assist nearly eight thousand Ugandan Asian refugees and applied a universal immigration policy when screening applicants. Moving beyond the initial years of resettlement, Ugandan Asian refugees established themselves permanently in Canada and embarked on the journey of becoming Canadian citizens.

CHAPTER 6

FROM REFUGEES TO CITIZENS:
Integration, Commemoration, and Identity Formation in Canada

When we first came, I think there was so much discrimination in Kamloops. You could feel it, you could see it. . . . It was a small city, but there were people [who] weren't as friendly, as welcoming at that time.

Amin Sunderji, 2015

However, more times than we encountered difficulties, we encountered friends. People opened up their homes and their hearts and gave generously of everything. The spirit of hospitality the state had extended to us from Uganda was repeated over and over again by the citizens of Brantford.

Zain Alarakhia, in Richard Saunders's *Journey into Hope*, 1994

If I had to choose between Canada and Uganda, I think I would choose Canada because this is the country that gave me a refuge when I needed it.

Sikandar, 2015

I am a Canadian, a Ugandan, an African, an Indian, and a Goan. You don't have to choose—except if one goes to war with another, then you might have to choose—but I don't have to. And I embrace all of them. They are all part of [my] psyche.

John Nazareth, 2015

The 1976 Immigration Act marked a new dynamic in Canadian immigration policy. It established three principal categories for applicants, including a designated category for refugees within the humanitarian class, alongside the family class and independent class. The formalization of refugee policy was spurred by the recent arrival of the Ugandan Asian refugees as well as Canada's commitment as a signatory of the 1951 Convention Relating to the Status of Refugees and the 1967 Protocol Relating to the Status of Refugees.[1] The Immigration Act formally acknowledged the principle of non-discrimination and emphasized collaboration "between all levels of government and the voluntary sector in the settlement of immigrants in Canadian society."[2] Cooperation between various government departments and the voluntary sector in particular was influenced by the success of the Uganda Asian Committees in providing positive social support for refugees. Based on government reports noted in the previous chapter, the resiliency of Ugandan Asian refugees and the general participation of Canadians in the committees facilitated the integration processes.

With the arrival of eighty thousand refugees from Vietnam, Cambodia, and Laos in the mid-1970s and early 1980s, Canadian immigration policy continued to promote the resettlement of refugees while balancing local and international concerns.[3] After the collapse of the Soviet Union, international governments shifted their politics onto the bodies of foreigners. As Cold War rhetoric subsided, governments used migrants to demonstrate their political alliances, by accepting or denying certain groups' entry or claims for asylum. The Canadian government focused on additional screening measures for migrants. Economic hardship in the 1980s was reflected in changes to immigration policy, as annual admission levels reached a decade low of eighty-four thousand in 1985.[4] In the 1990s immigration levels rose as the system favoured independent immigrants who would contribute to the Canadian labour market. A five-year immigration plan launched in 1990 promoted increased immigration during periods of poor economic growth.[5] During the 1990s Canada elected to admit roughly 250,000 immigrants per year, representing approximately 1 percent of the Canadian population. Within the same period, the number of asylum seekers continued to rise, along with anxieties about the legitimacy of asylum claims. The review of asylum claims created a backlog of refugees awaiting hearings while authorities failed to locate and deport those who were perceived to be "illegal" migrants, which fuelled public perceptions that immigration levels were too high.

As global conflicts, natural disasters, and other political crises had escalated in the late 1980s, the number of refugees worldwide had increased, reaching 14,914,160 by 1989.[6] A series of amendments to the 1976 Immigration Act occurred throughout the 1980s and 1990s, reflecting anxieties about terrorism and the validity of asylum claims. The arrival of two boats of refugees from Sri Lanka, in August 1986 and July 1987, reshaped Canadian immigration policy and started a process of criminalizing asylum seekers. The two groups of refugees, which included 155 Tamils and 174 Indians (mainly Sikhs from Punjab), respectively, were granted asylum in Canada, but their arrival led to the passing of Bill C-84, the Refugee Deterrents and Detention Bill. Although not all of the bill's provisions were implemented, political scientist Suha Diab argues that it prompted Canadians to form problematic links between refugees and terrorists. Moreover, Diab explains that the arrival of the Sikh refugees as well as "the highly publicized case of Mahmoud Muhammad Issa Muhammad," who was ordered to be deported after it was discovered that he lied on his permanent residence application and had links to the Popular Front for Liberation of Palestine but delayed the deportation by twenty-five years by filing a refugee claim and subsequent appeals, "were fortuitous moments that provided the government with the missing link and the legitimating discourse to demonstrate that the refugee determination system was broken, dangerous and in need of immediate intervention."[7]

Two years later, in 1989, another security measure was implemented, under the guise of permitting fair hearings for refugees. Bill C-55 established the Immigration and Refugee Board as a result of the precedent-setting *Singh v. Minister of Employment and Immigration*. The court case called into question whether the denial of Harbhajan Singh's and six others' requests for refugee status was unfair based on the procedures established in the 1976 Immigration Act. Claimants were denied an oral hearing based on the grounds that they were not entitled to due process under the Canadian Charter of Rights and Freedoms because they were noncitizens. The final unanimous

Supreme Court ruling said that once an asylum seeker arrived on Canadian soil they were entitled to protection under the Canadian Charter of Rights and Freedoms, and ordered the Department of Employment and Immigration to grant all asylum seekers the right to a formal hearing under section 7 of the Charter pertaining to the security of a person and fundamental justice.[8] The ruling ensured that all refugee claimants were entitled to appeal denied asylum claims. The Immigration and Refugee Board was mandated with determining the status of refugee claims, and governing authorities were prohibited from deporting prospective applicants without holding fair hearings. However, the same bill granted immigration officials the power to refuse applications from asylum seekers who submitted their request after coming through a "safe third country," which was arbitrarily defined. Any refugee claimant who applied for asylum in Canada but had first travelled through what was deemed a "safe country"—for example, the United States—would be sent back to the safe country or deported to their country of origin, where arguably "their lives would be in jeopardy."[9] Critics of the bill argue the "breadth of the provision could bar even very deserving claimants from receiving protection."[10] The Safe Third Country Agreement, a treaty between Canada and the United States that stipulates refugee claimants must apply to the first country they arrive in between these two countries, was enacted in 2004 to stem the number of refugee claims in both countries.

As Canada moved into the new millennium, concerns over security and terrorism became paramount in immigration policy. In the wake of 9/11, the Canadian government implemented the Immigration and Refugee Protection Act, which emphasized national security. The minister of citizenship and immigration at the time, Elinor Caplan, argued that the purpose of the latest act was to "close the back door to those who would abuse our rules, in order to open the front door wider to those who would come to us from around the world and help us build our country."[11] Caplan's statement aligned with rhetoric that smeared refugees as potential criminals, terrorists, and bogus claimants. The creation of the Canadian Border Services Agency in 2003 accentuated the primacy of security for government officials. The Immigration and Refugee Protection Act embodied a major shift in immigration policy towards a restrictive approach to the refugee determination process. As immigration historians Ninette Kelley and Michael Trebilcock argue, it differentiated itself from the specificity of the 1976 Immigration Act by "leaving considerable discretion to the executive to determine and implement immigration admission, exclusion, and removal policies through regulations."[12] Both Diab and political scientist Christopher Anderson contend that policy changes in the early 2000s emphasized the importance of the humanitarian-security nexus and the return of liberal nationalist discourse within immigration policy.

Major policy changes from the 1970s onwards encouraged increasing levels of immigration and diversified the source countries of newcomers. Prior to the creation of the points system, nearly 90 percent of all immigrants came from Europe; by 1990 immigrants from Asia and the Middle East represented more than 50 percent of all arrivals.[13] These figures continued to rise in the early 2000s, as arrivals from Asia and the Middle East grew to represent 58 percent of all immigrants, with China and India being the two largest source countries. By the turn of the new millennium, one in every five Canadian residents was born outside of the country.[14] Major shifts in Canadian immigration and refugee policy alongside changing demographics fostered the growth of both the South Asian and East African communities in Canada. The fallout from the expulsion decree in East Africa encouraged many other African Asians to migrate to other parts of the globe. This was complemented by further migrations of individuals of South Asian heritage from Fiji, the West Indies, Mauritius, and elsewhere in the 1970s. Although migration from the Indian subcontinent to Canada dates back to the late nineteenth century, South Asian migration during the 1970s and onwards represents a distinct wave. The number of South Asians living in Canada increased from 6,774 in 1961 to more than 300,000 by 1985.[15]

The Contested Grounds of Becoming Canadian

Ugandan Asian refugees experienced a range of interactions with Canadians during their initial years of settlement. Interviewees described how some Canadians were extremely helpful while others were more hesitant or prejudiced. For example, Shamim stated, "My experience was good. You know, I got lost, they helped me out. For me it was a good experience because they were there for me in my difficult time. When they found out my story, you know, I have a family, I'm looking after my family. I don't have a penny in my name. I'm broke. . . . I don't have money. I came from Uganda. When they heard, they were very sympathetic. . . . They started to understand me."[16] Shamim recalled how initially she had the shortest queue of customers at CIBC, where she worked as a bank teller, because people were reluctant to be served by a racialized woman. Her strong work ethic then resulted in her having the longest line, as she became known to process transactions quickly.[17] Tom and Joan, another set of oral history participants, said they did not personally face any prejudice:

> Joan: We never really had a bad experience. Honestly.
>
> Tom: No, we have not.
>
> Joan: With our neighbours or with our friends. . . . A lot of our [Ugandan Asian] friends say they had problems at work. . . . We never experienced that.
>
> Tom: And I think part of it . . . a lot of it was the university environment [where they both worked over the years at McGill, Guelph, and Western University]. But also, part of it I think is I think people don't understand Canadians. I think for me I found particularly among rural Canadians, sometimes they can seem to be standoffish, but actually they're shy. Once you start talking to them, they open up. But Canadians are shy, they're not like Americans. . . . You have to start the conversation, but you can sometimes perceive that to be discrimination, you know, or antagonism or something. It isn't—mostly they're just shy. So once we realized that, we would start the conversation and, you know, we made a lot of friends. I never, like Joan says, never really experienced discrimination. I'm sure there was, maybe people avoided us, but we never had any overt discrimination. We never had to feel like we didn't belong or anything like that.[18]

Like Shamim, Tom and Joan found that as time passed and relationships were formed with friends and neighbours, barriers to integration dissipated. They understood the reticence of Canadians to generate conversation as "shyness" as opposed to racial discrimination. They acknowledged that other Ugandan Asians faced discrimination in their

workplaces but they did not have the same experience. For Tom and
Joan, they consciously chose to dismiss prejudiced interactions as either
a failure to understand the "shyness of Canadians" or to misinterpret
the ignorance of society as purposeful discrimination.

Errol and Delphine also argued they were well received by members
of Canadian society:

> Errol: Even when I joined my golf club here at Markland
> Wood it was predominantly Caucasian.... Never felt like I
> didn't belong.
>
> Delphine: I would say that as well because, in my capacity
> as a teacher, I never ever would miss out at all, neither from
> the parents nor from the staff or anything. I did not feel that
> if I wanted to pursue and do something else would it have
> been a hindrance because I wasn't white Canadian. Now too
> ... I'm the golf captain of a little group.... I say little but
> there's about sixty of us seniors who play golf at Centennial,
> and I'm the only coloured person.... I don't *feel* that I'm the
> only one, I just notice it.[19]

Errol became president of a Canadian airline company in the 1980s.
He said he "didn't witness any discrimination or racism" in Canada and
felt his potential to advance was not hindered by his racial background.
He contrasted this with his experiences south of the border: "In the US
when I used to go in the early '80s, I'd go with my VPs who were all
Caucasian and you could see the presentations that were being made,
they were addressing them [the vice presidents].... And then they'd
soon find out that I was the president of the company and there would
be a sudden switch, and you could see that."[20] Shiraz also noted how
his initial interactions with Canadians at his first job in a factory in
Kitchener were cordial: "It was a little bit difficult in the beginning to
understand where they were coming from, what our values were and
what their values were.... We got caught up with them eventually. But
by and large, it was not very difficult dealing with them.... They were
mostly Germans in Kitchener."[21]

Some interviewees described regional differences in how they were
treated in Canada. Nimira recalled:

> Some of them [Canadians] were extremely nice, extremely helpful, more accepting, especially [in] Montreal. When we were in Montreal, we, because at the time we didn't realize this, but Montreal was the most cosmopolitan town in the country.... There were some that were snotty, but when we went to Toronto or Ottawa or anything, oh my god we used to feel so strange. They used to call us Paki [laughs], you know, words like that, but when you are amongst others who they themselves have been immigrants they don't make fun of you. Whereas we found that here [in Ottawa] they didn't have as many and they really made fun. And in Toronto it was the other extreme: they had too many so they didn't like it.[22]

Nimira's south shore neighbourhood in Montreal was composed of a large immigrant base. Her reflections coincided with those of other Ugandan Asians who permanently resettled in Ottawa and Toronto. At a commemorative event for Ugandan Asian refugees in 1994, Zain Alarakhia also described differences between the larger and smaller cities:

> I believe that those immigrants who chose to settle in the smaller cities had a significantly different experience than those who settled in the larger centres. In the smaller cities the Ugandan immigrants had to interact, largely, with the general population at all times. There was no sizeable Ugandan community to provide a buffer of sorts. Sometimes people didn't know what to make of us. At other times they preferred not to try. However, more times than we encountered difficulties, we encountered friends. People opened up their homes and their hearts and gave generously of everything. The spirit of hospitality the state had extended to us from Uganda was repeated over and over again by the citizens of Brantford.[23]

However, even couples who settled together, in the same region of Canada, could have different experiences. For example, after arriving in Ottawa with his wife, Zul explained that Canadians "were kinda cool at the beginning.... Like cold, I mean. They didn't accept us, you know. Most of the people at work were okay, people at my work were perfect and readily acceptable. But in Nilufar's [Zul's wife] work they were naturally [prejudiced]. If any positions came up for a promotion, it didn't happen easy, you had to work hard and show your work."[24]

Amin S. and Farida, who had moved to Kamloops, also remembered contrasting interactions with Canadians. "When we first came, I think there was so much discrimination in Kamloops. You could feel it, you could see it," recalled Amin S. "It was a small city, but there were people [who] weren't as friendly, as welcoming at that time."[25] Farida said she did not face the same prejudice that her husband did. She had attended a beauty and aesthetician school in London, England, and her exposure to British society made her more acceptable to Canadians. "It was good because I knew the London style and I did have a British accent at that time," she said. "So I got along really well and I didn't have a problem with any Canadians. In fact, they liked me and they loved to talk to me. And wherever I went, there wasn't any discrimination with me because I knew the weather, I knew what to wear."[26] To Canadians, Amin. S. embodied the traits of a "newcomer" in terms of his physical appearance and his accent. Scholars argue that accents are used as a basis for discriminating against others now that it is no longer socially acceptable to discriminate against people because of their race, ethnicity, and national origin.[27]

The idea of knowing what to wear was echoed by Munira, who argued that "prejudice will always be there. It was there, it is there.... When we first came here, we were always very culturally diversified. And when I say that, do you know in Uganda, we didn't walk around deliberately wearing traditional clothing or anything of that sort. And socially we always had what I call European dressing."[28] Both Munira and Farida had adopted Western clothing practices before arriving in Canada, which mitigated discrimination against them. According to historian G.S. Basran, adoption of Western styles of dress, along with other social customs and behaviours, in an effort to integrate into white Canadian society was common for Indo-Canadian families dating back to the 1930s.[29] However, this strategy did not guarantee that refugees would not encounter prejudice. Shamim, who initially felt welcomed at her place of work, faced a different environment when a new manager came in. "It was a guy this time," she said. "He would say, you know, 'You are so pretty. It's too bad you're brown. I can't take you out.' Things like that, like he told me on [to] my face, 'it's too bad you are brown, you are not white. I wish you were white because I would love to take you out.'"[30] In some instances, as noted in Shamim's testimony, racial discrimination was made explicit.

Many oral history participants described experiences of racism in the 1970s but considered them a product of the time, attributable to the small proportion of racialized people compared to the dominant white population at the time. For example, Shamim said that Canadians "didn't know what we were, right? They didn't have that many brown people at that time."[31] Aminmohamed recalled that "when I came to Ottawa, there were not too many immigrants. Even in the last like twenty years there has been a drastic change, you know. Before that, Rideau Centre [major shopping mall in Ottawa], you wouldn't see too many brown faces or too many black faces. There were more whites only."[32] Edmond described entering Toronto's Union Station in 1973 when "a young boy . . . spat in front of me before I could take the steps. He's looking at me and I didn't say anything, just walked past him."[33] He saw this incident as a product of the historical context, adding, "I don't know now but I'm sure things have changed a lot."[34] Sikandar remembered a threatening incident on the road: "I was driving a car and four guys . . . start yelling and screaming, 'Paki, go back to your country,' and so I gave them a finger, which is wrong on my part too. . . . They started chasing me with their car, so I said oh my god they are four and I am one. I am gonna get beat up. So I just drove my car right to where I used to work but before I could turn, they threw a big stick at my car and hit my car with a big stick."[35] Similar to Edmond and many others, Sikandar added, "But I've never had a problem for a long time."[36]

Being called a "Paki" in Canada was a racializing and demeaning act that exemplified the postcolonial subjectivity of Ugandan Asian refugees. In the eyes of Canadians, they were not East Africans, or even Indians. They were distinctly labelled as an inferior Other and robbed of the opportunity to self-identify. The dominant Anglo-Saxon majority situated them as Pakistani because of their physical appearance, ignoring their Ugandan upbringing and heritage. Avtar Brah argues, "Looks mattered because of the history of the racialization of 'looks'; they mattered because discourses about the body were crucial to the constitution of racisms."[37] Racial tensions continued to rise in the 1970s as "Paki-baiting"—where white Canadian youth would chase South Asians in cars and yell racial slurs at them—became more frequent in Vancouver, urban Ontario, Edmonton, Calgary, and Montreal. Discrimination against the South Asian community in Toronto culminated in the shooting of a fifteen-year-old South Asian boy on 14 April 1976. The shooter justified his actions by claiming that he "just shot the nigger. For every one you shoot, you leave a white girl with a broken heart."[38] Academic scholars Norman Buchignani, Doreen M. Indra, and Ram Srivastava argue that by 1977, general acts of racism against South Asians had become common in downtown Toronto and were spreading across Ontario and the Prairies.[39] Some refugees recalled instances of racialized bullying in public school. In St. Catharines, Ontario, Karim was made fun of at school. "I was the only brown person in my class," he said. "My name was Karim so people thought that 'cream in my coffee' would be a better name to call me. So, they would constantly tease me about that. They would call me chocolate because of my skin colour. They would call me chocolate milk."[40] For Amin V. bullying escalated into a physical confrontation when a classmate yelled at him, "Hey you fucking Paki." His friend ended up getting punched by the classmate. "I grabbed this guy and I just went nuts. I started punching him," said Amin V.[41]

Historian Hugh Johnston documents the prevalence of racial discrimination against the South Asian community in the 1970s and 1980s, and argues that the media presented biased reports relating to violence that purposefully drew attention to the ethnic backgrounds of South Asian suspects whereas the racial identities of whites were not disclosed.[42] The media reinforced negative stereotypes of South Asia as a whole by exclusively reporting on poverty, low levels of literacy, violence, natural disasters, and political repression in the region. Animosity towards the South Asian community manifested in several ways, from "racist signs and bumper stickers to acts of vandalism, assaults on individuals and, in a couple instances minor riots."[43] From 1972 to 1975 in Vancouver, racial tensions were so high that Vancouver police sanctioned the establishment of special neighbourhood patrols to reduce vandalism and violence targeted at Sikhs.

Canadians struggled to adjust to the arrival of a nonwhite refugee group amid a largely white population. As noted, some oral history participants chalked this up to a lack of exposure to different ethnic communities. Others pointed to the reluctance of some refugees to actively engage in Canadian society as a factor that may have fostered discrimination. Aminmohamed's spouse, Begum, said:

> I think now, looking back, it wasn't just the fault of the Canadians to call us names because in high school I remember hanging out with just Ismailis, right? And then we would sit and talk in Gujarati so no wonder they were calling us names. But at that time, we were like look at them, they were discriminating. But now I look back and I say no wonder they were discriminating.... That's human nature. When you are in a strange environment you look for comfort, and comfort is where something is familiar.[44]

Other participants said they understood Canadian anxieties and contended that "we would have been the same way if we were in their shoes and we saw all these new peoples coming into the country.... You do become defensive, you do care about your jobs, you do care about other things,... that it's the public money that's going into spending on these peoples and why are we using these energies and resources on people?"[45] Oral histories suggest that refugees were aware of public perceptions that their resettlement was a potential drain on social services, as noted in the previous chapter, and that ethnic clustering could spur discriminations. The possible danger of gathering in larger groups of South Asians was reiterated by Amin V., who argued that "you didn't want to be seen around them [other South Asians] because everyone was called Paki at that time.... If you really were gathering in batches of ten to twenty people, it becomes a scary phenomenon."[46] It is critical to note that these observations may be distorted by their recontextualizations of the past. Scholars argue that memories are continuously reconstructed as people try to understand their own histories.[47]

Oral history interviews give salience to historian Dirk Hoerder's argument that everyday cultural interactions, not race and ethnicity, defined inclusion and integration for immigrants. Day-to-day interactions, not top-down legislation in the form of the 1976 Immigration

Act or multiculturalism policy, influenced how Ugandan Asian refugees perceived Canadians. The majority of interviewees shared similar
recollections about their initial interactions in Canadian society. They
described Canadians as friendly, curious, and very helpful. Though many
experienced different forms of racism, publicly, institutionally, and sys-
temically, throughout their first ten to twenty years in the country, they
did not feel these instances were representative of the overall Canadian
population. They also indicated that these issues dissipated over time,
possibly due to the demographic shifts in Canada. However, ethnic
antagonism complicated the continuing processes of identity formation. Scholars maintain that one's sense of self is fluid, multifaceted,
and continuously reconstructed, but it is also significantly informed
by imposed identities. Academics Haideh Moghissi, Saeed Rahnema,
and Mark J. Goodman argue that "the assigned identity of others is
not a matter of choice. It is not fluid. It is fixed by forces of racism and
xenophobia, despite the possibility of social mobility and regardless of
the individual's wishes or desires . . . the 'ethnicity' of such groups is
absolute."[48] Regardless of the historical backgrounds of Ugandan Asian
refugees, they were subsumed within the category of South Asian by
the dominant white society.

Celebrating and Commemorating Life in Canada

As Ugandan Asian refugees became citizens of Canada, they began
to reflect on and commemorate their transition into Canadian society
through various events marking the anniversary of the resettlement
initiative. Through these commemorative events, they attempted to
ground the Ugandan Asian refugee experience within the Canadian
historical narrative, reaffirming the community's identity while also
solidifying their connection to Canada. Anniversary celebrations
were public demonstrations of their simultaneous membership in
Canadian society and the global diaspora of Ugandan Asian refugees.
Scholars contend that these events reinforced shared histories of
forced displacement, pain, resistance, and resilience, intrinsic features of both diaspora and indigenous communities.[49] The collective
memory of Ugandan Asian refugees plays a formative role in their
identity construction; social groups are responsible for the creation
of public memories. As French philosopher Maurice Halbwachs
argues, collective memories determine not only what ought to be

remembered by the community but also how memories should be recounted.[50] Establishing a formal historical narrative that privileged certain events as particularly worthy of remembrance allowed refugees to bond over shared experiences of resettlement. However, given the realities of social memory, it is crucial to be aware of how these shared memories are selective. Historian Peter Burke argues for remaining conscious of how these events are selected alongside who shapes the group's recollection of historical episodes.[51] Commemorative events are also manifestations of public history and hold high levels of significance for marginalized communities. While navigating the influences of race, class, ethnicity, sexual orientation, and gender, Ugandan Asian refugees established new identities, searching through their memories of previous events to capture victories and defeats, trauma and resilience, as a powerful means to define and redefine their identity in the present moment.

Three major commemorative events were held, in 1994, 1998, and 2002. A two-day symposium titled Journey Into Hope took place at the Canadian Museum of Civilization in Ottawa on 29 April 1994.[52] This event was initiated by the Canadian Immigration Historical Society and supported by Citizenship and Immigration Canada and the Ugandan Asian community. The organizers sought to promote Canadian multiculturalism while highlighting a specific group of refugees who were well integrated and grateful to the Canadian government. Over three hundred people attended the two-day event. Attendees included several dignitaries, such as Sergio Marchi, the minister of citizenship and immigration; Mwanyengela Ngali, high commissioner for Kenya; Aziz Bhaloo, president of the Ismaili Council for Canada; and several members of Uganda's immigration team, including Roger St. Vincent and Michael Molloy. Parts of the event, including the keynote speakers and several participants, were filmed for circulation among those refugees who were unable to attend.

The second event marked the twenty-fifth anniversary of the resettlement initiative. Flight of Courage was held in Vancouver on 30 May 1998 and featured several prominent speakers and members of the community.[53] This included speeches from Dr. Hedy Fry, the secretary of state for multiculturalism and the status of women; Sue Hammell, minister of women's equality; Dr. Charles Olweny, a professor of oncology at the University of Manitoba and president of Friends of Makerere in Canada (a charity dedicated to the advancement of higher education in Africa, particularly at Makerere University in Uganda); Sam Kuteesa, the minister of state for planning and investment for the Republic of Uganda; and several members of the refugee community such as Sultan Baloo and Umeeda Switlo. John Halani, an oral history participant who was the chair of the Canada Uganda Association and also served as an honorary consul to Uganda, organized the event. The event brought together members of the refugee community as well as others from Uganda to demonstrate the various ways in which Ugandans have made significant contributions to Canada. Flight of Courage was also used to promote philanthropic endeavours in Uganda and foster commercial and humanitarian connections to East Africa.

Building on the success of the previous two celebrations, another anniversary event was held in Ottawa. The event, 30th Anniversary Celebration, was held on 2 October 2002 in Parliament Hill's West Block to "celebrate the 30th anniversary of the South Asian Exodus from Uganda to Canada."[54] It was sponsored by the Pearson-Shoyama Institute (a think tank focused on a progressive future for the country), the Uganda 30 Committee (a group of organizers largely composed of Ugandan Asian refugees), and various others from within the Ugandan Asian community. In addition to promoting diversity and Canadian multiculturalism, the event aimed to bring attention to the resettlement of Ugandan Asian refugees as a "Canadian success story." The event featured speeches from Sheila Copps, minister of Canadian heritage; Mobina Jaffer, an oral history participant and the first and only Ugandan Asian refugee to become a senator in Canada; and St. Vincent and Molloy.

Reviewing the themes presented by each of these commemorative events provides a broader understanding of the ways in which refugees conceptualized their community, collective and personal identities, and histories of resettlement. Marking the anniversary of the Asian expulsion from Uganda provided a formal avenue for Ugandan Asian refugees in Canada to reassert their connections to East Africa while also reaffirming their allegiance to Canada. Honorary Consul to Uganda John Halani explained to attendees at the twenty-fifth anniversary that "President Museveni took a very courageous steps towards national reconciliation and reconstruction. These and other bold steps have marked a turning point in Uganda's revitalisation."[55] The president of Uganda at the time, Yoweri Museveni, had launched a campaign in the early 1990s to revitalize economic development by inviting expelled Ugandan Asians to return. An official campaign to return confiscated property had been announced under President Milton Obote in 1982, but it was not until 1992, when the World Bank threatened to withhold a $125-million USD loan, that the Ugandan government began processing land and business claims submitted by Ugandan Asian refugees.[56] As Uganda took steps towards reconciliation, Senator Jaffer reiterated the honorary consul's appeal. "All Ugandans," said the senator at the thirtieth anniversary, "though we may be here and Canada has been good to us, I ask you not to forget Uganda."[57] She encouraged refugees to make peace with the past and offer their skills and expertise to assist in the development of Uganda. Dr. Sudhir Ruparelia of the Kampala Goan Institute, founded in 1910 by Goans living in Kampala as a place for the Goan community to socialize, would later note that these celebrations served "the dual purpose of reviving a journey down the memory lane and at the same time provides a word of encouragement to our future generation—new settlers—of the opportunities that exist in Uganda. It will also be a strong reminder to them not to forsake the crucial rope of their culture and traditions."[58] Promoting opportunities for furthering the development of Uganda and creating transnational links was a central theme at the commemorative events.

Government representatives consistently emphasized the roots that refugees put down in Canada by applauding their contributions to the diversity of the country and to society as a whole. Minister Marchi expressed at the 1994 symposium that "among us this evening are representatives of the Ugandan Asians who are now proud Canadians. You have proved Pierre Elliott Trudeau's words to be right. You have made an immeasurable contribution to the richness and variety of our country and we are honoured and blessed to have you in our midst."[59] The resettlement of the Ugandan Asian refugees continued to be viewed as an overwhelming success by the government. Similarly, in a letter addressed to the Ugandan Asian community in Canada in commemoration of the twenty-fifth anniversary, Prime Minister Jean Chrétien noted in 1998 that "the strength and diversity of our society are vitally dependent on the continued cooperation of its diverse peoples, and events such as this anniversary celebration provide an excellent opportunity for Canadians of Ugandan origin to celebrate both their uniqueness and their valuable contributions to Canada's prosperity and cultural heritage."[60] Government officials emphasized the contributions of Ugandan Asian refugees while reinforcing their position as Canadian citizens.

UNHCR representatives in attendance at the celebrations also highlighted the contributions that refugees made in their countries of resettlement. Judith Kumin, the UNHCR representative in Canada during the thirtieth anniversary, stated that Ugandan Asian refugees "are active and productive in so many walks of life, and each of you is testimony to the fact that the courage, the energy, the hard work, the tenacity of refugees, refugees from all countries deserve our constant respect. Your remarkable economic and social success in Canada is, I think, a powerful example of the potential of refugees the world over to contribute to their new countries."[61]

Aziz Bhaloo reinforced the narrative of success among refugees in Canada at the symposium. He stated that "the once penniless refugees have blossomed into large and medium sized entrepreneurs, highly placed professionals, senior civil servants, and academics, all contributing actively to Canada's economic and social development and thereby enriching the Canadian Mosaic."[62] Although he may have been predisposed to offer a favourable review of his community as the president of the Ismaili Council for Canada, his comments articulated the strong connections between refugees and Canadian history.

Building on the government's recognition of Ugandan Asian refugees as contributing Canadian citizens, many refugees used the commemorative events as a platform for expressing their sincere gratitude. Zain Alarakhia concluded her speech at the 1994 banquet in Ottawa by stating, "I want you to know that we still carry a deep sense of gratitude to this country and its people. And that God willing, we shall somehow give back to this country a little of all that it has given us."[63] Her sentiments were echoed by Halani at Vancouver's celebration. In the welcoming brochure for the event, he wrote that "we [Ugandan Asian refugees] are extremely grateful to Canada for welcoming us with open arms and warm generosity. During this period, we have all faced challenges and with God's grace, most of us have done well."[64] These expressions of gratitude reflected the sentiments of refugees when they first arrived in Canada, as discussed in previous chapters. The theme of gratitude was prevalent among oral history participants, each of whom thanked the government for supporting them to resettle in Canada and become Canadian citizens. They emphasized the opportunities available to them in Canada. Delphine recalled returning from a trip to see her relatives abroad: "We always come back to Canada saying how fortunate . . . we were that Canada opened their doors. . . . Here were the opportunities, here you took advantage, education, jobs, everything, for us, for the next generation, and now for the next generation it has worked out just wonderful."[65] Nazir also described Canada as "a country of opportunity and adventure. It is a country that does let you as an individual gain as much as you wish to gain."[66] Other refugees emphasized their continued appreciation to the government and Canadians as a whole for their support. Aziz and his family members agreed that "we are always grateful to Canada because Canada really took care of us . . . like Canadians, initially when we came here, they really looked after us. Even the Canadian government, even the people, they really helped us to be what we are."[67] The entire family highlighted the collaborative efforts of the government and the public as a fundamental part of the resettlement initiative. Every interviewee within the study thanked the government for their efforts as they reflected on their personal life histories.

Ugandan Asian refugees who participated in the commemorative events recalled moments of catharsis and healing. Jalal, an oral history participant who spoke at the symposium in Ottawa, reflected on the atmosphere of the event. There were "representatives from the Bora community, for example, other Muslim communities, Goan communities. Everyone recounted their so-called success stories but in an unusual sense everybody's story had such a sense of hurt feelings and emotional baggage they were carrying," he said. "In the audience there wasn't a single dry eye. It was almost like a catharsis of sorts, complete letting down your emotional hurt feelings. It was quite a spectacle. So we heard so many stories in those two days."[68] Historian Mark Klempner argues that recounting trauma narratives in oral history interviews, or in this instance at a public gathering, enables survivors to "re-externalize" the event: "Through the therapeutic process of constructing a narrative and telling it to a listener, the event may be externalized once again, that is, re-externalized. In the process, its meaning changes, due in part to the empathy of the listener and the safety of the setting in which the narrative is shared."[69] Ugandan Asians

participated in a communal expression of re-externalization as they engaged in a therapeutic process amongst fellow refugees and government
officials who were sympathetic to their plight.

Commemorative events were also designed to reunite members of
the Ugandan diaspora in Canada and allow them to share their histories with the next generations. At the twenty-fifth anniversary event
in Vancouver, Halani noted the importance of learning from history:
"This occasion will hopefully remind us, our children, and our fellow
Canadians of the important lessons of our past—namely that racial and
religious intolerance hurts everybody and ultimately weakens the very
fabric of a nation and community."[70] Minister Copps echoed this idea
during the thirtieth anniversary celebration:

> After September 11, we have another message. Multi-
> culturalism is not enough. We also need to work on intercul-
> turalism—interculturalism so that the story of the Ugandan
> refugees is the story of building Canada . . . until we teach
> our children about religions, until our children carry the
> story of Uganda and you as refugees from Uganda as part of
> their story of Canada, until we manage through the instru-
> ments that are at our fingertips to see ourselves reflected on
> television and films, in books, in music. Our children will be
> strong in our cultures but not strong between cultures and
> one of the exceptional messages, I believe, of the Ugandan
> expatriates is that you can come to this country and you can
> build your community as you've done in an incredible fash-
> ion. But you also have something incredible to contribute
> to the community at large and these are stories that most
> Canadians do not know.[71]

Minister Copps advocated for embracing a pluralistic model in
Canadian society, using the case study of Ugandan Asian refugees who
resettled in Canada as a means of breaking down barriers to integration and countering Islamophobia. Furthermore, she emphasized the
necessity of situating the Ugandan Asian refugee experience within the
broader Canadian historical narrative, one of the central tenets of this
book. Her statement coincided with those made by other government
officials who acknowledged the transition of refugees into contributing

members of Canadian society and reaffirmed their status as Canadian citizens. Like Halani, Minister Copps vocalized the importance of sharing the life histories and contributions of Ugandan Asian refugees with the broader public.

A critical step towards educating the public and preserving this history for future generations was taken through the creation of the Uganda Collection at Carleton University. The Uganda Collection opened on 20 June 2014 as a collaborative effort between Carleton University, the Canadian Immigration Historical Society, and the Fakirani family. As the principal donors to the archive, the Fakirani family emphasized the significance of establishing a formal archive to solidify the place of Ugandan Asian refugees within Canadian history. The donation was made in honour of Hassanali and Sikinabai Fakirani, who passed away in Canada after ensuring that all nine of their children were resettled there. "It's very important because it allows the family to share some of the experiences that we'd been through during the time that we had to leave the country and also the experience of settling into Canada," said their son Nizar Fakirani at the opening of the archive. "We want to preserve this experience for the future generations. I hope that they will learn about it and extrapolate from it. That it will assist Canada, and our policy makers, to be able to respond to any future incidents of similar kind, where people have to be uprooted in large numbers."[72] Building on Nizar's comments, Senator Jaffer explained that the establishment of a permanent archive marked the "next stage in our evolution, and it's a very emotional stage, because now we have a place in history."[73] English professor Marianne Hirsch argues that archives serve as a site of "post-memory," which enables the survival of memories that can be carried on to future generations. Archives and major commemorative events also create public memories, according to communications professor Kendall Phillips, in this case encouraging all members of society to consciously investigate the historical roots of Ugandan Asian refugees and providing active spaces to share, discuss, and interact.

Ugandan Asian refugees have also celebrated milestones in Uganda's independence in collaboration with Ugandan Africans. In late September of 2012, an anniversary celebration was held in Toronto by the Uganda50Toronto committee. The intent was to commemorate the golden jubilee of Uganda's independence from British rule "from the viewpoint of the Ugandan Diaspora living in Canada."[74] The Uganda High Commission sponsored the main event, held on 8 September 2012, along with the creation of a souvenir book, *Uganda: 50 Years of Independence*. Activities concluded with a boat cruise in Toronto on 7 October 2012. Members of the organizing committee comprised a mix of Ugandan expatriates, including Dr. Munini Mulera, who escaped Uganda as a refugee in 1977 during Idi Amin's reign and resettled in Canada in 1981; Opiya Oloya, who came to Canada as a refugee fleeing Milton Obote's regime in the 1980s; and Persis Kavuma, who immigrated with her spouse after graduating from Makerere University in 1985. The events and souvenir book reasserted the deep historical roots of the Asian community in East Africa and emphasized the bonds that some Ugandan Asian refugees have formed with Ugandan Africans who have moved to Canada. Naresh Majithia, chairman of the committee, stated, "In a special way I would like to welcome all the children of those of us who came from Uganda. I hope this celebration will help you understand that our hearts are large enough to have love and gratitude for our adopted country Canada and the country we are honouring—Uganda."[75]

Recipes for Identity: Food as a Means of Belonging

Food embodies a wide range of social, cultural, and political elements of human life. The consumption of food is an intrinsic component of personal identity construction and, especially for immigrants and refugees, is dynamically informed by historical experiences. Sociologist Dwaine Plaza notes how food evokes each of the five senses to bring back memories from a specific geography or even a feeling of home. Sensory experiences are inextricably linked to the historical moments in people's lives. Other scholars note how food "holds emotional, social, community and cultural significance in the ways it can be used for comfort, to show love and affection (or the withholding of those), and to define individual identities and social relationships."[76] Several oral history participants discussed the importance of recreating familiar meals and the need to adjust to new foods in Canada.

Home-cooked food is an inherently gendered process. Women are viewed as the bastions of cuisine in many cultures. Academics

Svetlana Ristovski-Slijepcevic, Gwen E. Chapman, and Brenda L. Beagan argue that mothers are expected to care for their children's health, leading to an assumption that women determine family food choices and are responsible for preparing meals.[77] Two cookbooks created by Ugandan Asian refugee women in Canada and England reinforce the links between identity and food. Authors Lella Umedaly and Yasmin Alibhai-Brown describe how their recipes were passed down from their mothers, who continued traditional culinary practices in their lands of resettlement. Both articulate the expectations to replicate traditional cultural norms and the role they play in their respective families as experts in healthy dietary habits. For example, Umedaly recounts her father's retort when she requested flying lessons while growing up in Uganda: "Leila, you learn to pilot your pots and pans!"[78]

In *The Settler's Cookbook: A Memoir of Love, Migration and Food*, Alibhai-Brown, an Oxford-educated Ugandan Asian refugee whose family resettled in Britain, takes a historical approach to her recipes. Using autobiographical elements, she situates her family's experiences within the historical context of South Asians living in East Africa. Her work is written as a novel with recipes that relate to her life history interspersed throughout. She documents the ways in which many dishes reflect specific historical periods and the larger social impacts of food. The second cookbook, *Mamajee's Kitchen: Indian Cooking from Three Continents*, was written by Umedaly, a Ugandan Asian refugee who resettled in Canada.[79] It is similar to a traditional cookbook with recipes and photos. Umedaly captures important historical elements while following the standard pattern of detailed recipes supplemented by photos. Food and culture historian Marlene Epp argues that cookbooks act as historical sources that reveal how immigrant groups "maintain a public connection with homeland culture, reinforce ethnic identity, integrate into a new culture, and form new hybrid identities."[80] Investigating the themes presented in these two cookbooks illustrates the intersections among food, history, and identity.

The cookbooks show the ways in which Ugandan Asians fused South Asian and East African cuisine to produce hybrid or creolized snacks and entrees. For example, the propensity to deep-fry various South Asian snacks, from bhajias to pakoras, led to the creation of cassava chips. Cassava is a root vegetable found in East Africa, and migrants from the Indian subcontinent would thinly slice and deep-fry it, then add salt and chili powder for flavouring.[81] Another example is matoke with peanut curry. Matoke is a starchy banana that is popular in Uganda. The dish fuses this staple crop with South Asian flair through the addition of chili powder, garlic, tomatoes, and *dhana* and *jeera* powder seasoning (coriander and cumin).[82] Oral history participants spoke about the fusion of cuisines, noting that the culinary exchange went both ways. Rossbina recalled how Ugandan Asians "experienced cooking with African style. We had matoke, we had the plantain, the green bananas, and the *mogo* [cassava]. . . . Those were our favourites. . . . At the same time, the Africans learned how to make samosas and they became so creative. So instead of having meat or chicken samosas, they would start making chickpea samosas, or potato samosas."[83] Local Ugandan crops became favourites of Ugandan Asians. Laila discussed how staple crops signified her father's attachment to Uganda: "He loved the food over there, like matoke and all that. We loved it. Even I miss it."[84]

As Ugandan Asian refugees were resettled internationally, they had to adapt to changes in food and revise or improvise recipes. Those who moved to Canada had limited access to familiar spices and were forced to be creative, as Umedaly attests.[85] Many oral history participants said that eating Canadian food was difficult for them— mashed potatoes, hamburgers, meatloaf, baked fish, fast food, and other dishes lacked flavour. "We were eating all Canadian food, we found it very bland in the beginning," Shiraz remembered. "There is no Indian stores or anything and we would go in the grocery stores, Dutchboy was the big one at that time, and we would ask them for chilis or some spices. There were some spices . . . but not the spices that we use for our cooking."[86] Alibhai-Brown's mother came up with a way to combat the bland flavours of shepherd's pie, telling her daughter, 'Next time this will be my Indian shepherd's pie. With a bit of garam masala and magic we can repair the dish.'"[87] Historian Donna Gabaccia's pioneering work on ethnic foods in the United States details how immigrant mothers innovated with new ingredients to respond to changes in their geographical setting.[88] This is what Ugandan Asians did in actively adding flavour to recipes they found bland.

For families who relocated with young children or had children born in Canada, the issue of bland food took on another dimension. Tom explained how he and his spouse, Joan, adjusted to the food available in Canada but also adapted it for their children: "A lot of times we ate—for lack of a better word—bland food. We adapted to the Canadian thing and then occasionally on weekends and so on Joan would make something spicy, but we didn't have to have spicy food every single day. I mean, it was not a requirement in our house, and you know with kids a lot of other things, pasta, things like that, went over better. So yeah, it was a mix. It still is. We still have both types of food."[89] Tom and Joan had to adjust because certain spices they were used to could not be found in Canada, but they also integrated foods such as pasta into their diet for their children, who were not "accustomed to the spices."[90] Often, refugee mothers had to navigate between the appeals of their husbands and children. Historians Franca Iacovetta, Marlene Epp, and Valerie J. Korinek argue that immigrant men, or men from a culture that is not the dominant one in society, encourage their wives to create authentic traditional dishes to maintain that cultural connection, or to make more Canadian foods to demonstrate their integration into the cultural fabric of Canada. Canadian-born children made this dynamic increasingly complex for Ugandan Asian mothers as they pressured their mothers to "try" or "buy" Canadian foods such as hot dogs and hamburgers.

Not all food discoveries in Canada were disappointing though. For Azim and many other Ugandan Asian refugees, certain fruits like apples and grapes were items they "never saw in Uganda, you only got it as a treat."[91] In Canada these fruits were regularly available. Other novelties included processed and canned goods as well as time-saving cooking tools. Umedaly describes how she "developed one-pot, quick cooking techniques ... so I have been able to reduce my cooking time. Now I can cook a complex meal for family and friends in an hour and still stay true to traditional tastes."[92] Of course, whether these changes were ones to embrace depended on individual perspectives. For instance, Nimira said, "When we came here we had to buy ready-made stuff and ready-made this and ready-made that. It didn't taste the same. It was more than just adapting to another country and food, but more adapting to the taste of everything. Even if we were used to eating something—breads, we were used to eating bread, but bread here doesn't taste the same as bread over there. So, very different, it took a long time."[93] Adjusting to life in Canada was not a universal process for Ugandan Asian refugees.

Food is a powerful element of personal identity construction. As an African Canadian living in Nova Scotia aptly put it: "The way I eat it reflects who I am. I like hot meals, you know I like a lot of Soul food, it reflects who I am and I'm not changing that for nobody."[94] For Umedaly, writing each recipe brought back memories of "a person, a story and feeling. In this book I see so many colours, smell the spices, hear the laughter, and I feel the tears and the challenges that have made me who I am today."[95] Shamim echoed this sentiment, identifying how "green mangoes, sweet potatoes, for me that's my roots."[96] Other refugees argued that for them, food is home. Jitu explained that "in terms of food," the "huge, vast country" of India does not feel like home, "whereas when you go to Uganda, yes, this is my country. It just feels so good to be back."[97] Cookbooks, life histories, and various works interrogating the role of food in the lives of immigrants and refugees emphasize how history significantly impacts identity. Fusion recipes, Ugandan crops, and the need to adjust to the foods available in Canada all significantly contributed to the identities of Ugandan Asian refugees. The complexities surrounding food demonstrate the contested grounds of identity formation and how Ugandan Asian refugees in Canada express their sense of self.

Exploring the Identities of Ugandan Asian Refugees

Ugandan Asian refugees navigate multiple allegiances and attachments to Canada, Uganda, and South Asia. To understand the diverse ways they do this, I asked oral history participants how they identified themselves after living in Canada for over forty years. This is a personal question, and I consistently reminded participants that there was no right or wrong answer. I encouraged them to identify as they wished, and they were even welcome to challenge the question itself. Exploring one's sense of self requires the freedom to create an individual sense of personhood, which, for Ugandan Asian refugees, may not fall within the neat categories of Canadian, Ugandan, and Indian or Pakistani. National identities are not the only way of expressing one's sense of self. Historian Eric Hobsbawm argues that affiliation with a certain country, no matter how strong, is only one component of an individual's social being. Sociologist Avtar Brah similarly argues that making assumptions of national identities are inherently problematic because naming a single country identity can render every other aspect of one's personal affiliations invisible. This process ignores the fluid aspects of identity where someone can embody being part of a nation's citizenry while also holding ties to various other communities based on a myriad of categories. Identities are informed by numerous daily practices, such as the production and consumption of food, and by histories of migration as well as race, class, gender, age, ethnicity, and other categories of analysis.

The responses of Ugandan Asian refugees reveal the complexity of identity formation as well as a clear attachment to Canada and being Canadian. Some interviewees declared that they were quite simply Canadian. Aminmohamed stated, "I am Canadian . . . 100 per cent. I believe in the values of Canada."[98] Similarly, John H. noted that his identity is "simple": "We are citizens of this country, so our loyalty now is to Canada, and we play our role in the day-to-day affairs of this country and see where our input is required."[99] For Aminmohamed and John H., their identities as Canadians were clear and uncontested. Their formal citizenship confirmed their allegiance to Canada and authenticated their status as Canadians. When asked to explain what made him feel Canadian, Amin outlined "the freedom to express yourself, freedom of religion . . . respecting others' religions, tolerating other people's views."[100] This was a common theme, as several participants equated their membership in society to respecting Canadian values. For example, Zul, who also felt a strong sense of Canadian identity, said, "I appreciate the values of Canada from day one. . . . They let me practice my religion. . . . I can speak out."[101] In a special issue of *The Ismaili Canada* magazine celebrating the settlement of the Ismaili community in Canada, Abidah Lalani wrote that "Canada's respect and tolerance of other cultures, commitment to volunteerism, and dedication to freedom, equality and peace are values that have proven to be a natural fit for Ismailis, most of whom embody the same characteristics that our beloved country holds dear."[102] Lalani's article captured the breadth of Canadian values that significantly shaped Ugandan Asian refugees' interpretations of what it means to be Canadian. At the thirtieth anniversary event, Senator Jaffer also included "sharing and making spaces for all of us" as a

Canadian value.[103] Ideas of inclusivity and personal freedoms cemented Ugandan Asian refugees' feelings of being Canadian. Of course, it is imperative to nuance idealized notions of Canadian identity that ignore the country's long-standing history of colonialism. Traditional Canadian historical narratives portray the country as a tolerant and open society, ignoring, as sociologist James Frideres and many other scholars have noted, the destructive impacts of colonialization and how Indigenous "social, religious, kinship, and economic institutions were ignored, rejected and replaced by Euro-Canadian institutions."[104]

For other refugees, the peace and security of Canada was what mattered to them. Shamim connected her Canadian identity to the idea of safety: "It means that I don't have to worry about political situations, I don't have to be scared, I feel safe.... Personally, financially, it's better, I feel more safe than anything else."[105] Shamim's attachment to Canada is based on being protected from the instalment of an authoritarian regime and from random acts of violence. In a similar way, a Ugandan Asian quoted in the *Uganda: 50 Years of Independence* souvenir book said that "they [the Canadian government] give my children shelter, food, education. And the best part is security."[106] Again, these views must be set against the long history of cultural genocide and violent exploitation of Indigenous communities in Canada.[107] What it means to be Canadian is often romanticized because "Canadians have not yet had to deal substantively with the underside of their colonial past."[108]

Several oral history participants mentioned that the length of time they have lived in Canada contributed to their identity as Canadian. Diamond argued he is "Canadian and Ismaili and that's it. I mean, I'm at that age now where I've been here for a long time. Yeah, I'm from Uganda, but that was a long time ago."[109] Almas said she is "more Canadian than Ugandan because I lived in Uganda for twenty-five years and I've been here [in Canada] forty-three years. So, I think I've become more Canadian.... Ugandan can become ... part of it, but first is Canadian."[110] Others who arrived in Canada when they were young found that over time their memories of Uganda faded. Mumtaz stated that she does not "think of Uganda anymore because I was young when I came here. I was in high school. I went to high school here. I consider myself Canadian.... I kind of forget the Ugandan life. It's almost like a dream ... I really don't associate myself as Ugandan at all."[111]

Some refugees identified distinctive experiences that led them to prioritize their identity as Canadians while still recognizing their Ugandan roots. Sikandar explained that "I'm proud of being from Uganda but at the same time I think my priorities have changed. I feel I am more loyal to Canada. If I had to choose between Canada and Uganda, I think I would choose Canada because this is the country that gave me a refuge when I needed it.... What they did for us when we came here, they accepted us, it was fantastic. I think this is the best country to live in."[112] Nimira described how she became more accustomed to Canadian culture and then embraced it:

> turning point at which one time you stop thinking of your-self as an East African because suddenly you don't feel as at home ... in the East African ways, [which] you've outgrown from aging, from moving on, you know. We have a choice of picking the better things out of the Canadian life, out of the Western life.... Here you earned your own value, you earned your own respect, if you stay true to yourself, you are a hard worker. In East Africa, there was no opportunities. You could work to the bone, but life kept you at a certain level. If you were poor, you were sure to die poor. No opportunity could be given to you where you could—you have to struggle for everything, work very, very hard. Very few people make that transition from being poor to being rich, whereas in Canada, if you were willing to work hard, if you were willing to, you know, be good, be honest, be this, there was places to go.[113]

Primary Canadian values for Nimira were the idea of opportunity, hard work, and freedom from being judged by others. The notion of opportunity and breaking the cycle of poverty was common among all interviewees, who expressed that hard work and dedication led to their successful integration in Canada. Nimira also distinguished between specific societal norms in East Africa and Canada to emphasize how her Canadian identity developed. In addition to differences related to labour and opportunity, she emphasized different approaches to gender relations. She recalled a trip to East Africa:

> Somebody there made a comment, "Oh, you're Canadian."
> Yes, I am. I'm happy that I have an identity now. I don't want

to be one of you, haha. Because their attitude, you know—
like we accepted certain things there because some things
we brought from India. When I say "we," I mean as a group.
The culture that came from India to East Africa was mainly
the noneducated illiterates because they were the only ones
that were doing so badly in India that they were willing to
make that journey to Africa into the unknown and live there.
So really, they had no education, no nothing, so all they had
they just adopted from either somebody or the culture. "This
is how you are, this is how you should behave." So they were
the ones who came up with "if you're a male, you're a god;
if you're a woman, you're nothing." That sort of an attitude
was so accepted and then society was like that in East Africa
where it was a male chauvinist society. Males made all the
decisions. They treated women like dirt.[114]

Furthermore, when told by her uncle to wear an Indian dress to the local
jamatkhana when she visited Nairobi, she curtly responded, "No, you
can't tell me to do that. I'm over eighteen. I get to decide what I'm gonna
wear."[115] For Nimira, in particular, Canadian values also encompassed
gender equality and the right to carry herself as she deemed appropriate.

Other refugees built upon their roots and expressed hyphenated or
multiple identities that reflected their allegiance to Canada, Uganda,
and South Asia. "I am a Canadian, a Ugandan, an African, an Indian,
and a Goan," said John N. "You don't have to choose—except if one
goes to war with another, then you might have to choose—but I don't
have to. And I embrace all of them. They are all part of [my] psyche,
and when I am with Ugandan Africans something almost goes click
in my brain and I joke like a Ugandan."[116] The ability to pivot between
several identities coincides with the findings of sociologist Czarina
Wilpert and anthropologist Steven Vertovec, who argue that newcomers and their children can turn on and off specific affiliations and switch
between cultural codes. Zaina said, "If I look back from an identity
perspective, it is a mixture of all, it's a mélange of the two."[117] For Zaina,
identity is in a constant flux between Canadian and Ugandan that have
mixed together. Jalal stated that he is "certainly very Canadian, I've
got cultural heritage which is Indian—which I am not at all defensive
about—so I am a combination of all of that. . . . But to identify me or

put me in a narrow hole—'Are you Ismaili? Are you Canadian? What does Canadian mean?' Canadian to me incorporates all of these, the value system, the cultural background, the attitudes . . . whatever. So that's a long-winded answer to a simple question, but I'm questioning the question."[118] Jalal was the only interviewee to interrogate the question of identity itself, confirming Hobsbawm's assertion that personal identities are multifaceted and extend beyond notions of nationality.

However, these multitudes of identity could come with varying levels of conflict, especially given the historical context. John N. expressed the emotional and psychological hardships of possessing multiple allegiances: "When I was in Uganda, I considered myself an African. It took Amin to remind me that I was an Indian again."[119] John N.'s identity was ruptured forever after the expulsion decree. He recalled that after submitting his official resignation letter to the Ugandan government, he told officials, " 'I'm so thankful that you gave me a chance to really contribute to my country.'. . . When I wrote that and signed it, I really, I shed a few tears because that was a break [pause]. I can never think about that without breaking. I can't."[120] John N. experienced a psychological, physical, and emotional break from his self-constructed identity as a Ugandan. Several other Ugandan Asian refugees struggled with the realities of possessing multiple identities.

Regardless of their self-identity and citizenship, they faced numerous questions about their ethnic and racial backgrounds. Errol argued, "If you answer 'where are you from?' with 'I'm Canadian,' people . . . don't accept that as an answer, right? That unfortunately will last for the next umpteen generations . . . because people associate if you are Canadian you have to be Caucasian, right? I mean, that's how it will always be because they want to know your ancestry and they want to know where you actually come from."[121] Errol encountered resistance to identifying strictly as a Canadian due to restricted and racist definitions of what a Canadian is. This was echoed by others, including Altaf, a college professor, who recounted his difficulties in explaining his background to incoming students:

> [They] always think you're from India [laughs]. They say, "Where are you from?" And I say, "Where do you think I'm from?" [laughs]. They never think of me as from Africa. . . . You have to go back and say, you know, "I'm from Uganda."

Then I start explaining it to them. My thing was different, my dad was not born in India, he was born in Uganda. My grandfather came from India, so my dad was born in Uganda too, right. So it's a whole different stuff. We're Ugandans. My mom was only eight months when she came to Uganda, so she wasn't anything else except Ugandan. So it's hard to explain, right. "First and foremost, we are from Uganda." Then you have to start telling the story.[122]

Similar to the experience of Errol, Altaf's allegiance to a specific country—in this case, Uganda—was challenged by others who assumed he was originally from South Asia. Karim, a dentist, also described the perceptions of new patients and others meeting him for the first time:

[They] look at me and say, "So you're from—" and I'll say I'm Canadian. "No, no, no, but where are you from?" . . . I say Uganda. "Oh, not India?" No, I've never stepped foot in India. . . . I think what you want to hear is that my blood is East Indian. My grandfather was from India, but he moved to Uganda where my dad was born and I was born, so theoretically I'm African. And then I am now in Canada, and I was a refugee when I came here. So now I am by citizenship Canadian.[123]

Karim's roots are in Uganda and Canada, but society pushes against his assertions that he is Ugandan and Canadian. Although most oral history participants expressed strong Canadian identities, their membership in society was continually challenged based on their physical appearance. This supports writer Neil Bissoondath's arguments about the failure of multiculturalism policy in Canada based on how his skin colour is seen as representative of his identity: "To be simply Canadian untinged by the exoticism of elsewhere seems insufficient, even unacceptable, to many other Canadians."[124]

Four interviewees consciously severed their connections to Uganda. Amin V. explained, "I don't think of myself as a Canadian of Ugandan origin. . . . [I] have an affinity towards India because of the foundation that I've opened in India and plus I've taken the girls to India. . . . I don't think of myself as a Ugandan."[125] The experience of multiple migrations impacts how Ugandan Asian refugees articulate their sense of self. As historian Margret Frenz argues, their associations are blurred across both space and time.[126] Terrence stated, "I generally say to people I am a Canadian of Indian origin." When asked to elaborate on his answer, he explained that "one of the decisions I made early ... when I came out of Uganda, I shut the door and I had no interest in the country. ... It really was a great life [in Uganda], I enjoyed it. ... We just had a fairy-tale life in Uganda. But that door is shut, and I have no interest."[127] For Terrence, "closing the door" on his Ugandan identity was an effort to find closure. It allowed him to concentrate on starting life anew in Canada, which he believed helped his brothers and other refugees to prosper.[128] Edmond explained that "we are proud to be of Goan ancestry, and the culture is slightly different from the rest of the Indian community, we have our own culture. We are Christians. That is one other major difference."[129] Maria, Edmond's partner, built on his construction of identity, arguing that "we usually say we are Goan origin. Goan and brought up in Africa, and we live most of our life in Canada. So I always say that."[130] Similar to most Ugandan Asian refugees, Amin V., Terrence, Edmond, and Maria all expressed strong attachments to Canada. However, they purposefully dismissed their affiliations to Uganda. Their reasons for this disassociation varied, revealing their nuanced constructions of their sense of self.

Family was a central theme in all oral history interviews, and it played a critical role in how refugees connected to Uganda and Canada. Many participants commented on how their family was an integral part of their support structure and how East African family values were significantly stronger than Canadian ones. Nimira noted how kinship networks and society in Uganda were based on a larger sense of family and community: "You felt cared for no matter what [in Uganda]. Especially, if you were aged, you had respect. Everybody respected you. If you were a child, everybody cared for you. It's not like that here. Those are some of the negatives. Not big negatives, but still negatives. Neighbour to neighbour. You know in East Africa we were not able to travel. None of us had cars and we lived in little villages, so we didn't always have an opportunity to get together with others from the same family or something, so whoever was next to you was your brother. Your neighbour was your brother."[131] Zaina described family as a marker of home: "My identity is not Canadian or Ugandan. It really is more around that family growing up [in

Uganda] and this family being here [in Canada]."[132] Zaina's oral testimony reveals the complications of living "here" and remembering "there." It captures the everyday tension refugees experience between their physical place of residence and the homeland in their hearts and minds.

The final theme related to interviewees' personal identity construction was the ethic of volunteerism. Refugees mentioned an intrinsic belief in and commitment to volunteering within their local communities and religious organizations as well as internationally. Their desire to give back to those less fortunate was driven by their deep sense of gratitude for the efforts made by Canadians and the government. They also saw volunteering as an inherent component of being Canadian. As a member of the Rotary Club since 1977, Zul commented, "[What] makes you Canadian? It's just all the values, and you participate in Easter Seal campaigns. . . . Yeah, when you become part of all this you feel Canadian."[133] Rossbina echoed Zul's comments when she reflected on giving back to her religious community in Canada: "I think that if I ever wanted to say thank you spiritually, materially, this is what I'm gonna do, is I'm gonna volunteer my whole life now."[134] Volunteering in community-based organizations provides immigrants with a safe space to interact with Canadians and participate in society at large, according to scholars Baukje Miedema and Evangelia Tastsoglou, who have conducted oral histories with various immigrant communities. One of their participants explained that she "became a Canadian citizen by doing community work. A real Canadian citizen by doing Canadian work."[135]

Other public examples of Ugandan Asian refugees engaging in volunteerism include Pyarali and Gulshan Nanji, who aspired to give back to Canada once their family was established. They have made numerous donations to various hospitals in the Greater Toronto Area, including North York General Hospital, where the Gulshan and Pyarali G. Nanji Orthopaedic and Plastics Centre opened in 2006.[136] More recently, Pyarali and Gulshan made a $1 million dollar donation to UNHCR to support scholarships for refugees who are pursuing post-secondary degrees in the field of medicine.[137] Some refugees began to volunteer soon after arriving in Canada. Noordin Somji stated in his autobiography that "since having settled in Canada, I decided to volunteer giving blood demonstrating generosity and sincere interest in others and received a certificate from the Red Cross signed by the Governor General of Canada for 31 donations of blood for this noble cause during 1997."[138] In a 2012 consulate report, John Halani listed several major initiatives that refugees across the country have facilitated, including the Uganda Sustainable Clubfoot Care Project, which was founded by Dr. Shafique Pirani and received $1 million in funding from the Canadian International Development Agency and the University of British Columbia to treat over fifteen hundred Ugandan children with a congenital foot deformity; the Maternal Mortality project, which provided training for doctors, midwives, and birth attendants in the Kiboga District; and the Shanti Uganda Society, which collected funds to provide women's health programs in Uganda.[139]

Refugees have also created international aid organizations to provide services and support in India and Uganda. Amin Visram (an oral history participant) founded REACH Empowering Girls Through Education, which provides underprivileged girls in Pune, India, with housing, education, food, and access to health practitioners. Azim Sarangi (another oral history participant) founded Shukhar Philanthropic Foundation to help those living in poverty in Porbandar, India, to improve their living quarters. Vasant Lakhani (another oral history participant) founded the Indo-Africa Charitable Society, which promotes public health in rural areas of Uganda and India through mobile medical and dental clinics. This kind of international work reflects the transnational links of Ugandan Asian refugees in Canada. As sociologists Rina Cohen and Guida Man argue, transnational activities demonstrate how refugees integrate into Canadian life while also engaging in relationships in their home countries. These activities reinforce affiliations with Uganda and South Asia while solidifying refugees' sense of Canadian identity, represented by the ethic of giving back. Refugees were encouraged by community members to support Uganda, while government officials recognized the numerous contributions and citizen activism of Ugandan Asians. Citizenship and Immigration Canada researchers Tara Gilkinson and Genevieve Sauve argue that sustained recognition of citizenship reinforces a shared history and national identity, which is critical for immigrants who become Canadians.

Integration is an enduring process that requires efforts from newcomers and the host community. Ugandan Asians were the first major non-European refugee community to arrive in Canada, and they are regarded as a successful example of refugee resettlement by the government, the public, and the Ugandan Asian refugee community. Ugandan Asian refugees define themselves as Canadian and continue to express their gratitude to the government and the public for generously accepting them and their families. As Ugandan Asian refugees and their descendants continue to raise their families in Canada, it is imperative that the historical record reflect the diversity of Canadian peoples. It is at this juncture that we can begin to comprehend the numerous ways in which Ugandan Asian refugees have become full-fledged Canadians.

GIFTS THAT KEEP ON GIVING:
Ugandan Asian Canadians in the Twenty-First Century

The expulsion of Ugandan Asians in August of 1972 led to the forced displacement of thousands of people from East Africa. Under the guise of African nationalism and using postcolonial rhetoric, President Idi Amin justified his decision to remove all Ugandans of South Asian descent. According to Amin, Ugandan Asians were Britain's problem and he was going to put control of the economy back into the hands of Ugandan Africans. His dream did not come to fruition as he privileged those from the Kakwa and South Sudanese tribes for recruitment into military and economic positions. Further, Amin's regime condoned an atmosphere of mass killing in which three hundred thousand to five hundred thousand Ugandan Africans died. Uganda descended into an economic recession that required decades of reconstruction.

Canada admitted nearly eight thousand Ugandan Asian refugees in the early 1970s, the country's largest resettlement of a nonwhite and predominantly non-Christian population before the establishment of formal refugee policy in the 1976 Immigration Act. Through coordinated efforts between multiple government departments, voluntary agencies, and Canadians, Ugandan Asian refugees were offered various levels of social support, leading to a successful resettlement. Although they faced barriers as they confronted gatekeepers of integration, Ugandan Asian refugees who participated in this study firmly identified themselves as Canadians. As self-defined Canadians, they have claimed their place within the broader

Canadian historical narrative. With the fiftieth anniversary of their migration approaching in the fall of 2022, Ugandan Asian refugees continue to share their oral histories as part of the Uganda Collection at Carleton University. They hope to capture their lived experiences for future generations and have emphasized to me the importance of sharing their historical roots in East Africa and South Asia with their children and grandchildren. The first, second, and third generations are investing time and energy into understanding their histories of migration. For many youth, the navigation of multiple identities as racialized individuals who face consistent challenges to their place in society has been fraught. In response, Canada continues to critically examine multiculturalism policy and its utility in establishing an inclusive society. For a lot of second-generation youth—the children of immigrants—the largest impediment to having a sense of belonging is racial minority status. Numerous scholars describe the multiplicity of experiences that deny the connection of the second and third generations to their country of birth based on their appearance.[1]

The issue for racialized second-generation Canadians is that "they may feel Canadian, but nonetheless experience racism and prejudice that situate them as outsiders . . . the pressures to assimilate and 'belong' can result in denying aspects of one's own culture, feeling inferior, and internalizing the dominant ideology."[2] In several studies, second-generation Canadians have felt they will never be regarded as "true" citizens regardless of where they were born and the number of years they have spent in the country.[3] This is a pertinent issue for the Ugandan Asian refugee community as their children and grandchildren continue to fight to be recognized as Canadians. Exclusion of this kind has significant psychological consequences because lower levels of social integration into Canadian society lead to negative effects on well-being. This book presents a humble point of departure for the second and third generations by exploring the histories of their parents and grandparents, situating Ugandan Asian refugees within Canadian history, and reasserting their linkages to Canada. Most importantly, the book rejects the practice of ignoring the shared humanity of noncitizens and citizens, which has been reinforced by recent policy changes that criminalize asylum seekers and refugees.

In the first two decades of the twenty-first century, a considerable shift took place in the Canadian government's attitude towards migrants. Under the Conservative government of Stephen Harper (2006–15), barriers to refugee resettlement and restrictions on citizenship increased dramatically, particularly through Bills C-31 and C-24. Bill C-31 created a two-tiered system for refugee protection in Canada, where those who hail from a "safe" country are held to different standards within the refugee determination system. The minister for citizenship and immigration holds the power to determine which countries are "safe," overriding expert oversight and making asylum seekers more vulnerable to exploitation based on political considerations. Therefore, those deemed to be arriving from a "safe" country are not entitled to "a full, fair, and independent decision process to decide who is a refugee, based on the facts of their case and regardless of their countries of origin."[4] There are also tighter timelines governing when asylum seekers must present themselves in front of Canadian courts as well as mandatory detention for anyone that enters Canada as an "irregular arrival." These policy changes produce a dangerous association between asylum seekers and criminals, which ultimately exacerbates the vilification of refugees.

Bill C-24 created two classes of citizenship. One includes those who solely possess Canadian citizenship and are ineligible for citizenship elsewhere, and the other includes dual citizens and those who are eligible for citizenship elsewhere. Under Bill C-24 a citizenship officer could revoke a person's citizenship under various circumstances, including suspicion of treason or a reasonable belief that the individual did not intend to live in Canada. There was no opportunity for a formal hearing or an appeal if an officer revoked a person's citizenship. Bill C-24 violated the Universal Declaration of Human Rights and was vehemently denounced by the British Columbia Civil Liberties Association and the Canadian Association of Refugee Lawyers, which described the bill as "anti-immigrant, anti-Canadian, anti-democratic, and unconstitutional."[5] In 2019, under the Liberal government of Justin Trudeau, Bill C-24 was amended by Bill C-6, which repealed the provisions for the revocation of citizenship and the requirement that individuals must plan to keep living in Canada. Bill C-6 declares that "dual citizens living in Canada who are convicted of these crimes will face the Canadian justice system, like other Canadians who break the law."[6] While advocates welcomed this change, there remains a problematic association between newcomers and criminality.

Both Bill C-24 and C-31 promote the idea that "citizenship is not a right, it's a privilege," as articulated by former minister of citizenship and immigration Chris Alexander.[7] This is in line with Prime Minister William Lyon Mackenzie King's famous assertion in 1947: "It is not a 'fundamental human right' of any alien to enter Canada. It is a privilege."[8] As immigration scholars have noted, King's quote captures Canada's discriminatory immigration policy in the postwar period. Current political discourse shows a return to these prejudicial attitudes, which affect Canadian immigration and refugee policy. Although Justin Trudeau's Liberal government has made several changes to legislation, concerns over refugees, national security, and noncitizen rights persist.

Populists have leveraged xenophobic tendencies within communities that are based on a mixture of misinformation, prejudice, and general ignorance. A pertinent example of misinformation comes from a widely circulated social media post and email in 2015 that claimed refugees in Canada receive more social benefits than did retirees, concluding that "perhaps our senior citizens should ask for the Status of Refugees instead of applying for Old Age Pension."[9] It was fact-checked and disproved by the *Toronto Star* and CTV News, but the message was embraced by a large contingent of the public. So many Canadians believed the post that Citizenship and Immigration Canada dedicated a webpage to explaining that "refugees do not get more financial help from the federal government than Canadian pensioners. A commonly shared e-mail makes this false claim."[10] In the age of mass media, critical thinking alongside responsible reporting is required to combat dangerous rhetoric that vilifies refugees and perpetuates stereotypes of vulnerable individuals as drains on public funds.

On a global scale, recent political debates in the United States and in Europe have centred on deterrence policies to limit the movement of people and asylum claims from vulnerable populations. The rhetoric has continued to vilify refugees while grossly inflating the numbers of asylum seekers. Under the Trump administration's "America First" policy, a thinly veiled populist approach leveraging xenophobic attitudes, the United States pulled out of the United Nations Global Compact for Migration, dramatically reduced the number of refugees accepted into the country per year, and instituted a "Remain in Mexico" policy that forced refugees travelling through Mexico to stay there while their applications for asylum in the United States were processed. The government and the media continue to homogenize a diverse group of migrants seeking entry into the country. By lumping together asylum seekers, economic migrants, refugees, and immigrants with criminals and terrorists, the media and the Trump administration have distorted public perceptions of persecuted individuals. More recently, the Biden administration renewed the "Remain in Mexico" policy in December 2021. Furthermore, a public health law known as Title 42 implemented under the Trump administration has also carried over into the new administration. Under Title 42, the Biden administration continues to remove migrants under the guise of them presenting health risks due to the COVID-19 pandemic.[11] Although the Biden administration was elected on the premise of immigration reform and moving away from the position of the previous Republican government, immigration policies have remained largely the same under the Democrats. They have placed the blame on the victims of war, poverty, natural disasters, and racial, religious, and sexual intolerance for requesting shelter within their borders.

Similarly, the European Union (EU) remains divided on refugee policy but has moved to limit arrivals from North Africa and Turkey. The EU-Turkey Joint Action Plan, known more commonly as the EU-Turkey deal, was signed in March 2016.[12] According to the agreement, every "irregular migrant" crossing from Turkey to the Greek islands must be returned to Turkey. In exchange for the Turkish government's cooperation in accepting returnees and hosting nearly four million refugees, the EU will accept one recognized refugee from Turkey for every returnee and provide three billion euros to support refugee reception facilities in Turkey. If the plan were successful, an additional three billion euros would be mobilized by the EU to support Turkey's resettlement efforts.[13] Consequently, the Turkish government, under Recep Tayyip Erdoğan's leadership, has used refugees as a political tool to exert pressure on the EU and continue to secure large sums of funding. The same approach has been used in Libya, where the EU has funded militias and rebel groups to place potential asylum seekers in detention centres before they attempt to travel across the Mediterranean Sea to Italy, Greece, or Spain.

Building on deterrence policies, anti-immigrant sentiment has also fuelled the rise of populist governments in the EU. The Visegrád Group, composed of government leaders from the Czech Republic, Hungary, Poland, and Slovakia in partnership with Italy's interior minister, has vehemently opposed a universal EU refugee policy. Italy's reluctance to admit refugees is based on the historical failure of other EU member states to accept a proportional share of refugees. The Visegrád Group defended its stance on admitting few refugees based on the sovereignty of each country to determine who can enter its borders and fought the EU's proposal to disperse refugees equally throughout the region. The group claimed that the decision to resettle refugees was taken by the majority of EU member states without due consideration of the group's dissenting votes. Backed by Islamophobic and anti-immigrant sentiments in their countries, the populist governments of the Czech Republic, Hungary, Poland, and Slovakia linked their protests to the risk of terrorism and threats to local cultures and identities. This reveals the reality that the world is facing a crisis in migration management, not a "refugee crisis."

The first decade of the twenty-first century saw the number of displaced people around the world increase by 12 million for a total of 33.92 million people. A distinct increase occurred in 2013, when the total rose to 42.87 million. At the end of 2020, the total stood at 82.4 million.[14] In under a decade, the number of globally displaced people nearly doubled. In response, UNHCR called for a meeting of the international community. At the 2016 gathering in New York, a declaration was signed by 193 members of the United Nations General Assembly to "protect the human rights of all refugees and migrants, regardless of status. This includes the rights of women and girls and promoting their full, equal and meaningful participation in finding solutions."[15] In 2018 the United Nations General Assembly launched the Global Compact on Refugees. As defined by UNHCR, the compact "represents the political will and ambition of the international community as a whole for strengthened cooperation and solidarity with refugees and affected host countries."[16] The four key objectives are to reduce pressure on countries hosting refugees, facilitate pathways for refugees to become self-reliant, expand the number of pathways for refugees to be resettled internationally, and, lastly, ensure that safe and dignified conditions are restored in countries of origin prior to having refugees returned.

While the Global Compact on Refugees presents multiple pathways for international resettlement, including encouraging private refugee sponsorships and opening economic migration channels for refugee resettlement, several issues remain. Principally, the responsibility for hosting and supporting refugees falls on the shoulders of countries next to areas of conflict. This means that countries in Africa, the Middle East, South Asia, and Latin America are the largest receivers of refugees. As developing economies, many of these countries are not able to provide adequate services to refugees such as local integration, access to healthcare, sustained education, safety, or even quality food supplies. The compact leaves the bulk of resettlement work to the Global South and keeps refugees out of sight and out of mind for the Global North. These are the consequences of neoliberalism, economic inequality, war, ignorance, and climate change. United Nations Secretary General António Guterres aptly stated, "From climate change to migration to terrorism to the downsides of globalization—there is no doubt in my mind that global challenges require global solutions."[17] In an age where divisive political rhetoric, populism, and anti-immigrant sentiment are gaining momentum, an inclusive and truly global solution is required.

The Global Compact on Refugees does offer the prospect of a brighter future for displaced people. Canada became the leading nation for international resettlement at the end of 2018 while also being the only country in the world to offer a private sponsorship program for refugees, so both the government and the Canadian public can act as an example for the international community.[18] One need only look at the numerous examples of Canadians opening their hearts and homes to refugees in our recent history to see that a strong current of humanitarianism still exists among the public. Amid the current rise of displaced people and the recent arrival of Afghan and Ukrainian refugees, it is vital for Canadians and policymakers to comprehend the dynamic ways in which refugee communities have contributed to Canadian society. When given appropriate support from the government and the Canadian community, refugees can more readily make the transition to Canadian citizens. The case study of Ugandan Asian refugees serves as a means of enlightening public and government perceptions of refugees. This book fosters knowledge sharing on the impacts of public policy on refugee communities in the twenty-first century. Without addressing the global issues of warfare, climate change, and wealth inequalities, the numbers of displaced people will undoubtedly continue to rise. Under these circumstances, we as Canadians should be reminded that all refugee communities can be gifts that enrich our country's pluralistic nature.

ACKNOWLEDGEMENTS

This book would not have been possible without the endless support and guidance of several individuals and institutions. I am grateful for the opportunity to study at the University of Western Ontario to complete my doctoral dissertation, which forms the basis of this work. I would also like to acknowledge the financial support provided by both Western University and the Ontario government under the Ontario Graduate Scholarship program. The Migration and Ethnic Relations (MER) collaborative program at Western was critical to providing unique insights on the multidisciplinary and multifaceted elements of migration. I will always hold a special place in my heart for the MER program. Since I began my master's degree in the fall of 2011, the MER family has always been there for me. The faculty, graduate students, and guest speakers significantly added to my understanding of migration. These interdisciplinary perspectives were vital to the original dissertation and the final book.

I would also like to thank the entire team at Library and Archives Canada (LAC). Numerous staff members helped me throughout the archival research process to locate files and track down some particularly difficult boxes. The key starting point for my research at LAC was meeting with Michael Molloy. I cannot thank Mike enough for his continued support and encouragement throughout the project. Both Mike and Salim Fakirani helped connect me to countless Ugandan Asians and community resources, and shared their insights on the research I produced. The times we have spent together over the past few years have truly meant a lot to me.

Assistance and guidance from the dedicated staff and peer reviewers of the University of Manitoba Press allowed me to reshape the manuscript into a publishable scholarly work. Jill McConkey was instrumental in providing feedback on the flow of the book and offered numerous helpful suggestions to improve the quality of the writing. From our initial meeting at the Canadian Historical Association conference in 2017 and throughout the writing process, Jill continued to provide endless encouragement and positivity. Jill, I am truly grateful for the motivation you gave me to ensure this book would be published in time for the fiftieth anniversary of the resettlement of Ugandan Asian refugees in Canada.

Undoubtedly, I would not have been able to complete this book project without the support of my supervisor, Dr. Stephanie Bangarth. I cannot believe how far we have come from our very first meeting back in 2011 and your sound advice to write what you know. Without your dedication, vision, and guidance, the original dissertation would never have materialized. I am deeply indebted to you for your kindness, wisdom, and ability to motivate me throughout this journey. Of course, I am also very grateful for the home-cooked lunches, treats, and dinners we have had together over the years. You have been my mentor, my friend, and my guide. This book is a testament to your hard work and faith in me.

A large group of friends and family have also significantly contributed to this project. There are many whom I have not named directly but who kept me uplifted and inspired throughout this project. My close friends over the years, Adil, Omar, and Azhar, have all been pillars of strength and guidance. You have all shown me the meaning of living in the moment and the power of positivity, and you made sure I had endless nights of laughter and smiles during my graduate career. Each one of you has become my blood brother.

I am forever grateful to my family. Financial and emotional support from my father, mother, and grandmother enabled me to pursue this project to the best of my ability. You have worked tirelessly to provide for my two older brothers and me. The only reason I had the opportunity to attend graduate school and create this manuscript is because of your hard work and determination. Without these foundations, which you have also instilled in me, I would never have completed this project. To my two older brothers, Rizzy and Faiz, thank you from the bottom of my heart for keeping me zen and always being there for me. You have both given me sage advice in the moments when I needed it most, and you believed in me before I did. Your undying faith in me got me through the toughest parts of the research and writing phases.

Last, and most importantly, I must express my sincere gratitude to every single member of the Ugandan Asian refugee community in Canada. Your resiliency, humility, and perseverance in all facets of life consistently inspires me as both a researcher and a fellow Canadian. Many of you opened your homes and your hearts to me throughout the research project and I truly cannot thank you enough for sharing your life stories with me. These stories have made invaluable contributions to this project and will live on in the Uganda Collection at Carleton University. I continually struggle to find the words to describe the level of hospitality and honesty that has been extended to me by the community. I cannot thank you enough for the endless cups of chai, wonderful conversations, and countless meals that have profoundly changed my life in a very meaningful way. I hope that we may continue to honour the legacy of this community and of other immigrants and refugees that have settled in Canada. This book is dedicated to the wonderful community of Ugandan Asian refugees.

NOTES

Introduction

1 Library and Archives Canada (LAC), Records of the Immigration Branch, RG 76, vol. 1258, file 5850-3-5-650, A.E. Gotlieb, "Ugandan Asians—Press Briefing by British Community Relations Commission," 7 July 1975, 2.

2 Shamim Muhammedi, interviewed by S. Muhammedi, 2014.

3 "The Future of the Asians in Uganda," *Uganda Argus*, 5 August 1972, 1.

4 For more on mass violence in Uganda, see Avirgan and Honey, *War in Uganda*; Gwyn, *Death-Light of Africa*; Hansen, *Ethnicity and Military Rule*; Kyemba, *State of Blood*; Mazrui, *Soldiers and Kinsmen*; Melady and Melady, *Hitler in Africa*; Rice, *Teeth May Smile*; Smith, *Ghosts of Kampala*; Wooding and Barnett, *Uganda Holocaust*.

5 LAC, Records of the Immigration Branch, RG 76, vol. 1258, file 5850-3-5-650, A.E. Gotlieb, "Ugandan Asians—Press Briefing by British Community Relations Commission," 7 July 1975, 3.

6 Whitaker, *Double Standard*, 255. Although 1,250 Armenian refugees came to Canada during the Armenian genocide, this occurred gradually over nine years, from 1921 to 1930. For more, see Kaprielian-Churchill, "Armenian Refugees."

7 Over 60 percent of the Ugandan Asian refugee population were Muslim. The rest were Hindu, Sikh, or Christian. Pereira, "Study of the Effects."

8 United Nations High Commissioner for Refugees (UNHCR), *Convention and Protocol*, 14.

9 Major Canadian newspapers, including the *Globe and Mail*, *Toronto Star*, *Ottawa Citizen*, and *Vancouver Sun*, used the term "refugee" after the expulsion decree in 1972.

10 LAC, Records of the Immigration Branch, RG 76, vol. 990, file 5850-3-650, "Memorandum to the Minister - Meeting with the Aga Khan," 28 September 1972.

11 Laura Madokoro, *Elusive Refuge*, 7. See also Haddad, *Refugee in International Society*, and Hyndman, *Managing Displacement*, for thorough explorations of the global refugee regime and critical insights on forced displacement.

12 Madokoro, *Elusive Refuge*.

13 See Alibhai-Brown, *Settler's Cookbook*; Jamal, *Air Is Sweet*; Nanji, *Child of Dandelions*; Nazareth, *Brown Mantle*; Mamdani, *Citizen to Refugee*; Umedaly, *Mamajee's Kitchen*; and the Uganda Collection at Carleton University (https://arc.library.carleton.ca/exhibits/uganda-collection). Three major events, held in 1994, 1998, and 2002, have commemorated the resettlement of Ugandan Asian refugees in Canada.

14 LAC, Records of the Immigration Branch, RG 76, vol. 948, file sf-c-1-1, "Memoranda to Cabinet on Immigration Policy," 22 August 1972, 4.

15 Raska, *Czech Refugees*, xxi, 8.

16 See Bloemraad, "Citizenship and Immigration"; Maxwell, "Evaluating Migrant Integration"; Preston, Kobayashi, and Man, "Transnationalism"; and Wu, Schimmele, and Hou, *Social Integration of Immigrants*.

17 Hoerder, *Creating Societies*.

18 Iacovetta, *Gatekeepers*.

19 Dirks, *Canada's Refugee Policy*, 1977.

20 Epp, *Refugees in Canada*; Madokoro, *Elusive Refuge*; Raska, *Czech Refugees*.

21 Madokoro, "Belated Signing," 162.

22 Kelley and Trebilcock, *Making of the Mosaic*; Knowles, *Strangers at Our Gates*, 346, 366–68, 398.

23 For individual studies on the Hungarians, see Keyserlingk, *Breaking Ground*, and Thompson and Bangarth, "Transnational Christian Charity." For the Chileans, see Bangarth, "Citizen Activism"; Diab, "Fear and Vulnerability"; and Peddie, *Young, Well-Educated, and Adaptable*. For the Indochinese, see Adelman, *Canada and the Indochinese Refugees*; Beiser, *Strangers at the Gate*; Chan and Indra, *Uprooting, Loss and Adaptation*; and Tepper, *Southeast Asian Exodus*. For the Czechoslovaks, see Raska, *Czech Refugees*. For the Tibetans, see Raska, "Humanitarian Gesture."

24 Raska, *Czech Refugees*, xii, 7.

25 Raska, "Humanitarian Gesture," 541, 551.

26 For more, see Adelman, "Immigration Dream"; Dirks, "Canada and Immigration"; and Dreisziger, "Refugee Experience."

27 Anderson, *Canadian Liberalism*.

28 Diab, "Fear and Vulnerability."

29 Whitaker, *Double Standard*, 255.

30 Adams and Jesudason, "Employment," 464.

31 Kuepper, Lackey, and Swinerton, *Ugandan Asians*.

32 Frenz, "Transimperial Connections" and "Migration."

33 Herbert, "Oral Histories," "British Ugandan Asian Diaspora," and *Negotiating Boundaries*; Mawani, "Diasporic Citizens"; Tolia-Kelly, "Post-Colonial Geographies."

34 Morah, "Assimilation."

35 Pereira, "Study of the Effects."

36 Jamal, *Air Is Sweet*; Mamdani, *Citizen to Refugee*; Nanji, *Child of Dandelions*; Nazareth, *Brown Mantle*; Vassanji, *No New Land*.

37 Alibhai-Brown, *Settler's Cookbook*; Umedaly, *Mamajee's Kitchen*.

38 See Hajdukowski-Ahmed, Khanlou, and Moussa, *Not Born a Refugee Woman*; Hall et al., *Modernity*, 598; and Zembrzycki, *According to Baba*.

39 Bissoondath, *Selling Illusions*.

40 Maynes, Pierce, and Laslett, *Telling Stories*.

41 Klempner, "Life Review Interviews"; High, *Oral History*; Rogers, Leydesdorff, and Dawson, *Trauma*; Sheftel and Zembrzycki, "Only Human."

42 Field, "When the Interviewee Cries."

43 Freund, "Ethics of Silence," 224.

44 Frisch, *Shared Authority*.

45 See Buchignani, Indra, and Srivastava, *Continuous Journey*; and Johnston, *East Indians*.

46 High, *Oral History*.

47 LAC, Records of the Immigration Branch, RG 76, vol. 1258, file 5850-3-5-650, V.A. Latour, "Ugandan Expellees—Expenditures," 10 November 1972, 2. This document only captures data for the 4,420 Ugandan Asian refugees who flew into the Longue-Pointe military base in Montreal up to 8 November 1972. It does not include those who opted to pay for their own voyage from Uganda or the nearly 2,000 refugees who arrived between the end of 1972 and 1974.

48 Barnett and Noriega, introduction to *Communities of Color*, 15.

49 Ntzimane, "Tell My Story," 110.

50 UNHCR, "Less than 5 Per Cent."

51 Hyndman, *Managing Displacement*, 24.

52 Haddad, *Refugee in International Society*, 94.

53 Clarkson, *Room for All*, 21.

54 Aziz Fakirani, Khaerun Lalany, and Azad Lalany, interviewed by S. Muhammedi, 2015.

Chapter 1: Routes and Roots

1 Doornbos, "Ugandan Society and Politics," 3–4.

2 Doornbos, 4–5.

3 Denoon, "Historical Setting," 48.

4 Doornbos, "Ugandan Society and Politics," 15–16.

5 Doornbos, "Ugandan Society and Politics," 13; Turyahikayo-Rugyema, "Mass Nationalism," 255.

6 Turyahikayo-Rugyema, "Mass Nationalism," 246.

7 Doornbos, "Ugandan Society and Politics," 12–13.

8 Doornbos, 12.

9 King, Kasozi, and Oded, *Islam*, 50.

10 Ofcansky, *Tarnished Pearl*, 39.

11 Uzoigwe, introduction to *Dilemma of Nationhood*, xv.

12 Uzoigwe, xvi.

13 Ofcansky, *Tarnished Pearl*, 41.

14 Avirgan and Honey, *War in Uganda*, 4.

15 Avirgan and Honey, 503.

16 Kasozi, Musisi, and Sejjengo, *Social Origins*, 90.

17 Ofcansky, *Tarnished Pearl*, 42.

18   Omara-Otunnu, *Politics*, 95.

19   Avirgan and Honey, *War in Uganda*, 4.

20   Kasozi, Musisi, and Sejjengo, *Social Origins*, 106.

21   Kasozi, Musisi, and Sejjengo, 107–08.

22   Kasozi, Musisi, and Sejjengo, 106.

23   Kasozi, Musisi, and Sejjengo, 106.

24   Kasozi, Musisi, and Sejjengo, 104.

25   Kasozi, Musisi, and Sejjengo, *Social Origins*, 111; Darnton, "Idi Amin: A Savior Who Became the Creator of 8 Years of Horror," *New York Times*, 30 April 1979, A1.

26   Mittelman, *Ideology and Politics*, 245.

27   Kasozi, Musisi, and Sejjengo, *Social Origins*, 92.

28   Kasozi, Musisi, and Sejjengo, 91.

29   Kasozi, Musisi, and Sejjengo, *Social Origins*, 90; Mittelman, *Ideology and Politics*, 139.

30   Don Nanjira, *Status of Aliens*, 3; Forster, Hitchcock, and Lyimo, *Race and Ethnicity*, 76; Mangat, *History of the Asians*, 1; Melady and Melady, *Uganda*, 48.

31   Unlike the Atlantic slave trade, human trafficking in the Indian Ocean region lasted for over a thousand years. Prior to the eighth century, transiting of slaves throughout the region occurred on a smaller scale, then expanded during the height of the Arab Empire between the ninth and eleventh centuries. Vast slave trading networks continued to grow until the decline of the Arab Empire in the sixteenth century. As historian Shihan de Silva Jayasuriya argues, slaves from the entire East African coast were sold to countries in the East, including Egypt, Persia, and Arabia, prior to colonial expansion. European colonial powers revitalized the slave trade following the demise of the Arab Empire by purchasing 431,000 to 547,000 slaves from the Indian Ocean region and exporting them to other destinations in the region. For more, see Allen, "Labouring People"; Campbell, *Structure of Slavery*; Jayasuriya and Pankhurst, *African Diaspora*.

32   Melady and Melady, *Uganda*, 48.

33   Hirji, *Between Empires*, 32.

34   Hirji, 67.

35   Don Nanjira, *Status of Aliens*, 49.

36   Don Nanjira, 49.

37   Frenz, "Global Goans," 186–88.

38   Melady and Melady, *Uganda*, 50; Morah, "Assimilation," 9.

39   Don Nanjira, *Status of Aliens*, 4–5.

40   Don Nanjira, 4–5.

41   Kuper, "Goan Community in Kampala," 54.

42   Kuper, 56.

43   Frenz, "Global Goans," 190.

44   Edmond and Maria Rodrigues, interviewed by S. Muhammedi, 2015.

45   Edmond and Maria Rodrigues, interviewed by S. Muhammedi, 2015.

46   Azim Sarangi, interviewed by S. Muhammedi, 2015.

47   Forster, Hitchcock, and Lyimo, *Race and Ethnicity*, 84.

48   Jamal, "Asians in Uganda."

49   Don Nanjira, *Status of Aliens*, 11.

50   Kuepper, Lackey, and Swinerton, *Ugandan Asians*, 29.

51   Gregory, *South Asians*, 273; Jones, "Merchant-Kings and Everymen," 23.

52   Gregory, *South Asians*, 273–74.

53   Gregory, 249.

54   Gregory, 287.

55   Barungi, *Parliamentary Democracy*, 144.

56   Errol and Delphine Francis, interviewed by S. Muhammedi, 2015.

57   N. Rahemtulla, "Three Cheers!—Kenya Asian," *Vancouver Sun,* 2 September 1972, 5.

58   Kiwanuka, *Tragedy of Uganda*, 102.

59   Motani, "Ugandan Civil Service," 103.

60   Motani, 103.

61   Kiwanuka, *Tragedy of Uganda*, 103.

62   Mamdani, *Citizen to Refugee*, 16.

63   Jalal Jaffer, interviewed by S. Muhammedi, 2015.

64   See Amor, "Violent Ethnocentrism"; Morah, "Assimilation"; and Twaddle, *Expulsion of a Minority*.

65   Morah, "Assimilation," 10.

66   Tribe, "Economic Aspects," 154–55.

67   Morah, "Assimilation," 10–11.

68   Morah, 13. Several opinion pieces in the *Uganda Argus* demonstrate these views and are explored in Chapter 2. Some immediate examples include "Asian Question Answered," 4 August 1972, and "An Asian Dream is Ended," 18 August 1972.

69   Ocaya-Lakidi, "Black Attitudes," 85.

70   Ocaya-Lakidi, 89.

71   Ocaya-Lakidi, 89.

72   Ofcansky, *Tarnished Pearl*, 28.

73   Sathyamurthy, *Political Development*, 527.

74   Ofcansky, *Tarnished Pearl*, 27.

75   Mangat, *History of the Asians*, 175; Ofcansky, *Tarnished Pearl*, 27.

76   Tandon, "Political Survey," 88.

77   Rattansi and Abdulla, "Educational Survey," 132.

78   Gregory, *Rise and Fall*, 190–91.

79   Gregory, 192–93.

80   Thompson, "Ismailis in Uganda," 45.

81   Gregory, *Rise and Fall*, 206.

82   Gupta, "South Asians in East Africa," 122.

83   Somji, *Memoirs and Autobiography*, 27.

84   Mangat, *History of the Asians*, 175.

85   Adams, "Kin Network," 193.

86   Ojwang, "Exile and Estrangement," 529.

87   Nanji, *Child of Dandelions*, 184.

88   John Nazareth, interviewed by S. Muhammedi, 2015.

89   Karim Nanji, interviewed by S. Muhammedi, 2015.

90 Sikandar, interviewed by S. Muhammedi, 2015.

91 Sharma and Wooldridge, "Some Legal Questions," 398.

92 Amor, "Violent Ethnocentrism," 60.

93 LAC, Records of the Immigration Branch, RG 76, vol. 990, file 5850-3-650, "Memorandum to the Minister—Meeting with the Aga Khan," 28 September 1972, 1.

94 Reid, "Some Legal Aspects," 199.

95 Kasozi, Musisi, and Sejjengo, *Social Origins*, 92.

96 For more on the Common Man's Charter, Nakivubo Pronouncements, and the Trade Licensing Act, see Avirgan and Honey, *War in Uganda*; Kasozi, Musisi, and Sejjengo, *Social Origins*; and Ofcansky, *Tarnished Pearl*.

97 Ward and White, *East Africa*, 268.

98 Ghai, "Future Prospects," 188.

99 *The Nationalist*, 10 December 1968.

100 Ghai, "Future Prospects," 192.

101 Ward and White, *East Africa*, 259; Don Nanjira, *Status of Aliens*, 163.

102 LAC, Records of the Immigration Branch, RG 25, vol. 3146, file 1972/6, "Visit of UNHCR—The Future of Asians in East Africa," 2 February 1973, 1.

103 *Daily Nation*, 13 February 1967.

104 Ghai, "Future Prospects," 194.

105 *Spectator*, 4 December 1964, quoted in Wilson, "And Stay Out!," 570.

106 Herbert, "British Ugandan Asian Diaspora," 16.

107 "Uganda's New Military Ruler: Idi Amin," *New York Times*, 28 January 1971, 2.

108 Amin Visram, interviewed by S. Muhammedi, 2015.

109 1971 Statistical Abstract (Entebbe, Uganda: Government Printer, 1971), in Mittelman, *Ideology and Politics*, 228.

110 Patel, "General Amin," 12.

111 Nathan Epenu, "On the Eve of Census Day, A Look at Uganda's Asian Population," *Uganda Argus*, October 1971, 1.

112 Amin, "Speech," 211.

113 Sathyamurthy, *Political Development*, 619.

114 Amin, "Speech," 212.

115 Amin, 212.

116 Amin, 212–214.

117 Thompson, "Ismailis in Uganda," 45.

118 Amin, "Speech," 212.

119 Amin, 212.

120 Amin, 215.

121 Patel, "General Amin," 13.

122 Patel, 13.

123 Patel, 14.

124 Melady and Melady, *Uganda*, 74–75; Van Hear, *New Diasporas*, 72.

125 Melady and Melady, *Uganda*, 75.

126 "The Future of the Asians in Uganda," *Uganda Argus*, 5 August 1972, 1.

127 Mittelman, *Ideology and Politics*, 229.

Chapter 2: Dreams and Reality

1   Oded, "Israeli-Ugandan Relations," 66–67.

2   Oded, 67.

3   Oded, 71.

4   Oded, 74.

5   Kushner and Knox, *Refugees*, 267.

6   LAC, Records of the Immigration Branch, RG 76, vol. 990, file 5850-3-650, "Uganda: Expulsion of Asians," 10 August 1972.

7   Reid, "Some Legal Aspects," 201.

8   Reid, 201.

9   Kushner and Knox, *Refugees*, 267; Van Hear, *New Diasporas*, 71.

10   John Carnerio, "History of the KGI: Founding to Today," *Kampala Goan Institute 100th Anniversary*, June 2010, 15.

11   Nimira Charania, interviewed by S. Muhammedi, 2014.

12   Van Hear, *New Diasporas*, 65.

13   "All Asians Must Go," *Uganda Argus*, 21 August 1972, 1.

14   LAC, Records of the Immigration Branch, RG 76, vol. 990, file 5850-3-650, "Uganda: Asian Expulsion," 8 August 1972, 1.

15   "All Asians Must Go," *Uganda Argus*, 21 August 1972, 1.

16   "All Asians Must Go," 1.

17   Kotecha, "Short Changed," 3.

18   "There Will Be a Careful Check on Citizenship, Says the President. These Asians Can Stay," *Uganda Argus*, 23 August 1972, 1.

19   "Naburri on Why Asians Must Go," *Uganda Argus*, 15 August 1972, 1.

20   Kotecha, "Short Changed," 10.

21   John Nazareth, interviewed by S. Muhammedi, 2015.

22   Phillip Short, "Plight of the 23,000 Ugandans Made Stateless," *Times Newspapers*, 20 August 1972, in Lalani, *Ugandan Asian Expulsion*, 26.

23   Edmond and Maria Rodrigues, interviewed by S. Muhammedi, 2015.

24   Amin and Farida Sunderji, interviewed by S. Muhammedi, 2015.

25   Vasant and Sudra Lakhani, interviewed by S. Muhammedi, 2015.

26   Amor, "Violent Ethnocentrism," 64.

27   "All Shops Owned by Aliens to be Sold," *Uganda Argus*, 12 August 1972, 1.

28   "Amin Plans Check of Asians Left in Uganda," *Toronto Star*, 31 August 1972, 3.

29   Amor, "Violent Ethnocentrism," 62.

30   "The Declaration of Assets (Non-Citizen Asians) Decree, 1972," in Henckaerts, *Mass Expulsion*, 216.

31   "Government Directs on Cleared Asians Not More Than Two Days," *Uganda Argus*, 23 September 1972, 1.

32   "Government Directs on Cleared Asians Not More Than Two Days," 1.

33   "No Need for Money," *Uganda Argus*, 19 October 1972, 1; "Ugandans Seeking Bargains from Exiled Asians," *Toronto Star*, 31 August 1972, 3.

34 Michael Knipe, "Not a Single Ugandan Shilling to Leave, Airport Notice Says," *Times Newspapers*, 1 September 1972, in Lalani, *Ugandan Asian Expulsion*, 43.

35 "No Need for Money," *Uganda Argus*, 19 October 1972, 1.

36 Willy Mukasa, "Raid Uncovers 1.8m/- Asian 'Sandwiches,'" *Uganda Argus*, 25 September 1972, 1.

37 For more on the Makindye prison and violence under Amin's regime, see Rice, *Teeth May Smile*; Smith, *Ghosts of Kampala*; and Wooding and Barnett, *Uganda Holocaust*.

38 Willy Mukasa, "Raid Uncovers 1.8m/- Asian 'Sandwiches,'" *Uganda Argus*, 25 September 1972, 8.

39 "Kenya, Tanzania, and Zambia Asians to Quit," *Uganda Argus*, 10 October 1972, 8.

40 Frank Robertson, "Decision on Asians Final, Says Amin," *Daily Telegraph*, 7 August 1972, in Lalani, *Ugandan Asian Expulsion*, 3.

41 Brown, *Global South Asians*, 48.

42 Sir Edward Heath was not knighted until 1992. At the time he served as prime minister he did not hold this title.

43 Colin Legum, "Britain Will Reject Amin's Ultimatum on Asians," *The Observer*, 6 August 1972, in Lalani, *Ugandan Asian Expulsion*, 2.

44 Frank Robertson, "Decision on Asians Final, Says Amin," *Daily Telegraph*, 7 August 1972, in Lalani, *Ugandan Asian Expulsion*, 4.

45 Peter Thornton, "Amin Snubs Rippon on Asians," *Daily Telegraph*, 12 August 1972, in Lalani, *Ugandan Asian Expulsion*, 13.

46 Cosemans, "Politics of Dispersal," 101.

47 Cosemans, 102.

48 "Press Reactions," 10 August 1972, in Lalani, *Ugandan Asian Expulsion*, 7.

49 "Press Reactions," 7.

50 "Kibedi Defends Move on Asians," *Uganda Argus*, 1 September 1972, 1.

51 "London Threat to Uganda," *Uganda Argus*, 8 August 1972, 1.

52 "London Threat to Uganda," 1.

53 Kuepper, Lackey, and Swinerton, *Ugandan Asians*, 7.

54 Kuepper, Lackey, and Swinerton, 7.

55 "Tanzania Says No!" *News Compilation*, 10 August 1972, in Lalani, *Ugandan Asian Expulsion*, 7.

56 "Kenya Shuts the Door to Uganda Asians," *Daily Nation*, 9 August 1972, in Lalani, *Ugandan Asian Expulsion*, 5.

57 "New Warning by Moi," *Daily Nation*, 16 August 1972, in Lalani, *Ugandan Asian Expulsion*, 17.

58 Kuepper, Lackey, and Swinerton, *Ugandan Asians*, 7.

59 Kuepper, Lackey, and Swinerton, 8.

60 "Amin is More Racist—Vorster," 4 September 1972, in Lalani, *Ugandan Asian Expulsion*, 49.

61 Chris Serunjogi, "Ugandans Hail Move on Asians," *Uganda Argus*, 9 August 1972, 1.

62 Chris Serunjogi, 8.

63 "Asian Question Answered," *Uganda Argus*, 10 August 1972, 4.

64 Omugisha-Bukabbeha, "An Asian Dream Is Ended," *Uganda Argus*, 18 August 1972, 4.

65 Reverend Peter Ben Ocban, "An Asian Dream Is Ended," *Uganda Argus*, 18 August 1972, 4.

66 Dr. Mohan Kamarchand, "An Asian Dream Is Ended," *Uganda Argus*, 18 August 1972, 4.

67 Melady and Melady, *Uganda*, 75.

68 Omara-Otunnu, *Politics*, 136; Rice, *Teeth May Smile*, 12–13.

69 Jorgensen, *Uganda*, 313.

70 Chris Serunjogi, "Ugandans Hail Move on Asians," *Uganda Argus*, 9 August 1972, 1.

71 Melady and Melady, *Uganda*, 79.

72 Mobina Jaffer, interviewed by S. Muhammedi, 2015.

73 Nellie and Sadru Ahmed, interviewed by S. Muhammedi, 2015.

74 Saunders, *Journey into Hope*.

75 Terry Weiland, "'Any Asian Staying Here Is Stupid' UN Official Says," *Toronto Star*, 9 November 1972, 55.

76 John Nazareth, interviewed by S. Muhammedi, 2015.

77 Sathyamurthy, *Political Development*, 622.

78 Amin Visram, interviewed by S. Muhammedi, 2015.

79 Errol and Delphine Francis, interviewed by S. Muhammedi, 2015.

80 Mobina Jaffer, interviewed by S. Muhammedi, 2015.

81 Jalal Jaffer, interviewed by S. Muhammedi, 2015.

82 Edmond and Maria Rodrigues, interviewed by S. Muhammedi, 2015.

83 Mossadiq Umedaly, interviewed by S. Muhammedi, 2015.

84 Dennis Trudeau, "Ugandan Couple Like Canada Because She 'Really Wants to Help,'" *Calgary Herald*, 29 September 1972, in Lalani, *Ugandan Asian Expulsion*, 87.

85 Jalal Jaffer, interviewed by S. Muhammedi, 2015.

86 Amin Visram, interviewed by S. Muhammedi, 2015.

87 Edmond and Maria Rodrigues, interviewed by S. Muhammedi, 2015.

Chapter 3: "Thank you, Pierre"

1 Hawkins, *Canada and Immigration*, 151.

2 Knowles, *Strangers at Our Gates*, 192.

3 Knowles, 195.

4 Kelley and Trebilcock, *Making of the Mosaic*, 395.

5 Kelley and Trebilcock, 347.

6 Bumsted, *History*, 485.

7 Anderson and Black, "Political Integration," 45–46.

8 Kelley and Trebilcock, 351.

9 Bumsted, *History*, 442.

10 See Brodie, "Elusive Search"; Bumsted, *History*; Frideres, Burstein, and Biles, *Immigration and Integration*.

11 Belshaw, *Canadian History*, 715.

12 Belshaw, 716.

13 Belshaw, 720–21.

14 Brodie, "Elusive Search," 167–68.

15 Canada, *House of Commons Debates*, 28th Parliament, 3rd Session, Vol. 8, 8 October 1971, 8545. As argued by Richard J.F. Day, the foundations of Canadian multiculturalism long preceded the announcement of multiculturalism policy by Prime Minister Trudeau in 1971. By the turn of the twentieth century, progressive thinkers such as J.S. Woodsworth, Kate Foster, and John Murray Gibbon began to formulate discourses on Canadian diversity. Day argued that these texts "established a set of generic characteristics that have come to dominate thought, writing, and practice regarding the problem of Canadian diversity" (*Multiculturalism*, 8). For more, see Day, *Multiculturalism*, Chapters 6 and 7. See also the following works produced in the early 1900s: Woodsworth, *Strangers*; Foster, *Our Canadian Mosaic*; Gibbon, *Canadian Mosaic*.

16 Day, *Multiculturalism*, 441.

17 Bumsted, *History*, 440-441.

18 Forbes, "Trudeau," 28.

19 "Asian Airlift Soon," *Vancouver Sun*, 14 September 1972, 1.

20 LAC, Records of External Affairs, RG 25, vol. 3146, file 9-1973/1, Gerald Dirks, "Canada's Refugee Admissions Policy: Three Differing Responses," 1973, 13.

21 LAC, Records of the Immigration Branch, RG 76, vol. 1258, file 5850-3-4-650, "Uganda Asians in Canada," August 1973, 15.

22 Earle, "Hockey"; MacSkimming, *Cold War*.

23 Canada, *House of Commons Debates*, 28th Parliament, 4th Session, 1972, Vols. 1–4.

24 LAC, Records of the Immigration Branch, RG 76, vol. 948, file sf-c-1-1, "Ugandan Asians," 22 August 1972, 2.

25 LAC, "Ugandan Asians," 22 August 1972, 2.

26 Michael Lavoie, "Uganda Refugees May Have to Work Picking Fruit: PM," *Toronto Star*, 20 September 1972, 1.

27 Michael Lavoie, "Uganda Refugees May Have to Work Picking Fruit: PM," 4.

28 Terry Weiland, "Canada the Land of Hope for Asian Exiles of Uganda," *Toronto Star*, 20 October 1972, 39.

29 LAC, Records of the Immigration Branch, RG 76, vol. 1258, file 5850-3-5-650, "CLC says Ugandan Immigrants will Scarcely Affect Jobless Rate," 20 October 1972, 1.

30 Michael Lavoie, "Uganda Refugees May Have to Work Picking Fruit: PM," *Toronto Star*, 20 September 1972, 1.

31 "Metro's East Africans to help Asian Refugees," *Toronto Star*, 28 August 1972, 4. The Canadian Institute on Public Affairs is the oldest nonpartisan public affairs forum in Canada.

32 Norman Hartley, "Ugandans May Face Canadian Job Problem," *Globe and Mail*, 15 September 1972, 5.

33 LAC, Records of the Department of External Affairs, RG 25, vol. 8794, file 20-1-2-UGDA, "Uganda Situation Report," 25 September 1972, 4.

34 LAC, Records of the Immigration Branch, RG 76, vol. 990, file 5850-3-650, "Radio Station CKNW Vancouver Hotline Show—Asian Expellees from Uganda," 11 September 1972, 2.

35 H.G. Krinke, "Idi Amin Acted with Commonsense," *Vancouver Sun*, 31 October 1972, 5.

36 Philip Short, "Applications Mount for Canada Entry," *Globe and Mail*, 9 September

1972, 9. Other examples include Philip Short, "6,000 Asians in Uganda Seeking Entry to Canada," *Globe and Mail*, 7 September 1972, 1; Philip Short, "Asian Applications Soar, 11,000 Seeking to Enter," *Globe and Mail*, 8 September 1972, 1; and Norman Hartley, "Ugandans May Face Canadian Job Problem," *Globe and Mail*, 15 September 1972, 5.

37 LAC, Records of the Department of External Affairs, RG 25, vol. 8794, file 20-1-2-UGDA, "Uganda Situation Report," 5 October 1972, 3.

38 LAC, Pierre Elliott Trudeau Fonds, MG 26, vol. 748, file 840/U26, Mary Chadsey, "Letter to the Prime Minister," 6 October 1972, 1.

39 LAC, Pierre Elliott Trudeau Fonds, MG 26, vol. 748, file 840/U26, Derek Hayes, "Letter to the Prime Minister," 7 September 1972, 1.

40 LAC, Pierre Elliott Trudeau Fonds, MG 26, vol. 748, file, 840/U26, Jos Ain, "Letter to the Prime Minister," 4 October 1972, 1, and Eoin MacKay, "Letter to the Prime Minister," 25 August 1972, 1.

41 "Let Uganda's Asians Come to Canada," *Toronto Star*, 15 August 1972, 6.

42 "Friendly Welcome to Uganda Refugees," *Vancouver Sun*, 18 October 1972, 5.

43 "Mr. Amin's Racism Isn't Welcome Here," *Vancouver Sun*, 15 September 1972, 4.

44 James Eayrs, "Canada Has an Obligation to Admit Ugandan Expellees," *Toronto Star*, 21 August 1972, 6.

45 Quoted in Hawkins, *Critical Years*, 18. For more on racial discrimination against South Asian immigrants, see Chapter 1 in Hawkins.

46 Scott Bell, "Let UN expel Uganda for its Racist Action," *Toronto Star*, 26 August 1972, 9.

47 Anderson, *Canadian Liberalism*, 7.

48 LAC, Records of the Immigration Branch, RG 76, vol. 948, file sf-c-1-1, "Memoranda to Cabinet on Immigration Policy," 22 August 1972, 2.

49 Frank Jones, "Britain Appeals to Canada to Take Some Asians Expelled by Uganda," *Toronto Star*, 10 August 1972, 1.

50 LAC, Records of the Immigration Branch, RG 76, vol. 990, file 5850-3-650, "Press Conference by the Secretary of State for External Affairs, the Honourable Mitchell Sharp," 9 August 1972, 1.

51 LAC, Records of the Immigration Branch, RG 76, vol. 948, file sf-c-1-1, "Memoranda to Cabinet on Immigration Policy," 22 August 1972, 1–2.

52 Canada, *House of Commons Debates*, 28th Parliament, 4th Session, Vol. 4, 1 September 1972, 3937–38.

53 "Canada Opens Doors to Uganda Asians," *Windsor Star*, 26 August 1972.

54 Paul Jackson, "No Decision Yet on 'Ceiling' Here," *Vancouver Sun*, 25 August 1972, 2.

55 Canada, *House of Commons Debates*, 28th Parliament, 4th Session, Vol. 4, 1 September 1972, 3938.

56 "British Laud Canada on Offer to Asians: 'Thank you, Pierre,'" *Globe and Mail*, 26 August 1972, 1.

57 "British Laud Canada on Offer to Asians: 'Thank you, Pierre,'" 1.

58 Terrance Wills, "Ottawa May Be Prodding Others in Commonwealth to Admit Ugandan Asians," *Globe and Mail*, 26 August 26, 1972, 1.

59 Guy Demarino, "Canada Will Take Up to 5,000 Uganda Asians," *Southam News Service*, 25 August 1972, in Lalani, *Ugandan Asian Expulsion*, 33.

60 "Mackasey Fears Genocidal War," *South Ham News Service*, 25 August 1972, in Lalani, *Ugandan Asian Expulsion*, 33.

61 Trudeau Defends Admission of Uganda's Expelled Asians," *Toronto Star*, 25 September 1972, 1.

62 LAC, Records of the Immigration Branch, RG 76, vol. 948, file sf-c-1-1, "Memoranda to Cabinet on Immigration Policy," 22 August 1972, 1.

63 LAC, Records of the Immigration Branch, RG 76, vol. 145, file 5850-3-650, "Memorandum to the Minister," 22 August 1972, 1.

64 LAC, Records of the Immigration Brand, RG 76, vol. 990, file 5850-3-650, "Manpower Planning Unit Background Brief," 1 September 1972, 1–2.

65 LAC, Records of the Health Department, RG 29, vol. 3090, file 843-3-36, "East African Asians in the United Kingdom," 15 September 1972, 2.

66 LAC, Records of the Immigration Branch, RG 76, vol. 948, file sf-c-1-1, "Memorandum to Cabinet on Immigration Policy," 22 August 1972, 2–3.

67 St. Vincent, *Seven Crested Cranes*, viii.

68 LAC, Records of the Immigration Branch, RG 76, vol. 948, file sf-c-1-1, "Memorandum to Cabinet on Immigration Policy," 22 August 1972, 2.

69 UNHCR, *Convention and Protocol*, 14.

70 LAC, Records of the Immigration Branch, RG 76, vol. 990, file 5850-3-650, "East Indians in Uganda," 8 August 1972, 1.

71 LAC, RG 76, vol. 948, file sf-c-1-1, "Memoranda to Cabinet on Immigration Policy," 2.

72 LAC, Records of the Immigration Branch, RG 76, vol. 948, file sf-c-1-1, "Memorandum to Cabinet on Immigration Policy," 13 September 1972, 1.

73 LAC, "Memorandum to Cabinet on Immigration Policy," 13 September 1972, 3.

74 LAC, Records of the Health Branch, RG 29, vol. 3424, file 854-3-36, "Record of Cabinet Decision – Immigration to Canada of Asian Expellees from Uganda," 21 September 1972, 2.

75 LAC, Records of the Immigration Branch, RG 76, vol. 990, file 5850-3-650, "Memorandum to the Minister—Meeting with the Aga Khan," 28 September 1972, 1.

76 Letters between the two—contained in LAC, Pierre Elliott Trudeau fond, MG 26 O20 "Personal Correspondence 1965–1985"—demonstrate their close relations. They sent each other personal congratulations on the births of their children, wished each other happy new year, and often signed off letters with "in friendship." This friendship is not recorded in any major biographies of Trudeau.

77 Clarkson, *Room for All*, 23; John Geddes, "A Holy Man with an Eye for Connections," *Maclean's Magazine*, 27 October 2010, http://www2.macleans.ca/2010/10/27/a-holy-man.

78 LAC, Records of the Immigration Branch, RG 76, vol. 1214, file 5750-11, "Settlement of Ismailis from East Africa," 18 September 1972, 1–2.

79 LAC, Records of the Immigration Branch, RG 76, vol. 990, file 5850-3-650, "Background Paper," 2–3.

80 LAC, Records of the Immigration Branch, RG 76, vol. 1214, file 5750-11, "Letter to Prime Minister Trudeau from the Aga Khan," 23 August 1972, 1–3.

81 All quotations in this paragraph from LAC, Records of the Immigration Branch, RG 76, vol. 990, file 5850-3-650, "Aga Khan Meeting," 3–4.

82 LAC, Records of the Immigration Branch, RG 76, volume, 990, file 5850-3-650, "Memorandum to the Minister—Meeting with the Aga Khan," 1.

83 LAC, Records of the Immigration Branch, RG 76, vol. 990, file 5850-3-650, "Aga Khan Meeting," 3.

84 LAC, Records of the Immigration Branch, RG 76, vol. 990, file 5850-3-650, "Memorandum to the Minister—Meeting with the Aga Khan," 2.

85 LAC, Records of the Immigration Branch, RG 76, vol. 948, file sf-c-1-1, "Memoranda to Cabinet on Immigration Policy," 3.

86 LAC, Records from the Department of External Affairs, RG 25, volume 8794, file 20-1-2-UGDA "Uganda Situation Report," 5 October 1972, 4.

87 St. Vincent, *Seven Crested Cranes*, 82–102.

88 Roger St. Vincent, interviewed by S. Muhammedi, 2015.

89 LAC, Records of the Immigration Branch, RG 76, vol. 3424, file 854-3-36, "Phasing Out Operations, Kampala," 27 October 1972, 2.

90 "Michael Molloy—Uganda Asian Refugee Movement 1972," YouTube video, 1:31:49, 40th anniversary lecture on 18 October 2012, posted by Western University Migration and Ethnic Relations, https://www.youtube.com/watch?v=NtQPKNhxymY.

91 Michael Molloy, interviewed by S. Muhammedi, 2014.

92 John Nazareth, "How Hockey Determined the Number of Asian Refugees Accepted by Canada," *Kampala Goan Institute 100th Anniversary*, June 2010, 38–39.

93 Diab, "Fear and Vulnerability," 19–20.

Chapter 4: "His Dream Became My Nightmare"

1   St. Vincent, *Seven Crested Cranes*, 15.

2   Roger St. Vincent, interviewed by S. Muhammedi, 2015.

3   Raska, "Humanitarian Gesture," 557; St. Vincent, *Seven Crested Cranes*, 63.

4   LAC, Records of the Health Department, RG 29, vol. 3090, file 854-2-36, "Letter to Dr. Jacques Brunet from Dr. Maurice Leclaire," 27 September 1972, 1.

5   LAC, Records of the Health Department, RG 29, vol. 3090, file 854-3-36, "Ugandan Asian Program—Meeting with Commodore Roberts," 30 August 1972, 1.

6   LAC, Records of the Health Department, RG 29, vol. 3090, file 854-3-36, "Public Health Aspects of Ugandan Immigrant Program," 12 October 1972, 1 and LAC, Records of the Health Department, RG 29, vol. 3090, file 854-3-36, "200 Asians Screened Daily," 16 October 1972, 1.

7   LAC, Records of the Immigration Branch, RG 76, vol. 990, file 5850-3-650, "Uganda Meeting," 18 September 1972, 1.

8   LAC, Records of the Immigration Branch, RG 76, volume 990, file 5850-3-3-650, "Uganda Asians—Repayment of Assisted Passage Loans," 16 August 1973, 1.

9   LAC, Records of the Immigration Branch, RG 76, vol. 990, file 5850-3-3-650, "Final Report—Expellees Travelling on Charter Flights," 14 November 1972, 2.

10 LAC, Records of the Immigration Branch, RG 76, vol. 990, file 5850-3-3-650, "Report Respecting the Special Movement of Ugandan Asians," 5 December 1972, 2.

11 St. Vincent, *Seven Crested Cranes*, 37.

12 St. Vincent, 42.

13 Michael Molloy, interviewed by Heather LeRoux, 2014.

14 Michael Molloy, interviewed by Heather LeRoux, 2014.

15 Roger St. Vincent, interviewed by S. Muhammedi, 2015.

16 Mohamed and Almas Lalji, interviewed by S. Muhammedi, 2015.

17 Michael Molloy, interviewed by S. Muhammedi, 2014.

18 St. Vincent, *Seven Crested Cranes*, 93.

19 Granatstein and Bothwell, *Pirouette*, 283.

20 Jalal Jaffer, interviewed by S. Muhammedi, 2015.

21 Amin and Farida Sunderji, interviewed by S. Muhammedi, 2015.

22 Karim Nanji, interviewed by S. Muhammedi, 2015.

23 Shamim Muhammedi, interviewed by S. Muhammedi, 2014.

24 Raska, "Humanitarian Gesture," 550.

25 LAC, Records of the Immigration Branch, RG 76, vol. 948, file sf-c-1-1, "Memoranda to Cabinet on Immigration Policy," 22 August 1972, 1.

26 St. Vincent, *Seven Crested Cranes*, 62.

27 St. Vincent, 72.

28 St. Vincent, 72.

29 LAC, Records of the Immigration Branch, RG 76, vol. 990, file 5850-3-650, "Ugandan Asians," 27 October 1972, 1.

30 LAC, "Ugandan Asians," 27 October 1972, 1.

31 St. Vincent, *Seven Crested Cranes*, 41.

32 LAC, Records of the Immigration Branch, RG 76, vol. 1258, file 5850-3-3-650, "Ugandan Expellees—Expenditures," 10 November 1972, 3.

33 LAC, "Ugandan Expellees—Expenditures," 10 November 1972, 3.

34 LAC, Records of the Immigration Branch, RG 76, vol. 1258, file 5850-3-5-650, "Ugandan Asians," 15 May 1973, 1.

35 "United Nations Centre Advertisement," in Lalani, *Ugandan Asian Expulsion*, 115.

36 "How They Did It: Resettlement of Asians from Uganda in Europe and North America," Office of the United Nations High Commissioner for Refugees, May 1973, in Lalani, *Ugandan Asian Expulsion*, 165.

37 "4,000 Stateless Asians to Fly out to Europe," *Daily Nation*, 1 November 1972, in Lalani, *Ugandan Asian Expulsion*, 117.

38 Michael Knipe, "Only 800 Stateless Asians Left as Amin Deadline Expires," *The Times*, 9 November, 1972, in Lalani, *Ugandan Asian Expulsion*, 127.

39 Michael Knipe, "Only 800 Stateless Asians Left as Amin Deadline Expires," *The Times*, 9 November 1972; and "500 Expelled Asians Given Temporary Home at Malta," *Times of Malta*, 9 November 1972, in Lalani, *Ugandan Asian Expulsion*, 127–30.

40 Robert Chessyre, "Future of Uganda's Exiles Poses Problem for Countries Who Gave Them Refuge," *The Times*, 14 December 1972, in Lalani, *Ugandan Asian Expulsion*, 148.

41 Rune B. Axelsson, "Their Lives Begin in a Grey Barrack," December 13, 1972, in Lalani, *Ugandan Asian Expulsion*, 147.

42 All quotations in the paragraph come from Robert Chessyre, "Future of Uganda's Exiles Poses Problem for Countries Who Gave Them Refuge," in Lalani, *Ugandan Asian Expulsion*, 148.

43 Laila Jiwani, interviewed by S. Muhammedi, 2015.

44 Azim Sarangi, interviewed by S. Muhammedi, 2015. His uncle stayed behind in Uganda for two years following the expulsion, then joined family members in Canada as conditions for Ugandan Asian business owners deteriorated.

45 Mumtaz, interviewed by S. Muhammedi, 2015.

46 Nimira Charania, interviewed by S. Muhammedi, 2014.

47 LAC, Records of the Immigration Branch, RG 76, vol. 990, file 5850-3-650, "Uganda: Expulsion of British Asians," 9 August 1972, 1.

48 Adams and Bristow, "Expulsion Experiences," 201.

49 Jalal Jaffer, interviewed by S. Muhammedi, 2015.

50 Munira Dhanani, interviewed by S. Muhammedi, 2015.

51 Hundle, "Exceptions," 176–77.

52 Herbert, "Oral Histories," 28.

53 Herbert, 29.

54 Sikandar, interviewed by S. Muhammedi, 2015.

55 Other examples of harassment were described by the following oral history participants: Sadru and Nellie Ahmed, 2015; Munira Dhanani, 2015; Laila Jiwani, 2015; Shamim Muhammedi, 2014; Rossbina Nathoo, 2015; and Zaina and Altaf Sovani, 2015 (all interviewed by S. Muhammedi).

56 Sadru and Nellie Ahmed, interviewed by S. Muhammedi, 2015. Nellie told Michael Molloy, who had become a close friend, that she was helping women leave.

57 Nanji, *Child of Dandelions*, 167.

58 Nimira Charania, interviewed by S. Muhammedi, 2014.

59 "Mini Dress Girls Are Fined," *Uganda Argus*, 31 August 1972, 3.

60 LAC, Records of the Immigration Branch, RG 76, vol. 990, file 5850-3-650, "Uganda: Safety of Canadians," 24 September 1973, 5.

61 Hugh Davies, "Amin's Rampaging Soldiers Hold Asians to Ransom," *The Telegraph*, 25 September 1972, in Lalani, *Ugandan Asian Expulsion*, 81.

62 Aziz Dhalla, interviewed by S. Muhammedi, 2014.

63 Edmond and Maria Rodrigues, interviewed by S. Muhammedi, 2015.

64 Errol and Delphine Francis, interviewed by S. Muhammedi, 2015.

65 Amin Visram, interviewed by S. Muhammedi, 2015.

66 Nimira Charania, interviewed by S. Muhammedi, 2015.

67 Mobina Jaffer, interviewed by S. Muhammedi, 2015.

68 Van Hear, *New Diasporas*, 70.

69 Patrick Keatley, "Amin's Troops 'Spread Panic' in Kampala," *The Guardian*, 22 September 1972, in Lalani, *Ugandan Asian Expulsion*, 74.

70 "Medical Treatment for Asian Beaten by Soldier," *Daily Nation*, 2 October 1972, in Lalani, *Ugandan Asian Expulsion*, 97.

71 St. Vincent, *Seven Crested Cranes*, 41.

72 Iqbal, interviewed by S. Muhammedi, 2015.

73   Azim Sarangi, interviewed by S. Muhammedi, 2015.

74   Zul Devji, interviewed by S. Muhammedi, 2014.

75   Azim Sarangi, interviewed by S. Muhammedi, 2015.

76   Zabina Dossa, interviewed by S. Muhammedi, 2015.

77   Mohamed and Almas Lalji, interviewed by S. Muhammedi, 2015.

78   Munira Dhanani, interviewed by S. Muhammedi, 2015.

79   Examples came up in interviews with Mohamed and Almas Lalji, 2015, and Shamim Muhammedi, 2014 (all interviewed by S. Muhammedi).

80   Alibhai-Brown, *Settler's Cookbook*, 22.

81   Sadru and Nellie Ahmed, interviewed by S. Muhammedi, 2015.

82   Sadru and Nellie Ahmed, interviewed by S. Muhammedi, 2015.

83   Barnett and Noriega, introduction to *Communities of Color*, 17; Cruikshank, *Do Glaciers Listen?*, 9–10; Maynes, Pierce, and Laslett, *Telling Stories*, 12; Thompson, "Voice of the Past," 24–25; Yow, *Recording Oral History*, 11.

84   LAC, Records of the Immigration Branch, RG 76, vol. 1258, file 5850-3-3-650, "Cumulative Statistical Report on the Immigration Movement of Ugandan Expellees," 14 November 1972, 1.

Chapter 5: "An Honourable Place"

1   LAC, International Health Services, RG 29, vol. 3424, file 854-3-36, "Ugandan Asian Immigration Program," 20 September 1972, 2.

2   LAC, Records of the Immigration Branch, RG 76, vol. 1257, file 5850-3-650, "Final Report—Operation UGX," 8 January 1973, 1–4.

3   LAC, Records of the Immigration Branch, RG 76, vol. 1259, file 5850-3-8-650, "Letter to Mr. Rogers," 14 November 1972, 1.

4   LAC, Records of the Immigration Branch, RG 76, vol. 1258, file 5850-3-3-650, "Progress Report Respecting the Special Movement of Ugandan Asians," 19 October 1972, 4; Dennis Trudeau, "Ugandan Couple Like Canada Because She 'Really Wants to Help,'" *Calgary Herald*, 29 September 1972, in Lalani, *Ugandan Asian Expulsion*, 87.

5   LAC, Records of the Immigration Branch, RG 76, vol. 1257, file 5850-3-650, "Final Report—Operation UGX," 8 January 1973, 5–8.

6   LAC, Records of the Immigration Branch, RG 76, vol. 1258, file 5850-3-4-650, Freda Hawkins, "Uganda Asians in Canada," August 1973, 3.

7   Azim Sarangi, interviewed by S. Muhammedi, 2015.

8   LAC, Records of the Immigration Branch, RG 76, vol. 1258, file 5850-3-3-650, "Change in Immigration Policy Regarding Uganda Asians," 19 July 1973, 1.

9   LAC, "Change in Immigration Policy Regarding Uganda Asians," 17 July 1973, 1.

10   LAC, Records of the Immigration Branch, RG 76, vol. 1258, file 5850-3-3-650, "Uganda Asians—Repayment of Assisted Passage Loans," 16 August 1973, 1.

11   LAC, "Uganda Asians—Repayment of Assisted Passage Loans," 16 August 1973, 1.

12   Umedali Nanji, interviewed by S. Muhammedi, 2015.

13   Edmond and Maria Rodrigues, interviewed by S. Muhammedi, 2015.

14   Iqbal, interviewed by S. Muhammedi, 2015.

15   LAC, Records of the Immigration Branch, RG 76, vol. 1258, file 5850-3-3-650,

"Report Respecting the Special Movement of Ugandan Asians,"5 December 1972, 2.

16 LAC, Records of the Immigration Branch, RG 76, vol. 1258, file 5850-3-5-650, "Preliminary Report on UGX Information Centre,"31 October 1972, 2.

17 All information about Wilczur in this paragraph comes from LAC, Records of the Immigration Branch, RG 76, vol. 1258, file 5850-3-5-650, "Preliminary Report on UGX Information Centre,"31 October 1972, 1–4.

18 Norman Hartley, "Canadians Sacrifice Hockey to Receive Refugees," *Globe and Mail*, 29 September 1972, 10.

19 Hartley, "Canadians Sacrifice Hockey to Receive Refugees,"10.

20 Edmond and Maria Rodrigues, interviewed by S. Muhammedi, 2015.

21 Rossbina Nathoo, interviewed by S. Muhammedi, 2015.

22 Nazir Walji, interviewed by S. Muhammedi, 2015.

23 LAC, Records of the Immigration Branch, RG 76, vol. 1259, file 5850-3-8-650, "Letter to the Prime Minister,"31 October 1972, 1.

24 "Asian in Toronto Finds a Schoolmate," *Toronto Star*, 29 September 1972, in Lalani, *Ugandan Asian Expulsion*, 89.

25 LAC, Records of the Immigration Branch, RG 76, vol. 1258, file 5850-3-3-650, "Report Respecting the Special Movement of Ugandan Asians,"5 December 1972, 3.

26 LAC, Records of the Immigration Branch, RG 76, vol. 1259, file 5850-3-7-650, Bernard Ostry, "Letter to Dr. R.M. Adams,"24 October 1972, 3.

27 LAC, Records of the Immigration Branch, RG 76, vol. 1259, file 5850-3-7-650, "Regina Uganda Asian Committee," 18 October 1972, 1. For more examples, see "Committee Membership"in RG 76, vol. 1259, file 5850-3-7-650.

28 LAC, Records of the Immigration Branch, RG 76, vol. 1259, file 5850-3-7-650, Bernard Ostry, "Letter to Dr. R.M. Adams,"24 October 1972, 3. Bernard Ostry was an academic and public servant for over twenty-five years. He was the undersecretary of state from 1970 to 1973 before becoming the secretary general of National Museums of Canada for four years. He concluded his public service career in 1992 as the president of the Association for Tele-Education in Canada. For more, see Hillmer, "Bernard Ostry."

29 LAC, Records of the Immigration Branch, RG 76, vol. 1259, file 5850-3-7-650, "Progress Report Respecting the Special Movement of Ugandan Asians," 19 October 1972, 4.

30 LAC, Records of External Affairs, RG 25, vol. 3146, file 9-1973/1, Gerald Dirks, "Canada's Refugee Admissions Policy: Three Differing Responses,"31 January 1973, 8.

31 Wu, Schimmele, and Hou, *Social Integration*, 5–6.

32 Hoerder, *Creating Societies*, ix.

33 All quotations from the pamphlet come from LAC, Records of the Immigration Branch, RG 76, vol. 1259, file 5850-3-7-650, "Your First Few Months in Canada," 2–3.

34 LAC, Records of the Immigration Branch, RG 76, vol. 1259, file 5850-3-7-650, "The Uganda Asians," 27 September 1972, 5.

35 Zul Hirji and Shaffin Shariff, "Journey into Hope: A Chronicle of the Ugandan Asian Migration," *The Ismaili Canada*, Fall 1994, 12.

36 LAC, Records of the Immigration Branch, RG 76, vol. 1259, file 5850-3-7-650, "Committees to Assist the Uganda Asians," 7 December 1972, 6.

37 "Toronto Families Asked to Open Homes to Asians," *News Compilation*, 27 September 1972, in Lalani, *Ugandan Asian Expulsion*, 82.

38 LAC, Records of the Immigration Branch, RG 76, vol. 1259, file 5850-3-7-650, "Committees to Assist the Uganda Asians," 7 December 1972, 7.

39 LAC, "Committees to Assist the Uganda Asians," 7 December 1972, 7.

40 "Snow and Christmas Lights Delight Ugandans in City," *Edmonton Journal*, 26 December 1972, in Lalani, *Ugandan Asian Expulsion*, 152.

41 "Snow and Christmas Lights Delight Ugandans in City," 152.

42 LAC, Records of the Immigration Branch, RG 76, vol. 1259, file 5850-3-7-650, "Uganda Asian Committee—Newsletter Two," 24 January 1973, 10.

43 LAC, "Uganda Asian Committee—Newsletter Two," 10.

44 LAC, "Uganda Asian Committee—Newsletter Two," 27.

45 LAC, Records of the Immigration Branch, RG 76, vol. 1259, file 5850-3-7-650, Mr. J. Paproski, "Uganda Asian Committee," 19 February 1973, 1.

46 LAC, Records of the Immigration Branch, RG 76, vol. 1259, file 5850-3-7-650, J.W. Edmonds, "Uganda Asian Committees," 7 March 1973, 3.

47 LAC, Records of the Immigration Branch, RG 76, vol. 1259, file 5850-3-7-650, K.D. Allen, "Uganda Asian Committee," 20 February 1973, 2.

48 LAC, Records of the Immigration Branch, RG 76, vol. 1259, file 5850-3-7-650, "Uganda Asian Committee Newsletter Three," 23 March 1973, 1.

49 LAC, "Uganda Asian Committee Newsletter Three," 23 March 1973, 1.

50 LAC, Records of the Immigration Branch, RG 76, vol. 1257, file 5850-2-650, "Ugandan Expellees Visaed Kampala and Adjustment Assistance Expenditures Generally—Pacific Region," 17 July 1973, 1.

51 LAC, "Ugandan Expellees Visaed Kampala and Adjustment Assistance Expenditures Generally—Pacific Region," 17 July 1973, 1.

52 LAC, Records of the Immigration Branch, RG 76, vol. 1258, file 5850-3-5-650, "Overpayments of Adjustment Assistance to Ugandan Expellees," 1 October 1974, 1.

53 LAC, "Overpayments of Adjustment Assistance to Ugandan Expellees," 3.

54 LAC, Records of the Immigration Branch, RG 76, vol. 1259, file 5850-3-7-650, "Uganda Asian Committees—Evaluation Report," 14 March 1973, 3.

55 LAC, Records of the Immigration Branch, RG 76, vol. 1258, file 5850-3-5-650, "Overpayments of Adjustment Assistance to Ugandan Expellees," 1 October 1974, 1.

56 LAC, Records of the Immigration Branch, RG 76, vol. 1258, file 5850-3-5-650, "Ugandan Expellee Program—Auditor General's Report," 31 January 1975, 1.

57 LAC, Records of the Immigration Branch, RG 76, vol. 1259, file 5850-3-7-650, "Uganda Asian Committee," 25 January 1973, 5.

58 LAC, Records of the Immigration Branch, RG 76, vol. 1258, file 5850-3-4-650, Freda Hawkins, "Uganda Asians in Canada," August 1973, 15.

59 Shiraz Lalani, interviewed by S. Muhammedi, 2015.

60 "Toronto Families Asked to Open Homes to Asians," *News Compilation*, 27 September 1972, in Lalani, *Ugandan Asian Expulsion*, 82.

61 "Ugandan Refugees in Toronto Get Together," *News Compilation*, 10 October 1972, in Lalani, *Ugandan Asian Expulsion*, 100.

62 Terrence Francis, interviewed by S. Muhammedi, 2015.

63 "First Ugandans Arrive Today," *Montreal Gazette*, 28 September 1972, in Lalani, *Ugandan Asian Expulsion*, 83.

64 Patrick Best, "Government Won't Help Ugandans with Tuition Fees," *Ottawa Citizen*, 30 November 1972, in Lalani, *Ugandan Asian Expulsion*, 145.

65 LAC, Records of the Immigration Branch, RG 76, vol. 1259, file 5850-3-7-650, J.O. Swales, "Meeting of Ugandan-Asian Central Committee," 22 November 1972, 1.

66 Patrick Best, "Government Won't Help Ugandans with Tuition Fees," *Ottawa Citizen*, 30 November 1972, in Lalani, *Ugandan Asian Expulsion*, 145.

67 LAC, Records of the Immigration Branch, RG 76, vol. 1259, file 5850-3-7-650, James Cross, "Ugandan Expellee Teachers," 20 March 1973, 1.

68 Patrick Best, "Government Won't Help Ugandans with Tuition Fees," *Ottawa Citizen*, 30 November 1972, in Lalani, *Ugandan Asian Expulsion*, 145.

69 LAC, Records of the Immigration Branch, RG 76, vol. 1259, file 5850-3-7-650, "Uganda Asian Committee—Newsletter Two," 24 January 1973, 12.

70 LAC, Records of the Immigration Branch, RG 76, vol. 1257, file 5850-3-650, "Ugandan Expellee Teachers Following Professional Re-Orientation Courses at the Simon Fraser University," 14 March 1973, 1.

71 "Exiled Asians Need Help," *Edmonton Journal*, 2 November 1972, in Lalani, *Ugandan Asian Expulsion*, 118.

72 Edmond and Maria Rodrigues, interviewed by S. Muhammedi, 2015.

73 Zabina Dossa, interviewed by S. Muhammedi, 2015.

74 Errol and Delphine Francis, interviewed by S. Muhammedi, 2015.

75 LAC, Records of the Immigration Branch, RG 76, vol. 1257, file 5850-3-650, "UNHCR's Request for a Report on the Ugandan Asians Resettled in Canada," 27 April 1973, 3.

76 Dennis Trudeau, "Ugandan Couple Like Canada Because She 'Really Wants to Help,'" *Calgary Herald*, 29 September 1972, in Lalani, *Ugandan Asian Expulsion*, 87.

77 Gerald Utting, "Asian Children Here from Uganda Long to See Snow for the First Time," *Toronto Star*, 14 October 1972, 10.

78 "Ugandan Refugees in Toronto Get Together," *News Compilation*, 10 October 1972, in Lalani, *Ugandan Asian Expulsion*, 100.

79 "Asian Who Left Everything He Owned," *Toronto Star*, 29 September 1972, in Lalani, *Ugandan Asian Expulsion*, 86.

80 LAC, Records of the Immigration Branch, RG 76, vol. 1258, file 5850-3-4-650, J.S. McIntosh, "Meeting on the Ugandan Asian Immigrant Study," 20 June 1973, 1.

81 "Refugee Dies after Flight," in Lalani, *Ugandan Asian Expulsion*, 75.

82 Carol Hogg, "Finding a Job Is Biggest Worry for Ugandan Immigrant," *Calgary Herald*, 4 October 1972, in Lalani, *Ugandan Asian Expulsion*, 98.

83 Glen Allen, "Ugandans See Canada Life as Welcome Challenge," *The Gazette*, 30 September 1972, in Lalani, *Ugandan Asian Expulsion*, 91.

84 "Ugandan Refugees in Toronto Get Together," *News Compilation*, 10 October 1972, in Lalani, *Ugandan Asian Expulsion*, 100.

85 LAC, Records of the Immigration Branch, RG 76, vol. 1258, file 5850-3-4-650, "Ugandan Asian Expellees: The First Twelve Months in Canada," October 1976, 12.

86 Adams and Jesudason, "Employment," 472.

87 Adams and Jesudason, 472.

88 LAC, Records of the Immigration Branch, RG 76, vol. 1257, file 5850-3-650, J. McMaster, "Memorandum to the Chief of the Procedures Division," 24 January 1973.

89 Bonikowska and Hou, "Reversal of Fortunes," 320–53; Buzdugan and Halli, "Labor Market Experiences," 366–86; Picot, Hou, and Coulombe, "Poverty Dynamics," 393–424.

90 LAC, Records of the Immigration Branch, RG 76, vol. 1258, file 5850-3-4-650, J.S. McIntosh, "Meeting on the Ugandan Asian Immigrant Study," 20 June 1973, 1.

91 Vasant and Sudha Lakhani, interviewed by S. Muhammedi, 2015.

92 Sikandar, interviewed by S. Muhammedi, 2015.

93 Jalal Jaffer, interviewed by S. Muhammedi, 2015.

94 Vinnay Dattani, interviewed by S. Muhammedi, 2015.

95 Aziz Fakirani, Khaerun Lalany, and Azad Lalany, interviewed by S. Muhammedi, 2015.

96 Terrence Francis, interviewed by S. Muhammedi, 2015.

97 Iqbal, interviewed by S. Muhammedi, 2015.

98 K.U. Chandra, *Racial Discrimination in Canada* (San Francisco: R and E Research Associates, 1973), cited in Buchignani, Indra, and Srivastava, *Continuous Journey*, 211.

99 LAC, Records of the Immigration Branch, RG 76, vol. 1258, file 5850-3-4-650, "Ugandan Asian Expellees: The First Twelve Months in Canada," October 1976, 14.

100 John Stackhouse, "Aga Khan: 'Without a Doubt, I Am Seriously Worried' about the World," *The Globe and Mail*, 1 March 2014, http://www.theglobeandmail.com/news/world/aga-khan-without-a-doubt-i-am-seriously-worried-about-the-world/article17185492/.

101 Pereira, "Study of the Effects," 188.

102 LAC, Records of the Immigration Branch, RG 76, vol. 1258, file 5850-3-4-650, "Ugandan Asian Expellees: The First Twelve Months in Canada," October 1976, 2.

103 Canada, "Surge of Women."

104 LAC, Records of the Immigration Branch, RG 76, vol. 1258, file 5850-3-4-650, "Ugandan Asian Expellees: The First Twelve Months in Canada," October 1976, 1–2.

105 Errol and Delphine Francis, 2015; Shamim Muhammedi, 2014 (all interviewed by S. Muhammedi).

106 Almas and Mohamad Lalji, interviewed by S. Muhammedi, 2015.

107 Remtulla, "Educational and Social Adjustment," 34.

108 Rossbina Nathoo, interviewed by S. Muhammedi, 2015.

109 Amin and Farida Sunderji, interviewed by S. Muhammedi, 2015.

110 Sikandar, interviewed by S. Muhammedi, 2015.

111 Amin Visram, interviewed by S. Muhammedi, 2015.

112 Nimira Charania, interviewed by S. Muhammedi, 2014.

113 Karim Nanji, interviewed by S. Muhammedi, 2015.

114 Vinnay Dattani, interviewed by S. Muhammedi, 2015.

115 Nimira Charania, interviewed by S. Muhammedi, 2014.

116 Examples include Nimira Charania, 2014; Vinnay Dattani, 2015; Vasant and Sudha Lakhani, 2015; Shamim Muhammedi, 2014; Karim Nanji, 2015; and Amin Visram, 2015 (all interviewed by S. Muhammedi).

117　LAC, Records of the Immigration Branch, RG 76, vol. 1258, file 5850-3-4-650, J.S. McIntosh, "Meeting on the Ugandan Asian Immigrant Study," 20 June 1973, 1.

118　"Ugandan Asians Find Canadian Winter Cold but People Very Warm," *Ottawa Citizen*, 23 December 1972, in Lalani, *Ugandan Asian Expulsion*, 150.

119　Amin and Farida Sunderji, interviewed by S. Muhammedi, 2015.

120　Munira Dhanani, interviewed by S. Muhammedi, 2015.

121　Diamond Akbarali, interviewed by S. Muhammedi, 2015.

122　Gerald Utting, "Asian Children Here from Uganda Long to See Snow for the First Time," *Toronto Star*, 14 October 1972, 10.

123　Edmond and Maria Rodrigues, interviewed by S. Muhammedi, 2015.

124　Shiraz Lalani, interviewed by S. Muhammedi, 2015.

125　Sikandar, interviewed by S. Muhammedi, 2015.

126　LAC, Records of the Immigration Branch, RG 76, vol. 1258, file 5850-3-4-650, "Ugandan Asian Expellees: The First Twelve Months in Canada," October 1976, 68 and 72.

127　LAC, "Ugandan Asian Expellees," 8.

128　LAC, Records of the Immigration Branch, RG 76, vol. 1259, file 5850-9-650, "Ugandan Expellees," 12 March 1973, 1.

129　LAC, Records of the Immigration Branch, RG 76, vol. 1257, file 5850-3-650, "Background Note on Asians of Undetermined Nationality from Uganda," 1 January 1973, 3.

130　LAC, Records of the Immigration Branch, RG 76, vol. 1257, file 5850-3-650, "Ugandan Asians in the United Kingdom," 15 January 1973, 2.

131　LAC, Records of External Affairs, RG 25, vol. 13668, file 47-4-UNHCR-1-AFR, Robert M. Adams, "Letter to Mr. Hathway," 30 November 1972, 1.

132　LAC, Robert M. Adams, "Letter to Mr. Hathway," 30 November 1972, 1.

133　LAC, Records of External Affairs, RG 25, vol. 3146, file 9-1972/6, "Ugandan Expellee Program—Possible Visit of U.N. High Commissioner for Refugees," 25 January 1973, 1.

134　LAC, Records of External Affairs, RG 25, vol. 13668, file 47-4-UNHCR-1-AFR, "Canadian Immigration Policy for Refugees," 29 September 1972, 2.

135　LAC, Records of the Immigration Branch, RG 76, vol. 1257, file 5850-3-650, "Ugandan Expellee Program—Possible Visit of U.N. High Commissioner for Refugees," 25 January 1973, 3.

136　LAC, Records of the Immigration Branch, RG 76, vol. 1257, file 5850-3-650, "Visit of United Nations High Commissioner of Refugees," 31 January 1972, 2. "Hard-core cases" included anyone who failed to meet the selection criteria by a significant degree.

137　LAC, Records of the Immigration Branch, RG 76, vol. 1257, file 5850-3-650, "Further Assistance to Ugandan Asian Expellees," 16 February 1973, 1.

138　LAC, Records of External Affairs, RG 25, vol. 3146, file 9-1972/6, "Ugandan Expellee Program—Possible Visit of U.N. High Commissioner for Refugees," 25 January 1973, 2.

139　LAC, Records of the Immigration Branch, RG 76, vol. 1259, file 5850-3-7-650, "Ugandan Expellee Program," 15 November 1972, 1.

140　LAC, "Ugandan Expellee Program," 15 November 1972, 1.

141 LAC, Records of the Immigration Branch, RG 76, vol. 1257, file 5850-3-650, "Background Note on Asians of Undetermined Nationality from Uganda," 1 January 1973, 2.

142 LAC, Records of the Immigration Branch, RG 76, vol. 1258, file 5850-3-5-650, "Ugandan Asians," 15 May 1973, 2.

143 LAC, Records of the Immigration Branch, RG 76, vol. 1257, file 5850-3-650, "Visit of UNHCR to CDA—Ugandan Refugees," 26 January 1973, 1.

144 LAC, Records of the Immigration Branch, RG 76, vol. 1214, file 5750-11, "Telex to Immigration Office in Beirut," 18 November 1972, 1.

145 LAC, Records of the Immigration Branch, RG 76, vol. 1257, file 5850-3-650, "Visit of UNHCR to CDA—Ugandan Refugees," 26 January 1973, 1.

146 LAC, "Visit of UNHCR to CDA—Ugandan Refugees," 26 January 1973, 1–2.

147 LAC, "Visit of UNHCR to CDA—Ugandan Refugees," 26 January 1973, 1.

148 LAC, Records of the Immigration Branch, RG 76, vol. 1214, file 5750-11, "Question Regarding Processing of Ismaelis Already Answered in Nairobi," 22 November 1972, 1.

149 LAC, Records of the Immigration Branch, RG 76, vol. 1214, file 5750-11, Pierre Elliott Trudeau, "Letter to the Aga Khan," 21 March 1974, 2.

150 LAC, Pierre Elliott Trudeau, "Letter to the Aga Khan," 21 March 1974, 2–3.

151 LAC, Records of the Immigration Branch, RG 76, vol. 1214, file 5750-11, Aga Khan, "Letter to Prime Minister Trudeau," 16 April 1974, 1.

152 LAC, Records of the Immigration Branch, RG 76, vol. 1259, file 5850-3-9-650, "Narrative Report," 7 May 1972, 2.

153 LAC, Records of the Immigration Branch, RG 76, vol. 1214, file 5750-11, "Visits to Beirut, Nairobi, and Lagos," 26 June 1974, 1.

154 LAC, Records of the Immigration Branch, RG 76, vol. 1257, file 5850-3-650, "Settlement in Canada," 16 January 1973, 1.

155 LAC, Records of the Immigration Branch, RG 76, vol. 1257, file 5850-3-650, "Stateless Ugandan Asian Expellees in European Transit Camps with Relatives in Canada," 22 March 1973, 1. The National Interfaith Immigrant community was formally established in 1960 as several church groups across Canada shared mandates to assist with the integration of newcomers.

156 LAC, Records of the Immigration Branch, RG 76, vol.1257, file 5850-3-650, "Ugandan Asian Expellees," 8 March 1973, 1.

157 LAC, Records of the Immigration Branch, RG 76, vol. 1257, file 5850-3-650, "Stateless Ugandan Asian Expellees in European Transit Camps with Relatives in Canada," 22 March 1973, 3.

158 Diamond Akbarali, interviewed by S. Muhammedi, 21 July 2015.

159 Nimira Charania, interviewed by S. Muhammedi, 2014.

160 Nimira Charania, interviewed by S. Muhammedi, 2014.

161 Sikandar, interviewed by S. Muhammedi, 2015.

162 Aziz Fakirani, Khaerun Lalany, and Azad Lalany, interviewed by S. Muhammedi, 2015.

163 LAC, Records of the Immigration Branch, RG 76, vol. 1258, file 5850-3-5-650, A.E. Gotlieb, "Ugandan Asians—Press Briefing by British Community Relations Commission," 7 July 1975, 3.

164　LAC, A.E. Gotlieb, "Ugandan Asians—Press Briefing by British Community Relations Commission," 7 July 1975, 3.

165　Molloy, "Personal Memoir," 73.

166　"Humanity Requires Admitting the Weak Too," *Globe and Mail*, 26 August 1972, 6.

167　LAC, Records of the Immigration Branch, RG 76, vol. 1257, file 5850-3-650, Gerry Campbell, "Contingencies of the Kampala Operation," 22 March 1973, 5.

168　St. Vincent, *Seven Crested Cranes*, 42.

169　All quotations from Campbell in this paragraph come from LAC, Records of the Immigration Branch, RG 76, vol. 1257, file 5850-3-650, Gerry Campbell, "Contingencies of the Kampala Operation," 22 March 1973, 5, 11.

170　LAC, Gerry Campbell, "Contingencies of the Kampala Operation," 11–12.

171　LAC, Gerry Campbell, "Contingencies of the Kampala Operation," 11–12. See also Appendix A of Campbell's report.

172　Molloy, "Personal Memoir," 73.

173　LAC, RG 76, vol. 1257, file 5850-3-650, "Contingencies of the Kampala Operation," 13.

174　Michael Molloy, interviewed by S. Muhammedi, 2015; Roger St. Vincent, interviewed by S. Muhammedi, 2015; "Michael Molloy—Uganda Asian Refugee Movement 1972," YouTube video, 1:31:49, 40th anniversary lecture on 18 October 2012, posted by Western University Migration and Ethnic Relations, https://www.youtube.com/watch?v=NtQPKNhxymY; St. Vincent, *Seven Crested Cranes*, 94.

175　Information about Dirks's assessment and all quotations in this paragraph come from LAC, Records of External Affairs, RG 25, vol. 3146, file 9-1973/1, Gerald Dirks, "Canada's Refugee Admissions Policy: Three Differing Responses," 31 January 1973, 13, 16, and 17.

176　LAC, Records of the Immigration Branch, RG 76, vol. 1258, file 5850-3-4-650, "Ugandan Asian Expellees: The First Twelve Months in Canada," October 1976, 75.

177　Adams and Jesudason, "Employment," 464.

178　Ross Henderson, "Canada Took in Cream of Asian Refugees from Uganda Sociologists Report," *Globe and Mail*, 5 July 1975, 1.

179　Dirks, *Canada's Refugee Policy*, 243.

180　Whitaker, *Double Standard*, 255.

181　Henderson, "Canada Took in Cream of Asian Refugees from Uganda Sociologists Report," 1.

182　Peter Desberats, "Asian Airlift Efficient, Humane," *Vancouver Sun*, 7 November 1972, 10.

183　LAC, Records of the Immigration Branch, RG 76, vol. 1258, file 5850-3-5-650, A.E. Gotlieb, "Ugandan Asians—Press Briefing by British Community Relations Commission," 7 July 1975, 3.

184　Canada Showed Heart on Ugandans," *Toronto Star*, 27 July 1978, in Lalani, *Ugandan Asian Expulsion*, 160.

185　Henderson, "Canada Took in Cream of Asian Refugees from Uganda Sociologists Report," 1.

186　Henderson, "Canada Took in Cream of Asian Refugees from Uganda Sociologists Report," 1.

187 LAC, Records of the Immigration Branch, RG 76, vol. 990, file 5850-3-650, "Report Respecting the Special Movement of Ugandan Asians," 19 October 1972, 6.

188 One could speculate that since Ismailis made up a large proportion of arrivals, they would sponsor a large number of family members in transit centres.

189 LAC, Records of the Immigration Branch, RG 76, vol. 1258, file 5850-3-5-650, V.A. Latour, "Ugandan Expellees—Expenditures," 10 November 1972, 2.

Chapter 6: From Refugees to Citizens

1 Knowles, *Strangers at Our Gates*, 208.

2 Knowles, 208.

3 Knowles, 217.

4 Kelley and Trebilcock, *Making of the Mosaic*, 380.

5 Kelley and Trebilcock, 415.

6 Kelley and Trebilcock, 221–23.

7 Diab, "Fear and Vulnerability."

8 Casswell, "Singh," 356–60; Lamey, *Frontier Justice*.

9 Knowles, *Strangers at Our Gates*, 288.

10 Kelley and Trebilcock, *Making of the Mosaic*, 441.

11 Kelley and Trebilcock, 425.

12 Kelley and Trebilcock, 457.

13 Kelley and Trebilcock, 380–81.

14 Kelley and Trebilcock, 418–19.

15 Buchignani, Indra, and Srivastava, *Continuous Journey*, 205; Johnston, *East Indians*, 16.

16 Shamim Muhammedi, interviewed by S. Muhammedi, 2014.

17 Shamim Muhammedi, interviewed by S. Muhammedi, 2014.

18 Tom and Joan Francis, interviewed by S. Muhammedi, 2015.

19 Errol and Delphine Francis, interviewed by S. Muhammedi, 2015.

20 Errol and Delphine Francis, interviewed by S. Muhammedi, 2015.

21 Shiraz Lalani, interviewed by S. Muhammedi, 2014.

22 Nimira Charania, interviewed by S. Muhammedi, 2014.

23 Saunders, *Journey into Hope*.

24 Zul Devji, interviewed by S. Muhammedi, 2014.

25 Amin and Farida Sunderji, interviewed by S. Muhammedi, 2015.

26 Amin and Farida Sunderji, interviewed by S. Muhammedi, 2015.

27 Murray J. Munro argues that accent discrimination in Canada manifests in three dynamic ways, including biased hiring decisions, denial of access to employment or rental properties, and harassment or ridicule of the speaker's pronunciation. See Munro, "Primer." For more on the impacts of accent discrimination, see Creese and Kambere, "What Colour," and Norton, *Identity and Language Learning*.

28 Munira Dhanani, interviewed by S. Muhammedi, 2015.

29 Basran, "Indo-Canadian Families," 345.

30 Shamim Muhammedi, interviewed by S. Muhammedi, 2014.

31 Shamim Muhammedi, interviewed by S. Muhammedi, 2014.

32   Aminmohamed Jamal, interviewed by S. Muhammedi, 2014.

33   Edmond and Maria Rodrigues, interviewed by S. Muhammedi, 2015.

34   Edmond and Maria Rodrigues, interviewed by S. Muhammedi, 2015.

35   Sikandar, interviewed by S. Muhammedi, 2015.

36   Sikandar, interviewed by S. Muhammedi, 2015.

37   Brah, *Cartographies of Diaspora*, 3.

38   Brah, 3.

39   Buchignani, Indra, and Srivastava, *Continuous Journey*, 215.

40   Karim Nanji, interviewed by S. Muhammedi, 2015.

41   Amin Visram, interviewed by S. Muhammedi, 2015.

42   Johnston, *East Indians*, 21.

43   Johnston, 21.

44   Aminmohamed and Begum Jamal, interviewed by S. Muhammedi, 2014.

45   Karim Nanji, interviewed by S. Muhammedi, 2015.

46   Amin Visram, interviewed by S. Muhammedi, 2015.

47   Agnew, introduction to *Diaspora, Memory, and Identity*, 9.

48   Moghissi, Rahnema, and Goodman, *Diaspora by Design*, 7.

49   Agnew, introduction to *Diaspora, Memory, and Identity*, 3.

50   Burke, "History as Social Memory," 98.

51   Burke, 100.

52   Zul Hirji and Shaffin Shariff, "Journey into Hope: A Chronicle of the Ugandan Asian Migration," *The Ismaili Canada*, Fall 1994, 14.

53   Halani, "Flight of Courage," 8.

54   Crowl, *30th Anniversary Celebration*.

55   Halani, "Flight of Courage," 9.

56   Drummond, "Asians Return to Hope and Hostility in Uganda," *Los Angeles Times*, 17 August 1993, in Lalani, *Ugandan Asian Expulsion*, 161.

57   Drummond, 161.

58   Sudhir Ruparelia, "From the Kampala Institute, 2010," *Kampala Goan Institute 100th Anniversary*, June 2010, 7.

59   Zul Hirji and Shaffin Shariff, "Journey into Hope: A Chronicle of the Ugandan Asian Migration," *The Ismaili Canada*, Fall 1994, 14.

60   Halani, "Flight of Courage," 11.

61   Crowl, *30th Anniversary Celebration*.

62   Zul Hirji and Shaffin Shariff, "Journey into Hope: A Chronicle of the Ugandan Asian Migration," *The Ismaili Canada*, Fall 1994, 14.

63   Saunders, *Journey into Hope*.

64   Halani, "Flight of Courage," 9.

65   Errol and Delphine Francis, interviewed by S. Muhammedi, 2015.

66   Nazir Walji, interviewed by S. Muhammedi, 2015.

67   Aziz Fakirani, Khaerun Lalany, and Azad Lalany, interviewed by S. Muhammedi, 2015.

68   Jalal Jaffer, interviewed by S. Muhammedi, 2015.

69   Klempner, "Life Review Interviews," 201.

70   Halani, "Flight of Courage," 9.

71   Crowl, *30th Anniversary Celebration*.

72   Catherine Kitts, "Carleton Thanks the Fakirani Family for Its Donation to the Ugandan Asian Archives," Carleton University, https://futurefunder.carleton.ca/carleton-thanks-the-fakirani-family-for-its-donation-to-the-ugandan-asian-archives.

73   Catherine Kitts, "Carleton Thanks the Fakirani Family."

74   John Nazareth, "Celebrating Ugandans Who Have Excelled in Canada," *Uganda 50 Years of Independence*, 2012, 4.

75   Naresh Majithia, "Welcome From the Chairman," *Uganda 50 Years of Independence*, 2012, 3.

76   Ristovski-Slijepcevic, Chapman, and Beagan, "Good Mother."

77   Ristovski-Slijepcevic, Chapman, and Beagan, 469.

78   Umedaly, *Mamajee's Kitchen*, 178.

79   Regrettably, Umedaly was unable to do an interview with me as she was out of the country during the time of my research. She did, however, participate in an oral history interview conducted by Emily Burton in 2014. See Canadian Museum of Immigration at Pier 21, "Oral History 14.02.21USLU with Umeeda Switlo and Lella Umedaly," https://pier21.ca/content/oral-history-140221uslu-with-umeeda-switlo-and-lella-umedaly.

80   Epp, "Eating Across Borders," 51.

81   Alibhai-Brown, *Settler's Cookbook*, 49.

82   Alibhai-Brown, 62.

83   Rossbina Nathoo, interviewed by S. Muhammedi, 2015.

84   Laila Jiwani, interviewed by S. Muhammedi, 2015.

85   Umedaly, *Mamajee's Kitchen*, 168.

86   Shiraz Lalani, interviewed by S. Muhammedi, 2015.

87   Alibhai-Brown, *Settler's Cookbook*, 165.

88   Gabaccia, *We Are What We Eat*.

89   Tom and Joan Francis, interviewed by S. Muhammedi, 2015.

90   Tom and Joan Francis, interviewed by S. Muhammedi, 2015.

91   Azim Sarangi, interviewed by S. Muhammedi, 2015.

92   Umedaly, *Mamajee's Kitchen*, 2.

93   Nimira Charania, interviewed by S. Muhammedi, 2014.

94   Ristovski-Slijepcevic, Chapman, and Beagan, "Healthy Eating," 171.

95   Umedaly, *Mamajee's Kitchen*, 178.

96   Shamim Muhammedi, interviewed by S. Muhammedi, 2014.

97   Jitu Tanna, interviewed by S. Muhammedi, 2015.

98   Aminmohamed Jamal, interviewed by S. Muhammedi, 2014.

99   John Halani, interviewed by S. Muhammedi, 2015.

100 Aminmohamed Jamal, interviewed by S. Muhammedi, 2014.

101 Zulfikar Devji, interviewed by S. Muhammedi, 2014.

102 Abidah Lalani, "Ours to Discover: Toronto," *The Ismaili Canada*, Summer 2014, 59.

103 Crowl, *30th Anniversary Celebration.*

104 Frideres, "Aboriginal Identity," 318.

105 Shamim Muhammedi, interviewed by S. Muhammedi, 2014.

106 John Nazareth, "Celebrating Ugandans Who Have Excelled in Canada," *Uganda 50 Years of Independence*, 2012, 21.

107 See Frideres, "Aboriginal Identity"; Green, "Complexity"; and Medina and Whitla, "(An)Other Canada."

108 Medina and Whitla, "(An)Other Canada," 19.

109 Diamond Akbarali, interviewed by S. Muhammedi, 2015.

110 Mohamed and Almas Lalji, interviewed by S. Muhammedi, 2015.

111 Mumtaz, interviewed by S. Muhammedi, 2015.

112 Sikandar, interviewed by S. Muhammedi, 2015.

113 Nimira Charania, interviewed by S. Muhammedi, 2014.

114 Nimira Charania, interviewed by S. Muhammedi, 2014.

115 Nimira Charania, interviewed by S. Muhammedi, 2014.

116 John Nazareth, interviewed by S. Muhammedi, 2015.

117 Zaina and Altaf Sovani, interviewed by S. Muhammedi, 2015.

118 Jalal Jaffer, interviewed by S. Muhammedi, 2015.

119 John Nazareth, interviewed by S. Muhammedi, 2015.

120 John Nazareth, interviewed by S. Muhammedi, 2015.

121 Errol and Delphine Francis, interviewed by S. Muhammedi, 2015.

122 Zaina and Altaf Sovani, interviewed by S. Muhammedi, 2015.

123 Karim Nanji, interviewed by S. Muhammedi, 2015.

124 Bissoondath, *Selling Illusions*, 105.

125 Amin Visram, interviewed by S. Muhammedi, 2015.

126 Frenz, "Global Goans," 185.

127 Terrence Francis, interviewed by S. Muhammedi, 2015.

128 Terrence Francis, interviewed by S. Muhammedi, 2015.

129 Edmond and Maria Rodrigues, interviewed by S. Muhammedi, 2015.

130 Edmond and Maria Rodrigues, interviewed by S. Muhammedi, 2015.

131 Nimira Charania, interviewed by S. Muhammedi, 2014.

132 Zaina and Altaf Sovani, interviewed by S. Muhammedi, 2015.

133 Zulfikar Devji, interviewed by S. Muhammedi, 2014.

134 Rossbina Nathoo, interviewed by S. Muhammedi, 2015.

135 Tastsoglou and Miedema, "But Where Are You From," 87.

136 Somji, *Memoirs and Autobiography*, 42.

137 UNHCR, "Refugee Family Makes $1 Million Gift to UNHCR as They Commemorate Their 50 Years in Canada."

138 Somji, 42. Further examples of his voluntary commitments include serving on North Vancouver District Council's Local Court of Revision Committee for twelve years, being a member of the Social Planning and Advisory Committee in North Vancouer and part of the Public Involvement Program.

139 Halani, "Consulate of Uganda," 5–12.

Conclusion

1   For further reading, see Abouguendia and Noels, "Daily Hassles"; Beharry and Crozier, "Using Phenomenology"; Chariandy, "Fiction of Belonging"; Chuang and Moreno, *Immigrant Children*; Faulkner, *Economic Mobility*; Kasinitz, Mollenkopf, and Waters, *Becoming New Yorkers*; Plaza, "Construction"; and Reitz and Zhang, "National and Urban Contexts."

2   Beharry and Crozier, "Using Phenomenology."

3   Abouguendia and Noels, "Daily Hassles"; Beharry and Crozier, "Using Phenomenology"; Brettell and Nibbs, "Lived Hybridity"; Chariandy, "Fiction of Belonging"; Plaza, "Construction."

4   "Canada Rolls Back Refugee Protection: Bill C-31 Receives Royal Assent," Canadian Council for Refugees, 29 June 2012, http://ccrweb.ca/en/bulletin/12/06/29.

5   Debra Black, "Legal Advocacy Groups Launch Constitutional Challenge Thursday, Arguing Bill C-24 Creates Discriminatory 'Two-tier Citizenship Regime,'" *Toronto Star*, 20 August 2015, http://www.thestar.com/news/immigration/2015/08/20/court-challenge-slams-new-citizenship-act-as-anti-canadian.html.

6   Canada, "Changes to the Citizenship Act."

7   Bahrami, "Critical Review."

8   Canada, *House of Commons Debates*, 20th Parliament, 3rd Session, Vol. 3, 1 May 1947, 2644–46.

9   "No, Refugees in Canada Do Not Receive More Money from the Government Than Retired Citizens," AFP Fact Check, 16 October 2018, https://factcheck.afp.com/no-refugees-canada-do-not-receive-more-money-government-retired-citizens.

10 Canada, "Do Government-Assisted Refugees."

11 David Agren, "Remain in Mexico: Migrants Face Deadly Peril as Biden restores Trump Policy," *Guardian*, 3 December 2021, https://www.theguardian.com/world/2021/dec/03/remain-in-mexico-migrants-face-deadly-peril-as-biden-restores-trump-policy.

12 For more on the EU-Turkey deal, see "EU-Turkey Joint Action Plan," European Commission, 15 October 2015, https://ec.europa.eu/commission/presscorner/detail/en/MEMO_15_5860.

13 "EU-Turkey Statement, 18 March 2016 - Consilium," European Commission, 18 March 2016, https://www.consilium.europa.eu/en/press/press-releases/2016/03/18/eu-turkey-statement; "Texts Adopted—The Situation in the Mediterranean and the Need for a Holistic EU Approach to Migration," European Parliament, 12 April 2016, http://www.europarl.europa.eu/doceo/document/TA-8-2016-0102_EN.html.

14 UNHCR, *Global Trends*, 1.

15 UN General Assembly, Resolution 71/1.

16 UN General Assembly, *Report of the United Nations High Commissioner for Refugees*.

17 UNHCR, "Press Conference by Secretary-General António Guterres."

18 Jynnah Radford and Philip Connor, "Canada Now Leads the World in Refugee Resettlement, Surpassing the U.S.," *Pew Research Center*, 19 June 2019, https://www.pewresearch.org/fact-tank/2019/06/19/canada-now-leads-the-world-in-refugee-resettlement-surpassing-the-u-s.

BIBLIOGRAPHY

Archival Sources

Library and Archives Canada. Department of External Affairs fonds. RG 25, vol. 3146. "Visit of Prince Sadruddin Aga Khan, United Nations High Commissioner for Refugees—Briefing Notes."

———. Department of External Affairs fonds. RG 25, vol. 8794. "Political Affairs—Policy Background - Canadian External Policy and Relations—Uganda."

———. Department of External Affairs fonds. RG 25, vol. 13668. "Refugees—Organization and Conferences—United Nations High Commission for Refugees (UNHCR)—Policy and Programmes—Africa."

———. Department of External Affairs fonds. RG 25, vol. 13668. "Refugees—Organization and Conferences—United Nations High Commission for Refugees (UNHCR)—Executive Committee—23rd to 25th Sessions."

———. Department of National Health and Welfare fonds. RG 29, vol. 3090. "Medical Examination of Immigrants—Uganda."

———. Department of National Health and Welfare fonds. RG 29, vol. 3424. "Immigration Medical Service—Medical Examination of Immigrants—Uganda."

———. Immigration Branch fonds. RG 76, vol. 948. "Submission to Cabinet."

———. Immigration Branch fonds. RG 76, vol. 990. "Selection and Processing—General Series—Immigration from Uganda."

———. Immigration Branch fonds. RG 76, vol. 1214. "Ismailis."

———. Immigration Branch fonds. RG 76, vol. 1257. "Uganda."

———. Immigration Branch fonds. RG 76, vol. 1258. "Transportation."

———. Immigration Branch fonds. RG 76, vol. 1258. "Uganda Research."

———. Immigration Branch fonds. RG 76, vol. 1258. "Publicity."

———. Immigration Branch fonds. RG 76, vol. 1259. "Statistics."

————. Immigration Branch fonds. RG 76, vol. 1259. "Uganda Asian Committees."

————. Immigration Branch fonds. RG 76, vol. 1259. "Letters of Appreciation."

————. Immigration Branch fonds. RG 76, vol. 1259. "Selection and Processing—General Series—Uganda—Political Refugees."

————. Immigration Branch fonds. RG 76, vol. 1386. "Refugees—General."

————. Pierre Elliott Trudeau fonds. MG 26, vols. 481. "1969–1985 PMO General Correspondence."

————. Pierre Elliott Trudeau fonds. MG 26, vol. 45. "Correspondence 1972."

————. Pierre Elliott Trudeau fonds. MG 26, vol. 54. "Subject 131-140."

————. Privy Council Fonds. RG 2, vol. 6395. "Immigration to Canada of Asian Expellees from Uganda."

Interviews

Ahmed, Nellie, and Sadru Ahmed. Interviewed by S. Muhammedi. Vancouver, 24 June 2015.

Akbarali, Diamond. Interviewed by S. Muhammedi. Calgary, 21 July 2015.

Charania, Nimira. Interviewed by S. Muhammedi. Ottawa, 6 August 2014.

Dattani, Vinnay. Interviewed by S. Muhammedi. Calgary, 29 July 2015.

Devji, Zulfikar. Interviewed by S. Muhammedi. Ottawa, 20 August 2014.

Dhalla, Aziz. Interviewed by S. Muhammedi. Ottawa, 24 December 2014.

Dhanani, Munira. Interviewed by S. Muhammedi. Toronto, 15 February 2015.

Dossa, Zabina. Interviewed by S. Muhammedi. Ottawa, 10 June 2015.

Fakirani, Aziz, Khaerun Lalany, and Azad Lalany. Interviewed by S. Muhammedi. Vancouver, 8 July 2015.

Francis, Delphine, and Errol Francis. Interviewed by S. Muhammedi. Toronto, 17 April 2015.

Francis, Joan, and Tom Francis. Interviewed by S. Muhammedi. Toronto, 8 May 2015.

Francis, Terrence. Interviewed by S. Muhammedi. Vancouver, 3 July 2015.

Gomes, Pio. Interviewed by S. Muhammedi. Toronto, 12 May 2015.

Halani, John. Interviewed by S. Muhammedi. Vancouver, 21 June 2015.

Iqbal [pseud.]. Interviewed by S. Muhammedi. Edmonton, 9 August 2015.

Jamal, Aminmohamed. Interviewed by S. Muhammedi. Ottawa, 13 August 2014.

Jaffer, Jalal. Interviewed by S. Muhammedi. Vancouver, 7 July 2015.

Jaffer, Mobina. Interviewed by S. Muhammedi. Vancouver, 13 July 2015.

Jiwani, Laila. Interviewed by S. Muhammedi. Toronto, 14 May 2015.

Lakhani, Sudha, and Vassant Lakhani. Interviewed by S. Muhammedi. Vancouver, 13 July 2015.

Lalani, Shiraz. Interviewed by S. Muhammedi. Toronto, 25 April 2015.

Lalji, Almas, and Mohamed Lalji. Interviewed by S. Muhammedi. Toronto, 12 May 2015.

Molloy, Michael. Interviewed by Heather LeRoux. Ottawa, 13 August 2014. The Ugandan Asian Archive Oral History Project, Archives and Research Collections, Carleton University Library. https://arc.library.carleton.ca/sites/default/files/audio/UAC_Molloy_Transcript_0.pdf.

Molloy, Michael. Interviewed by S. Muhammedi. Ottawa, 13 August 2014.

Muhammedi, Shamim. Interviewed by S. Muhammedi. Ottawa, 21 August 2014.

Mumtaz [pseud.]. Interviewed by S. Muhammedi. Calgary, 29 July 2015.

Nanji, Karim. Interviewed by S. Muhammedi. Toronto, 24 April 2015.

Nathoo, Rossbina. Interviewed by S. Muhammedi. Calgary, 20 July 2015.

Nazareth, John. Interviewed by S. Muhammedi. Toronto, 21 March 2015.

Rodrigues, Edmond, and Maria Rodrigues. Interviewed by S. Muhammedi. Toronto, 11 May 2015.

Sarangi, Azim. Interviewed by S. Muhammedi. Vancouver, 15 July 2015.

Sikandar [pseud.]. Interviewed by S. Muhammedi. Edmonton, 4 August 2015.

Sovani, Altaf, and Zaina Sovani. Interviewed by S. Muhammedi. Ottawa, 16 February 2015.

St. Vincent, Roger. Interviewed by S. Muhammedi. Montreal, 30 October 2015.

Sunderji, Amin, and Farida Sunderji. Interviewed by S. Muhammedi. Vancouver, 22 June 2015.

Tanna, Jitu. Interviewed by S. Muhammedi. Toronto, 9 May 2015.

Umedali, Nanji. Interviewed by S. Muhammedi. Calgary, 27 July 2015.

Umedaly, Mossadiq. Interviewed by S. Muhammedi. Vancouver, 30 June 2015.

Visram, Amin. Interviewed by S. Muhammedi. Kitchener, 2 March 2015.

Walji, Nazir. Interviewed by S. Muhammedi. Calgary, 29 July 2015.

Magazines

The Ismaili Canada

Kampala Goan Institute 100th Anniversary

Maclean's

Newspapers

Daily Nation (Kenya)

Globe and Mail (Canada)

Nationalist (Kenya)

New York Times (USA)

Toronto Star (Canada)

Uganda Argus (Uganda)

Uganda Herald (Uganda)

Vancouver Sun (Canada)

Windsor Star (Canada)

Government and United Nations Publications

Canada. *House of Commons Debates.* 20th Parliament, 3rd Session. Vol. 3.

———. *House of Commons Debates.* 28th Parliament, 3rd Session. Vol. 8.

———. *House of Commons Debates.* 28th Parliament, 4th Session. Vols. 1–4.

———. "Changes to the Citizenship Act as a Result of Bill C-6." Immigration, Refugees and Citizenship Canada. 22 August 2018. https://www.canada.ca/en/immigration-refugees-citizenship/news/2017/10/changes_to_the_citizenshipactasaresultofbillc-6.html.

———. "Do Government-Assisted Refugees Get More Income Support and Benefits than Canadian Pensioners Do?" Immigration, Refugees and Citizenship Canada. 7 November 2012. http://www.cic.gc.ca/english/helpcentre/answer.asp?qnum=105&top=11.

———. "The Surge of Women in the Workforce." Statistics Canada, 17 December 2015. http://www.statcan.gc.ca/pub/11-630-x/11-630-x2015009-eng.htm.

UN General Assembly. *Report of the United Nations High Commissioner for Refugees: Part II Global Compact on Refugees.* 2018. https://www.unhcr.org/gcr/GCR_English.pdf.

———. Resolution 71/1, New York Declaration for Refugees and Migrants, A/RES/71/1. 3 October 2016. https://www.un.org/en/ga/search/view_doc.asp?symbol=A/RES/71/1.

UNHCR. *Convention and Protocol Relating to the Status of Refugees.* 2010. https://www.unhcr.org/protection/basic/3b66c2aa10/convention-protocol-relating-status-refugees.html.

———. *Global Trends: Forced Displacement in 2020.* 2021. https://www.unhcr.org/60b638e37/unhcr-global-trends-2020.

———. "Less than 5 Per Cent of Global Refugee Resettlement Needs Met Last Year." 6 February 2021. https://www.unhcr.org/news/briefing/2019/2/5c6bc9704/5-cent-global-refugee-resettlement-needs-met-year.html.

———. "Press Conference by Secretary-General António Guterres at United Nations Headquarters," 18 January 2019. https://www.un.org/press/en/2019/sgsm19436.doc.htm.

———. "Refugee Family Makes $1 Million Gift to UNHCR as They Commemorate Their 50 Years in Canada." 14 April 2022. https://www.unhcr.ca/news/refugee-family-gift-unhcr-commemorate-50-years-in-canada/.

Other Primary Sources

Crowl, Victor, dir. *30th Anniversary Celebration: Ugandan Refugees A Canadian Success Story.* Ottawa: S.M.F. Productions, 2002, DVD.

Halani, John. "Consulate of Uganda 2012 Annual Report." Vancouver, BC: Consulate of Uganda, 2012.

———. "Flight of Courage: Commemorating 25 Years of Ugandan Settlement in Canada." Canada Uganda Association. 30 May 1998.

Lalani, Z. *Ugandan Asian Expulsion: 90 Days and Beyond Through the Eyes of the International Press.* Tampa, FL: Expulsion Publications, 1997.

Saunders, Richard, dir. *Journey into Hope*. Ottawa: 1994, videocassette.

Somji, Noordin. *Memoirs and Autobiography of Noordin Somji*. Vancouver, BC: self-published, 2006.

Secondary Sources

Abouguendia, Mona, and Kimberly A. Noels. "General and Acculturation-Related Daily Hassles and Psychological Adjustment in First- and Second-Generation South Asian Immigrants to Canada." *International Journal of Psychology* 36, no. 3 (2001): 163–73.

Adams, Bert N. "The Kin Network and the Adjustment of the Ugandan Asians." *Journal of Marriage and Family* 36, no. 1 (1974): 190–95.

Adams, Bert, and Mike Bristow. "Ugandan Asian Expulsion Experiences: Rumour and Reality." *Journal of Asian and African Studies* 14, no. 3 (1979): 191–203.

Adams, Bert N., and Victor Jesudason. "The Employment of Ugandan Asian Refugees in Britain, Canada, and India." *Ethnic and Racial Studies* 7, no. 4 (1984): 462–76.

Adelman, Howard. *Canada and the Indochinese Refugees*. Regina, SK: L.A. Weigl Educational Associates, 1982.

———. "An Immigration Dream: Hungarian Refugees Come to Canada—An Analysis." In *Breaking Ground: The 1956 Hungarian Refugee Movement to Canada*, edited by Robert H. Keyserlingk, 25–41. Toronto: York Lanes Press, 1993.

Agnew, Vijay, ed. *Diaspora, Memory, and Identity: A Search for Home*. Toronto: University of Toronto Press, 2005.

Alibhai-Brown, Yasmin. *The Settler's Cookbook: A Memoir of Love, Migration and Food*. London: Portobello Books, 2012.

Allen, Richard B. "Satisfying the 'Want for Labouring People': European Slave Trading in the Indian Ocean, 1500–1850." *Journal of World History* 21, no. 1 (March 2010): 45–73.

Amin, Idi. "Speech at Meeting of Asian Leaders in Uganda." In *Case Studies on Human Rights and Fundamental Freedoms: A World Survey*, Vol. 4, edited by Willem Adriaan Veenhoven and Winifred Crum Ewing, 211–215. The Hague, Netherlands: Nijhoff, 1975.

Amor, Meir. "Violent Ethnocentrism: Revisiting the Economic Interpretation of the Expulsion of Ugandan Asians." *Identity: An International Journal of Theory and Research* 3, no. 1 (2003): 53–66.

Anderson, Christopher G. *Canadian Liberalism and the Politics of Border Control, 1867–1967*. Vancouver: UBC Press, 2013.

Anderson, Christopher G., and Jerome H. Black. "The Political Integration of Newcomers, Minorities, and the Canadian Born: Perspectives on Naturalization, Participation, and Representation." In *Immigration and Integration in Canada in the Twenty-First Century*, edited by John Biles, Meyer Burstein, and James Frideres, 45–75. Kingston, ON: McGill-Queen's University Press, 2008.

Avirgan, Tony, and Martha Honey. *War in Uganda: The Legacy of Idi Amin*. Westport, CT: Lawrence Hill, 1982.

Bahrami, Somayeh. "Critical Review of the New Canadian Citizenship Law Bill C-24." *Bilingual Corner* (blog). Simon Fraser University, 6 December 2014. http://www.sfu.ca/education/cels/bilingual/bilingual-corner/bill-c-24.html.

Bangarth, Stephanie. "Citizen Activism, Refugees, and the State: Two Case-Studies in Canadian Immigration History." In *Modern Canada: 1945 to the Present,* edited by Catherine Briggs, 17–30. Toronto: Oxford University Press, 2014.

Barnett, Teresa, and Chon A. Noriega, eds. *Oral History and Communities of Color.* Los Angeles: UCLA Chicano Studies Research Center Press, 2013.

Barungi, Baganchwera. *Parliamentary Democracy in Uganda: The Experiment That Failed.* Bloomington, IN: AuthorHouse, 2011.

Basran, G.S. "Indo-Canadian Families: Historical Constraints and Contemporary Contradictions." *Journal of Comparative Family Studies* 24, no. 3 (October 1993): 339–52.

Beharry, Pauline, and Sharon Crozier. "Using Phenomenology to Understand Experiences of Racism for Second-Generation South Asian Women." *Canadian Journal of Counselling* 42, no. 4 (2008): 262–77.

Beiser, Morton. *Strangers at the Gate: The "Boat People's" First Ten Years in Canada.* Toronto: University of Toronto Press, 1999.

Belshaw, John Douglas. *Canadian History: Post-Confederation.* Victoria: BCcampus, 2016. https://opentextbc.ca/postconfederation/.

Bissoondath, Neil. *Selling Illusions: The Cult of Multiculturalism in Canada.* Rev. ed. Toronto: Penguin, 2002.

Bloemraad, Irene. "Citizenship and Immigration: A Current Review." *Journal of International Migration and Integration* 1, no. 1 (2000): 9–37.

Bonikowska, Aneta, and Feng Hou. "Reversal of Fortunes or Continued Success? Cohort Differences in Education and Earnings of Childhood Immigrants." *The International Migration Review* 44, no. 2 (2010): 320–53.

Brah, Avtar. *Cartographies of Diaspora: Contesting Identities.* London: Routledge, 1996.

Brettell, Caroline B., and Faith Nibbs. "Lived Hybridity: Second-Generation Identity Construction Through College Festival." *Identities: Global Studies in Culture and Power* 16, no. 6 (2009): 678–99.

Brodie, Janine. "An Elusive Search for Community: Globalization and the Canadian National Identity." *Review of Constitutional Studies* 7, no. 1–2 (2002): 155–78.

Brown, Judith M. *Global South Asians: Introducing the Modern Diaspora.* Cambridge: Cambridge University Press, 2006.

Buchignani, Norman, Doreen Marie Indra, and Ram Srivastava. *Continuous Journey: A Social History of South Asians in Canada.* Toronto: McClelland and Stewart, 1985.

Bumsted, J.M. *A History of the Canadian Peoples.* 4th ed. Toronto: Oxford University Press, 2011.

Burke, Peter. "History as Social Memory." In *Memory: History, Culture and the Mind,* edited by Thomas Butler, 97–113. Oxford: Basil Blackwell, 1989.

Buzdugan, Raluca, and Shiva S. Halli. "Labor Market Experiences of Canadian Immigrants with Focus on Foreign Education and Experience." *The International Migration Review* 43, no. 2 (2009): 366–86.

Campbell, Gwyn, ed. *The Structure of Slavery in Indian Ocean Africa and Asia.* London: Frank Cass, 2004.

Casswell, Donald G. "Singh v. Minister of Employment and Immigration Case Comments and Notes." *Alberta Law Review* 24 (1986): 356–60.

Chan, Kwok B., and Doreen Marie Indra, eds. *Uprooting, Loss and Adaptation: The Resettlement of Indochinese Refugees in Canada*. Ottawa: Canadian Public Health Association, 1987.

Chariandy, David. " 'The Fiction of Belonging': On Second-Generation Black Writing in Canada." *Callaloo* 30, no. 3 (2007): 818–29.

Chuang, Susan S., and Robert P. Moreno, eds. *Immigrant Children: Change, Adaptation, and Cultural Transformation*. Lanham, MD: Lexington Books, 2011.

Churchill, Winston. *My African Journey*. London: Hodder and Stoughton, 1908.

Clarkson, Adrienne. *Room for All of Us: Surprising Stories of Loss and Transformation*. Toronto: Allen Lane Canada, 2011.

Cohen, Rina, and Guida Man, eds. *Engendering Transnational Voices: Studies in Family, Work, and Identity*. Waterloo, ON: Wilfrid Laurier University Press, 2015.

Cosemans, Sara. "The Politics of Dispersal: Turning Ugandan Colonial Subjects into Postcolonial Refugees (1967-76)." *Migration Studies*, 6, no.1 (March 2018): 99–199.

Creese, Gillian, and Edith Ngene Kambere. " 'What Colour Is Your English?' " *Canadian Review of Sociology* 40, no. 5 (2003): 565–73.

Cruikshank, Julie. *Do Glaciers Listen?: Local Knowledge, Colonial Encounters, and Social Imagination*. Vancouver: UBC Press, 2005.

Denoon, Donald. "The Historical Setting to 1900." In *Uganda: The Dilemma of Nationhood*, edited by G.N. Uzoigwe, 17–56. New York: NOK Publishers International, 1982.

Diab, Suha. "Between Fear and Vulnerability: The Emergence of the Humanitarian Security-Nexus in the Canadian Refugee Protection Regime." PhD diss., Carleton University, 2014.

Dirks, Gerald E. "Canada and Immigration: International and Domestic Considerations in the Decade Preceding the 1956 Hungarian Exodus." In *Breaking Ground: The 1956 Hungarian Refugee Movement to Canada*, edited by Robert H. Keyserlingk, 3–12. Toronto: York Lanes Press, 1993.

———. *Canada's Refugee Policy: Indifference or Opportunism?* Montreal: McGill-Queen's University Press, 1977.

Don Nanjira, Daniel D.C. *The Status of Aliens in East Africa: Asians and Europeans in Tanzania, Uganda, and Kenya*. New York: Praeger, 1976.

Doornbos, Martin R. "Ugandan Society and Politics: A Background." In *Uganda: The Dilemma of Nationhood*, edited by G.N. Uzoigwe, 3–16. New York: NOK Publishers International, 1982.

Dreisziger, N.F. "The Refugee Experience in Canada and the Evolution of the Hungarian Canadian Community." In *Breaking Ground: The 1956 Hungarian Refugee Movement to Canada*, edited by Robert H. Keyserlingk, 65–85. Toronto: York Lanes Press, 1993.

Earle, Neil. "Hockey as Canadian Popular Culture: Team Canada 1972, Television and the Canadian Identity." *Journal of Canadian Studies* 30, no. 2 (1995): 107–23.

Epp, Marlene. "Eating across Borders: Reading Immigrant Cookbooks." *Social History* 48, no. 96 (2015): 45–65.

————. *Refugees in Canada: A Brief History*. Immigration and Ethnicity in Canada Series, booklet no. 35. Ottawa: Canadian Historical Association, 2017.

Faulkner, Caroline L. *Economic Mobility and Cultural Assimilation among Children of Immigrants*. El Paso, TX: LFB Scholarly Publishing, 2011.

Field, Sean. " 'What Can I do When the Interviewee Cries?': Oral History Strategies for Containment and Regeneration." In *Oral History in a Wounded Country: Interactive Interview in South Africa*, edited by Philippe Denis and Radikobo Ntsimane, 144–68. Scottsville, South Africa: University of KwaZulu-Natal Press, 2008.

Forbes, Donald Hugh. "Trudeau as the First Theorist of Canadian Multiculturalism." In *Multiculturalism and the Canadian Constitution*, edited by Stephen Tierney, 27–42. Vancouver: UBC Press, 2007.

Forster, Peter G., Michael Hitchcock, and F.F. Lyimo. *Race and Ethnicity in East Africa*. Basingstoke, UK: Macmillan Press, 2000.

Foster, Kate A. *Our Canadian Mosaic*. Toronto: Dominion Council, 1926.

Frenz, Margret. "Global Goans: Migration Movements and Identity in a Historical Perspective." *Lusotopie* 15, no. 1 (2008): 183–202.

————. "Migration, Identity and Post-Colonial Change in Uganda: A Goan Perspective." *Immigrants and Minorities* 31, no. 1 (2013): 48–73.

————. "Transimperial Connections: East African Goan Perspectives on 'Goa 1961.'" *Contemporary South Asia* 22, no. 3 (2014): 240–54.

Freund, Alexander. "Toward an Ethics of Silence? Negotiating Off-the-Record Events and Identity in Oral History." In *Oral History Off the Record: Toward an Ethnography of Practice*, edited by Anna Sheftel and Stacey Zembrzycki, 223–238. New York: Palgrave MacMillan, 2013.

Frideres, James. "Aboriginal Identity in the Canadian Context." *Canadian Journal of Native Studies* XXVII, no. 2 (2008): 313–42.

Frideres, James S., Meyer Burstein, and John Biles, eds. *Immigration and Integration in Canada in the Twenty-First Century*. Kingston, ON: McGill-Queen's University Press, 2008.

Frisch, Michael. *A Shared Authority: Essays on the Craft and Meaning of Oral and Public History*. Albany: State University of New York Press, 1990.

Gabaccia, Donna R. *We Are What We Eat: Ethnic Food and the Making of Americans*. Cambridge, MA: Harvard University Press, 1998.

Ghai, Yash P. "The Future Prospects." In *Portrait of a Minority: Asians in East Africa*, revised edition, edited by Dharam P. Ghai and Yash P. Ghai, 170–227. Nairobi: Oxford University Press, 1970.

Gibbon, John Murray. *Canadian Mosaic: The Making of a Northern Nation*. Toronto: McClelland and Stewart, 1938.

Gilkinson, Tara, and Genevieve Sauve. *Recent Immigrants, Earlier Immigrants and the Canadian Born: Association with Collective Identities*. Ottawa: Citizenship and Immigration Canada, 2010.

Granatstein, J.L., and Robert Bothwell. *Pirouette: Pierre Trudeau and Canadian Foreign Policy*. Toronto: University of Toronto Press, 1990.

Green, Joyce. "The Complexity of Indigenous Identity Formation and Politics in Canada: Self-Determination and Decolonisation." *International Journal of Critical Indigenous Studies* 2, no. 2 (2009): 36–46.

Gregory, Robert G. *The Rise and Fall of Philanthropy in East Africa: The Asian Contribution.* Piscataway, NJ: Transaction Publishers, 1992.

———. *South Asians in East Africa: An Economic and Social History, 1890–1980.* Boulder, CO: Westview Press, 1993.

Gupta, Desh. "South Asians in East Africa: Achievement and Discrimination." *South Asia: Journal of South Asian Studies* 21, no. 1 (January 1, 1998): 103–36.

Gwyn, David. *Idi Amin: Death-Light of Africa.* Boston: Little, Brown and Company, 1977.

Haddad, Emma. *The Refugee in International Society: Between Sovereigns.* Cambridge: Cambridge University Press, 2008.

Hajdukowski-Ahmed, Maroussia, Nazilla Khanlou, and Helene Moussa, eds. *Not Born a Refugee Woman: Contesting Identities, Rethinking Practices.* New York: Berghahn Books, 2008.

Hall, Stuart, David Held, Don Hubert, and Kenneth Thompson, eds. *Modernity: An Introduction to Modern Societies.* Cambridge, MA: Wiley-Blackwell, 1996.

Hansen, Holger Bernt. *Ethnicity and Military Rule in Uganda.* Uppsala: Scandinavian Institute of African Studies, 1977.

Hawkins, Freda. *Canada and Immigration: Public Policy and Public Concern.* Kingston, ON: McGill-Queen's University Press, 1988.

———. *Critical Years in Immigration: Canada and Australia Compared.* Montreal: McGill-Queen's University Press, 1991.

Henckaerts, Jean-Marie. *Mass Expulsion in Modern International Law and Practice.* Dordrecht: Martinus Nijhoff Publishers, 1995.

Herbert, Joanna. "The British Ugandan Asian Diaspora: Multiple and Contested Belongings." *Global Networks* 12, no. 3 (2012): 296–313.

———. *Negotiating Boundaries in the City: Migration, Ethnicity, and Gender in Britain.* Studies in Migration and Diaspora. Aldershot, UK: Ashgate, 2008.

———. "Oral Histories of Ugandan Asians in Britain: Gendered Identities in the Diaspora." *Contemporary South Asia* 17, no. 1 (2009): 21–32.

High, Steven. *Oral History at the Crossroads: Sharing Life Stories of Survival and Displacement.* Vancouver: UBC Press, 2014.

Hillmer, Norman. "Bernard Ostry." In *The Canadian Encyclopedia.* Article published 2 December 2007; last modified 16 December 2013. http://www.thecanadianencyclopedia.ca/en/article/bernard-ostry/.

Hirji, Zulfikar Amir. *Between Empires: Sheikh-Sir Mbarak Al-Hinawy, 1896–1959.* London: Azimuth Editions, 2012.

Hirsch, Marianne. *Family Frames: Photography, Narrative, and Postmemory.* Cambridge, MA: Harvard University Press, 1997.

Hobsbawm, E. J. *Nations and Nationalism since 1780: Programme, Myth, Reality.* Cambridge: Cambridge University Press, 1992.

Hoerder, Dirk. *Creating Societies: Immigrant Lives in Canada.* Montreal: McGill-Queen's University Press, 1999.

Hundle, Anneeth Kaur. "Exceptions to the Expulsion: Violence, Security and Community among Ugandan Asians, 1972–79." *Journal of Eastern African Studies* 7, no. 1 (2013): 164–82.

Hyndman, Jennifer. *Managing Displacement: Refugees and the Politics of Humanitarianism.* Minneapolis: University of Minnesota Press, 2000.

Iacovetta, Franca. *Gatekeepers: Reshaping Immigrant Lives in Cold War Canada.* Toronto: Between the Lines, 2006.

Iacovetta, Franca, Marlene Epp, and Valerie Joyce Korinek, eds. *Edible Histories, Cultural Politics: Towards a Canadian Food History.* Toronto: University of Toronto Press, 2012.

Jamal, Tasneem. *Where the Air Is Sweet.* Toronto: HarperCollins, 2014.

Jamal, Vali. "Asians in Uganda, 1880–1972: Inequality and Expulsion." *Economic History Review* 29, no. 4 (1976): 602–16.

Jayasuriya, Shihan de S., and Richard Pankhurst, eds. *The African Diaspora in the Indian Ocean.* Trenton, NJ: Africa World Press, 2003.

Johnston, Hugh. *The East Indians in Canada.* Ottawa: Canadian Historical Association, 1982.

Jones, Stephanie. "Merchant-Kings and Everymen: Narratives of the South Asian Diaspora of East Africa." *Journal of East African Studies* 1, no. 1 (2007): 16–33.

Jorgensen, Jan Jelmert. *Uganda: A Modern History.* New York: St. Martin's Press, 1981.

Kaprielian-Churchill, Isabel. "Armenian Refugees and Their Entry into Canada, 1919–30." *Canadian Historical Review* 71, no. 1 (1990): 80–108.

Kasinitz, Philip, John H. Mollenkopf, and Mary C. Waters, eds. *Becoming New Yorkers: Ethnographies of the New Second Generation.* New York: Russell Sage, 2004.

Kasozi, A.B.K., Nakanyike Musisi, and James Mukooza Sejjengo. *The Social Origins of Violence in Uganda, 1964–1985.* Montreal: McGill-Queen's University Press, 1994.

Kelley, Ninette, and Michael Trebilcock. *The Making of the Mosaic: A History of Canadian Immigration Policy.* Toronto: University of Toronto Press, 2010.

Keyserlingk, Robert H., ed. *Breaking Ground: The 1956 Hungarian Refugee Movement to Canada.* North York, ON: York Lanes Press, 1993.

King, Noel Quinton, A.B.K. Kasozi, and Arye Obed. *Islam and the Confluence of Religions in Uganda, 1840–1966.* Tallahassee, FL: American Academy of Religion, 1973.

Kiwanuka, Semakula. *Amin and the Tragedy of Uganda.* Munich: Weltforum Verlag, 1979.

Klempner, Mark. "Navigating Life Review Interviews with Survivors of Trauma." In *Oral History Reader*, edited by Robert Perks and Alistair Thomson, 202–208. New York: Routledge, 1998.

Knowles, Valerie. *Strangers at Our Gates: Canadian Immigration and Immigration Policy, 1540–2006.* Toronto: Dundurn Press, 2007.

Kotecha, K.C. "The Short Changed: Uganda Citizenship Laws and How They Were Applied to Its Asian Minority." *International Lawyer* 8, no. 1 (1975): 1–29.

Kuepper, William G., G. Lynne Lackey, and E. Nelson Swinerton. *Ugandan Asians in Great Britain: Forced Migration and Social Absorption.* London: Croom Helm, 1975.

Kuper, Jessica. "The Goan Community in Kampala." In *Expulsion of a Minority: Essays on Ugandan Asians*, edited by Michael Twaddle, 53–69. London: Athlone Press, 1975.

Kushner, Tony, and Katharine Knox. *Refugees in an Age of Genocide: Global, National, and Local Perspectives during the Twentieth Century.* New York: Frank Cass, 1999.

Kyemba, Henry. *A State of Blood: The Inside Story of Idi Amin.* New York: Ace Books, 1977.

Lamey, Andy. *Frontier Justice: The Global Refugee Crisis and What to Do about It.* Toronto: Doubleday Canada, 2011.

MacSkimming, Roy. *Cold War: The Amazing Canada-Soviet Hockey Series of 1972.* Vancouver, BC: Greystone Books, 1996.

Madokoro, Laura. " 'Belated Signing': Race Thinking and Canada's Approach to the 1951 Convention Relating to the Status of Refugees." In *Dominion of Race: Rethinking Canada's International History,* edited by Laura Madokoro, Francine McKenzie, and David Meren, 160–82. Vancouver: UBC Press, 2017.

———. *Elusive Refuge: Chinese Migrants in the Cold War.* Boston: Harvard University Press, 2016.

Mamdani, Mahmood. *From Citizen to Refugee: Uganda Asians Come to Britain.* Cape Town: Pambazuka Press, 2011.

Mangat, J.S. *A History of the Asians in East Africa, c. 1886 to 1945.* Oxford: Clarendon Press, 1969.

Mawani, Zehra. "Diasporic Citizens: Ugandan Asians and Identity Formation; Facebook Photographs as a Method of Creating and Sharing Identity." Master's thesis, Carleton University, 2014.

Maxwell, Rahsaan. "Evaluating Migrant Integration: Political Attitudes across Generations in Europe." *International Migration Review* 44, no. 1 (2010): 25–52.

Maynes, Mary Jo, Jennifer L. Pierce, and Barbara Laslett. *Telling Stories: The Use of Personal Narratives in the Social Sciences and History.* Ithaca, NY: Cornell University Press, 2008.

Mazrui, Ali Al'Amin. *Soldiers and Kinsmen in Uganda: The Making of a Military Ethnocracy.* Beverly Hills: Sage Publications, 1975.

Medina, Néstor, and Becca Whitla. "(An)Other Canada Is Possible: Rethinking Canada's Colonial Legacy." *Horizontes Decoloniales / Decolonial Horizons* 5 (2019): 13–42.

Melady, Thomas Patrick, and Margaret Badum Melady. *Idi Amin Dada: Hitler in Africa.* Kansas City: Universal Press Syndicate, 1977.

———. *Uganda: The Asian Exiles.* New York: Orbis Books, 1976.

Mittelman, James H. *Ideology and Politics in Uganda: From Obote to Amin.* New York: Cornell University Press, 1975.

Moghissi, Haideh, Saeed Rahnema, and Mark J. Goodman. *Diaspora by Design: Muslims in Canada and Beyond.* Toronto: University of Toronto Press, 2009.

Molloy, Michael. "The Ugandan Asian Expulsion, 1972: A Personal Memoir." In *Finding Refuge in Canada: Narratives of Dislocation,* edited by George Melnyk and Christina Parker, 65–78. Athabasca, AB: Athabasca University Press, 2021.

Morah, Benson Chukwuma. "The Assimilation of Ugandan Asians in Calgary." Master's thesis, University of Calgary, 1974.

Motani, Nizar. "The Ugandan Civil Service and the Asian Problem 1894–1972." In *Expulsion of a Minority: Essays on Ugandan Asians*, edited by Michael Twaddle, 98–111. London: Athlone Press 1975.

Munro, Murray J. "A Primer on Accent Discrimination in the Canadian Context." *TESL Canada Journal* 20, no. 2 (2003): 38–51.

Nanji, Shenaaz. *Child of Dandelions*. Toronto: Second Story Press, 2008.

Nazareth, John, ed. *Uganda: 50 Years of Independence*. Toronto: Chandaria Family and Conros Corporation, 2012.

Nazareth, Peter. *In a Brown Mantle*. Nairobi: East African Literature Bureau, 1972.

Norton, Bonny. *Identity and Language Learning: Gender, Ethnicity and Educational Change*. New York: Longman, 2000.

Ntsimane, Radikobo. " 'Why Should I Tell My Story?': Culture and Gender in Oral History." In *Oral History in a Wounded Country: Interactive Interviewing in South Africa*, edited by Philippe Denis and Radikobo Ntsimane. Scottsville, South Africa: University of KwaZulu-Natal Press, 2008.

Ocaya-Lakidi, Dent. "Black Attitudes to the Brown and White Colonizers of East Africa." In *Expulsion of a Minority: Essays on Uganda Asians*, edited by Michael Twaddle, 81–97. London, Athlone Press 1975.

Oded, Arye. "Israeli-Ugandan Relations in the Time of Idi Amin." *Jewish Political Studies Review* 18, no. 3/4 (2006): 65–79.

Ofcansky, Thomas P. *Uganda: Tarnished Pearl of Africa*. Boulder, CO: Westview Press, 1996.

Ojwang, Dan. "Exile and Estrangement in East African Indian Fiction." *Comparative Studies of South Asia, Africa and the Middle East* 32, no. 3 (2012): 523–42.

Omara-Otunnu, Amii. *Politics and the Military in Uganda, 1890–1985*. Basingstoke, UK: Macmillan Press, 1987.

Patel, Hasu H. "General Amin and the Indian Exodus from Uganda." *Issue: A Journal of Opinion* 2, no. 4 (1972): 12–22.

Peddie, Francis. *Young, Well-Educated, and Adaptable: Chilean Exiles in Ontario and Quebec, 1973–2010*. Winnipeg: University of Manitoba Press, 2014.

Pereira, Cecil Patrick. "A Study of the Effects of the Ethnic and Non-Ethnic Factors on the Resettlement of the Ugandan Asian Refugees in Canada." PhD diss., University of Wisconsin–Madison, 1981.

Phillips, Kendall R., ed. *Framing Public Memory*. Rhetoric, Culture, and Social Critique. Tuscaloosa: University of Alabama Press, 2004.

Picot, Garnett, Feng Hou, and Simon Coulombe. "Poverty Dynamics among Recent Immigrants to Canada." *The International Migration Review* 42, no. 2 (2008): 393–424.

Plaza, Dwaine. "The Construction of a Segmented Hybrid Identity among One-and-a-Half-Generation and Second-Generation Indo-Caribbean and African Caribbean Canadians." *Identity* 6, no. 3 (2006): 207–29.

Preston, Valerie, Audrey Kobayashi, and Guida Man. "Transnationalism, Gender, and Civic Participation: Canadian Case Studies of Hong Kong Immigrants." *Environment and Planning A* 38, no. 9 (2006): 1633–51.

Raska, Jan. *Czech Refugees in Cold War Canada: 1945–1989*. Winnipeg: University of Manitoba Press, 2018.

———. "Humanitarian Gesture: Canada and the Tibetan Resettlement Program, 1971–5." *Canadian Historical Review* 97, no. 4 (2016): 546–75.

Rattansi, P.M., and M. Abdulla. "An Educational Survey." In *Portrait of a Minority: Asians in East Africa*, revised edition, edited by Dharam P. Ghai and Yash P. Ghai, 128–50. Nairobi: Oxford University Press, 1970.

Reid, James S. "Some Legal Aspects of the Expulsion." In *Expulsion of a Minority: Essays on Ugandan Asians*, edited by Michael Twaddle, 193–209. London: Athlone Press 1975.

Reitz, Jeffrey, and Ye Zhang. "National and Urban Contexts for the Integration of the Immigrant Second Generation in the United States and Canada." In *The Next Generation: Immigrant Youth in a Comparative Perspective*, edited by Richard Alba and Mary C. Waters, 207–28. New York: New York University, 2011.

Remtulla, Mehdi. "Educational and Social Adjustment of Francophone and Anglophone Khoja Ismailis in Montreal." Master's thesis, McGill University, 1979.

Rice, Andrew. *The Teeth May Smile but the Heart Does Not Forget: Murder and Memory in Uganda*. New York: Metropolitan Books, 2009.

Ristovski-Slijepcevic, Svetlana, Gwen Chapman, and Brenda Beagan. "Being a 'Good Mother': Dietary Governmentality in the Family Food Practices of Three Ethnocultural Groups in Canada." *Health* 14, no. 5 (2010): 467–83.

———. "Engaging with Healthy Eating Discourse(s): Ways of Knowing about Food and Health in Three Ethnocultural Groups in Canada." *Appetite* 50, no. 1 (2008): 167–78.

Rogers, Kim Lacy, Selma Leydesdorff, and Graham Dawson. *Trauma: Life Stories of Survivors*. New Brunswick, NJ: Transaction Publishers, 2004.

Sathyamurthy, T.V. *The Political Development of Uganda: 1900–1986*. Aldershot, UK: Gower Publishing, 1986.

Sharma, Vishnu D., and F. Wooldridge. "Some Legal Questions Arising from the Expulsion of the Ugandan Asians." *The International Comparative Law Quarterly* 23, no. 2 (1974): 397–425.

Sheftel, Anna, and Stacey Zembrzycki. "Only Human: A Reflection on the Ethical and Methodological Challenges of Working with 'Difficult' Stories." *Oral History Review* 37, no. 2 (2010): 191–214.

Smith, George Ivan. *Ghosts of Kampala*. London: George Weidenfeld and Nicolson, 1980.

St. Vincent, Roger. *Seven Crested Cranes: Asian Exodus from Uganda; The Role of Canada's Mission to Kampala*. Ottawa: Canadian Immigration and Historical Society, 1993.

Tandon, Yash. "A Political Survey." In *Portrait of a Minority: Asians in East Africa*, revised edition, edited by Dharam P. Ghai and Yash P. Ghai, 68–97. Nairobi: Oxford University Press, 1970.

Tastsoglou, Evangelia, and Baukje Miedema. " 'But Where Are You From, Originally?' Immigrant Women and Integration in the Maritimes." *Atlantis: Critical Studies in Gender, Culture and Social Justice* 24, no. 2 (2000): 82–91.

Tepper, Elliot, ed. *Southeast Asian Exodus: From Tradition to Resettlement; Understanding Refugees from Laos, Kampuchea, and Vietnam in Canada.* Ottawa: Canadian Asian Studies Association, 1980.

Thompson, Andrew S., and Stephanie Bangarth. "Transnational Christian Charity: The Canadian Council of Churches, the World Council of Churches, and the Hungarian Refugee Crisis, 1956–1957." *The American Review of Canadian Studies* 38, no. 3 (2008): 295–316.

Thompson, Gardner. "The Ismailis in Uganda," in *Expulsion of a Minority: Essays on Uganda Asians*, edited by Michael Twaddle, 30–52. London: Athlone Press, 1975.

Thompson, Paul. "The Voice of the Past: Oral History." In *The Oral History Reader*, edited by Robert Perks and Alistair Thomson, 21–28. New York: Routledge, 1998.

Tolia-Kelly, Divya P. "Materializing Post-Colonial Geographies: Examining the Textural Landscapes of Migration in the South Asian Home." *Geoforum* 35, no. 6 (2004): 675–88.

Tribe, M.A. "Economic Aspects from the Expulsion of Asians from Uganda." In *Expulsion of a Minority: Essays on Ugandan Asians*, edited by Michael Twaddle, 140–76. London: Athlone Press, 1975.

Turyahikayo-Rugyema, Benoni. "The Development of Mass Nationalism, 1952–1962." In *Uganda: The Dilemma of Nationhood*, edited by G.N. Uzoigwe, 217–255. New York: NOK Publishers International, 1982.

Twaddle, Michael, ed. *Expulsion of a Minority: Essays on Ugandan Asians.* London: Athlone Press, 1975.

Umedaly, Lella. *Mamajee's Kitchen: Indian Cooking From Three Continents.* Vancouver, BC: UP Umedaly, 2006.

Uzoigwe, G.N., ed. *Uganda: The Dilemma of Nationhood.* Studies in East African Society and History. New York: NOK Publishers International, 1982.

Van Hear, Nicholas. *New Diasporas: The Mass Exodus, Dispersal and Regrouping of Migrant Communities.* London: University Colleges London Press, 1998.

Vassanji, M.G. *No New Land.* Toronto: McClelland and Stewart, 1991.

Vertovec, Steven. *Transnationalism.* London: Routledge, 2009.

———. "Young Muslims in Keighley, West Yorkshire: Cultural Identity, Context, and 'Community.'" In *Muslim European Youth: Reproducing Ethnicity, Religion, Culture*, edited by S. Vertovec and A. Rogers, 87–101. Aldershot, UK: Ashgate, 1998.

Ward, W.E.F., and L.W. White. *East Africa: A Century of Change, 1870–1970.* New York: Africana Publishing, 1972.

Whitaker, Reginald. *Double Standard: The Secret History of Canadian Immigration.* Toronto: Lester and Orpen Dennys, 1987.

Wilpert, Czarina. "Ethnic and Cultural Identity: Ethnicity and the Second Generation in the Context of European Migration." In *New Identities in Europe: Immigrant Ancestry and the Identity of Youth*, edited by K. Liebkind, 6–24. Aldershot, UK: Gower, 1989.

Wilson, Kevin C. "And Stay Out! The Dangers of Using Anti-Immigrant Sentiment as a Basis for Social Policy: America Should Take Heed of Disturbing Lessons from Great Britain's Past." *Georgia Journal of International and Comparative Law* 24, no. 3 (1995): 567–92.

Wooding, Dan, and Ray Barnett. *Uganda Holocaust*. London: Pickering and Inglis, 1980.

Woodsworth, J.S. *Strangers within Our Gates: Or, Coming Canadians*. Toronto: F.C. Stephenson, 1909.

Wu, Zheng, Christoph M. Schimmele, and Feng Hou. *Social Integration of Immigrants and Their Children in Canada's Urban Neighbourhoods*. Vancouver: Metropolis British Columbia, 2010.

Yow, Valerie Raleigh. *Recording Oral History: A Guide for the Humanities and Social Sciences*. Lanham, MD: Rowman and Littlefield, 2015.

Zembrzycki, Stacey. *According to Baba: A Collaborative Oral History of Sudbury's Ukrainian Community*. Vancouver: UBC Press, 2014.

INDEX